Storytellers

At its best, journalism helps make sense of the world and connects us to each other. In more than thirty interviews with some of Australia's most celebrated media professionals, Leigh Sales takes us behind the scenes, to explore how stories are discovered, pursued, crafted and delivered.

In ten sections – from news reporting to editing, via investigative journalism, commentary and of course interviewing – we tour the profession. A who's-who of Australian journalism talks candidly and directly about their greatest lessons and trade secrets: how they get leads, survive in war zones, write a profile, tell a story with pictures, and think on their feet when everything that can go wrong does go wrong.

Storytellers is more than just a masterclass in the tradecraft of journalism, it's also an invaluable guide to clear, concise and honest communication for anyone who has a story to tell.

Storytellers

Leigh Sales
Storytellers

questions, answers and the craft of journalism

SCRIBNER

First published in Australia in 2023 by Scribner, an imprint of
Simon & Schuster Australia
Suite 19A, Level 1, Building C, 450 Miller Street, Cammeray, NSW 2062

Sydney New York London Toronto New Delhi
Visit our website at www.simonandschuster.com.au

SCRIBNER and design are registered trademarks of The Gale Group, Inc., used under
licence by Simon & Schuster Inc.

10 9 8 7 6 5 4 3

A catalogue record for this
book is available from the
National Library of Australia

9781761106965 (paperback)
9781761106972 (ebook)

Cover design by Laura Thomas
Typeset by Midland Typesetters in 12.5/17 pt Adobe Garamond Pro
Printed and bound in Australia by Griffin Press

The paper this book is printed on is certified
against the Forest Stewardship Council® Standards.
Griffin Press – a member of the Opus Group holds
chain of custody certification SCS-COC-001185.
FSC® promotes environmentally responsible, socially
beneficial and economically viable management
of the world's forests.

Detainee 002: The Case of David Hicks

On Doubt

*Any Ordinary Day: Blindsides, Resilience and
What Happens After the Worst Day of Your Life*

Well Hello: Meanderings from the World of Chat 10 Looks 3
(with Annabel Crabb)

Contents

Storytellers

Introduction

When I was twenty-one and a shiny new journalist in Brisbane, I was assigned to cover the Boxing Day sales for the evening ABC TV News bulletin. A cameraman and I navigated the bargain-crazed hoards at Myer and then returned to the newsroom, where I inserted our camera tape into a Betacam and watched it in fast forward (and yes, the only thing that could have made that sentence sound more 1994 was a reference to Boyz II Men). 'It's just footage of shoppers,' my thinking went, 'no need to suffer the tedium of watching it in real time.'

Dave English, a gruff ex-newspaperman with a bald head and a white goatee, was the line-up producer that day – the senior journalist in charge of ordering the bulletin, editing the reporters' scripts, and putting the news to air from the studio control room. He was a generous mentor, known for his wit and economy with words, along with an intolerance of fools and time-wasters. As I watched my material on high speed, Dave marched over and smacked the toggle on the tape machine to pause it.

'You're missing every good line in this script,' he barked.

I had no idea what he was talking about because I hadn't started writing.

Dave rewound the tape and played it at normal speed. He hit pause again after a shot of a woman picking up a shoe, inspecting it, and then putting it back on the table before walking away.

'"Not every looker was a buyer" is the opening line,' Dave said before returning to his seat at the head of the news desk.

Dave was schooling me in what is known as 'writing to pictures' (choosing your words to complement, but not describe, the shots), as opposed to 'wallpapering' (writing the script without tailoring it to specific images). It is a tool I have used thousands of time at work in the twenty-nine years since.

That was not my first lesson in how to write for television, and certainly far from the last, but it illustrates something that was evident from my first day in a newsroom: almost everything worthwhile is learned on the job. For all its transition to a university-qualified profession in the past fifty years, journalism is, and always will be, a trade. As with all trades, an apprentice learns either directly, through the instruction of experienced craftspeople, or indirectly through observation and imitation.

For much of journalism's history, people left school, joined newspapers as copy kids, or radio and television newsrooms as cadets, and worked their way up through a grading system, starting at D until they became fully-fledged A-grade journalists. The occasional well-educated type may have strolled into a newsroom via an arts or law degree but journalism itself was not something that anybody spent three years studying at university.

In the 1980s, the professionalisation of journalism took hold and it rapidly became difficult to get an entry-level job without a degree, even if that job mostly involved making cups of tea and answering the phone. In 1991, I started a journalism course at the

Queensland University of Technology. Our teachers were experienced journalists who loved the media and were well-connected in the industry. Employers viewed the QUT course favourably because it was heavily practical compared to more academic offerings elsewhere. Even with my useful foundation from QUT, I still learned 95 per cent of how to be a journalist once I actually joined a newsroom, in my case Channel 9 Brisbane in 1993.

My first job was on a local news feature program called *Brisbane Extra*. I was responsible for any junior task that needed to be done: answering the phone to viewers with story ideas or complaints, printing out scripts for that night's program and distributing them through the control room, rolling the autocue for the presenter, assigning crews to reporters, organising library footage for stories, helping with research if asked. Some of the staff had a lot of experience and others were only slightly older than me but already knew much more than I did. I was lucky because almost all of them took the time to educate me in aspects of television production. I was especially fortunate when one of the senior producers, Elizabeth Egan, let me work with her on some stories. She was generous with her time and advice, but more importantly, made me feel that she believed I could become a proper journalist.

When I moved to the ABC in 1994 for an on-air reporting role, colleagues such as Dave English and others gave me the same time and help. Often it was camera operators with whom I filmed stories, and editors sitting at their consoles afterwards in darkened suites, who explained what could have been done better: I needed more shots like this, I should have asked the talent that, my voice would sound less forced if I relaxed. One of the more nerve-shredding experiences occurred when the Queensland ABC News Director, John Cameron, formerly the network's Washington Bureau Chief, occasionally replaced the line-up producer on the news desk so he could personally subedit reporters' scripts. He was known for his frank feedback – sometimes brutal, always spot-on – about flabby writing and poor structure. He was no stranger to an early morning phone call either, to let you know that in the previous night's bulletin you had mispronounced the word 'ceremony' as the Americanised 'ce-re-moan-ee', instead of the correct 'ce-re-munny', and that he would not care to hear it repeated.

Those formative experiences still inform my values as a journalist: if a reporter doesn't care about a correct word, or using the best possible shots, how can the viewer trust that they care about getting the basic facts right, not to mention fairness or balance?

I learned a lot too when I was a D-grade by watching my competitors in the field, particularly the fearless way senior reporters in the Queensland press gallery of the 1990s would grill the premier. The lesson that stayed with me forever was that hardworking Australians pay politicians' salaries, so journalists shouldn't be afraid to ask tough questions and hold them accountable on behalf of the voters at home.

Learning from colleagues on the job has continued, no matter how experienced I have become. When I was Washington Correspondent for the ABC in the early 2000s, my daily newspaper reading included *The New York Times*, *The Wall Street Journal* and *The Washington Post*. Immersion in blue-ribbon journalism every day taught me a great deal about clear writing, thorough investigation, and finding fresh angles on stories. When I anchored *Lateline* from 2007 onwards, observing the urbane and rigorous way my colleague Tony Jones interviewed politicians and world figures helped me find my own style. Studying the non-fiction of Helen Garner, unpicking her minimalist writing style and the way she dissects issues, has given me a goal for my own books.

The years have flown by and now I am the crusty old-timer passing on knowledge. I've also discovered, to my delight, that teaching is a two-way street. I learn as much in return from young producers and reporters. They know so much more than I do about the latest technology, new storytelling techniques, and how to best adapt material for different platforms. They often bring new perspectives on issues and events because of their age and life experience. I love being assigned to work with journalists in their twenties because while I've heard all the stereotypes about pampered millennials who prioritise their yoga classes above all else, I've found most of them to be the opposite. The ones with whom I've worked have inspired me with their creativity, empathy and work ethic.

Though I am fascinated by new ways of thinking about and practising journalism, I also unashamedly believe that regardless of evolving technology and values, the basics of the craft are unchanged and remain critical to effectively reporting on the world in which we live. Skills such as active listening, close observation, clear communication and sparse writing are always essential, whether you are filing for TikTok or *Four Corners*.

Journalists are professional storytellers, but every single one of us is an amateur storyteller in our own lives. Giving order to the world around us and making sense of it through storytelling is the way we connect to each other, be it telling your partner what happened at work or chatting to a neighbour over the fence. When we write a Facebook post we are telling a story. When a lawyer tries to persuade a jury, they are telling a story. When an engineer unveils new technology to a client, they are telling a story. A patient consulting a doctor, a pilot explaining a flight delay, a real estate agent selling a property: every day, every encounter we have is rich in character, plot, narrative and meaning. The basic skills of journalism are the same tools anyone could use to become better at communicating with others. That's one reason I've written this book.

The second is to pass on knowledge and tricks of the trade to a new generation of journalists, because I'm concerned that opportunities for that are dwindling due to the huge changes in the media industry during the past twenty-five years.

The arrival of the internet and the information it offers on tap decimated the traditional media business model and drastically reduced profitability. To save money, many senior, well-paid reporters were made redundant and replaced with less experienced, cheaper staff. The downsizing and closure of newsrooms happened at the exact moment that news on-demand took hold with the rise of the 24/7 news cycle and social media. That means there are fewer journalists left to produce more content. Those who remain are constantly swamped by information and besieged by deadlines. Burnout from ludicrous workloads and paltry pay has caused still more journalists to leave the industry; they can earn more in public relations or corporate communications. Others have become disillusioned with the direction of the media and the trend in some organisations towards open ideological bias. As a result, an extraordinary amount of experience and knowledge has drained from newsrooms.

The combination of more work and fewer people to do it means finding the time for proper training, or to even trade tips with colleagues, is almost impossible. Technology is playing a role too: newsrooms used to be noisy places where you could overhear colleagues' phone patter and the way they winkled out stories or pursued leads. Now they are largely silent, either because journalists rely more on email or texting, or because people are working from home post-covid. I know also that some older journalists are anxious about providing critical feedback to young reporters for fear of being accused of bullying or sexism. In the age of cancel culture, they also worry that they might step on a landmine they don't know exists and find themselves reported to Human Resources. Equally, I know some young reporters are irritated by sanctimonious 'back in the day' lectures from old-timers and can't stand being treated as if they're snowflakes who have it easier today than people in newsrooms did twenty years ago.

One consequence of all of this is declining quality. I recently saw a tabloid headline about myself that read: 'Can't Bare It: Leigh Sales Reveals Reason She Can't Return to ABC Studio'. I hadn't in fact been angling to perform a striptease on live television: I had written an Instagram post about the death of a very close colleague. Amusing mistakes like this appear on every media website almost every day of the week, but there are more serious offences that arise from a lack of understanding of journalism basics and an insufficient monitoring of standards. Opinion and activism are dressed up as objective reporting; deliberate bias, misinformation and the skewing of facts are common. These things cause readers and viewers to either become bored and tune out or, worse, to lose trust. Data shows that there is growing disengagement from the news and it is driven by a number of factors: an overwhelming volume of information, constant negativity that has a detrimental effect on mental health, and a distrust in the 'facts' the media presents. All of those things would be improved by reporters paying better attention to fundamentals: synthesise information and make it clear, don't catastrophise and exaggerate, tell the truth and set aside your own agenda.

When I was studying journalism, our bible was *News Sense* by Bob Jervis. I recently asked a friend who lectures in journalism in Sydney what is used today. She said there isn't anything comparable and that students are mostly assigned academic readings.

She sent me a few samples. They were full of phrases such as 'hegemonic epistemologies and ontologies', 'pedagogical predicaments' and 'conceptual frameworks'. I don't know what any of that means but I can tell you this: it has zero to do with learning to be a good journalist. I have nothing against university journalism courses – as I've said, my own was excellent. Academia is about theory and that serves a purpose, but my view is that if you want to *practise* journalism, it is best viewed as a trade learned by observation and experience.

I don't hold myself up as an exemplar of journalism; and more broadly, the media regularly falls short of community expectations as well as the standards we claim to set for ourselves. I see plenty of one-sided reporting for which I have contempt – to be frank, increasingly so. I often find the self-congratulatory tone of the media nauseating. Books could, and should, be written about media ethics; the lack of diversity in journalism; cosying up to power and 'access' journalism; declining quality; the loss of public trust in the media as an institution; the infiltration of 'woke' thinking into newsrooms; the tension between activist journalists and legacy journalists; the tendency of much media reporting to unnecessarily stoke anxiety, depression and division; the erosion of free speech and the rise of cancel culture; blatant opinion masquerading as news coverage; audience disengagement; the rise of fake news and the concentration of ownership in the hands of barons such as Rupert Murdoch.

This is not any of those books.

My focus in this book is entirely on the practicalities of the craft: where do story ideas come from? How do you make contacts? What does a good voiceover sound like? How do you make a one-minute video story compelling? How do you know when to interrupt a politician during an interview? How do you structure fifty thousand words of research into a narrative? What makes the perfect photograph to illustrate a story?

More than thirty media professionals, widely considered to be among Australia's finest, are answering those questions and more in these pages. Many are household names. Between them they have hundreds of years of experience covering some of the biggest stories of the past fifty years. You could fill a garage with their collected awards. But they are by no means the definitive list of Australia's best: the choice of who to include was subjective and limited by space and a desire to include diverse experience. I wanted voices from many different types of media: public broadcasting to commercial television to tabloid newspapers, digital entrepreneurs to old-school newspaper hounds, serious investigative reporters to brilliant camera operators. Each person offers insights based on their own experience: nothing more, nothing less. Their views can be contradictory and open to interpretation. One might argue with the choice of who is included and one might approve or disapprove of their work, but each has attained a level of mastery of a particular aspect of journalism that makes their insights worth hearing.

This book is not a manual of universal truths or a set of rules to follow. What it offers is many subjective opinions on becoming a great storyteller. My ideas about what constitutes journalism's first principles are not necessarily the same as those of another reporter. As the cliché goes, there's more than one way to skin a cat, and it has been exhilarating in this project to discover them. One reporter might think it's ludicrous to start writing without having first plotted a structure. Another might think it's best to just start typing and see what comes out.

While the careers of the journalists featured here vary wildly, as do their techniques and practices, they also share many traits.

They are passionate and enthusiastic about their work. They have a great deal of natural curiosity about what makes people tick. Most are compulsively persistent and detail-oriented. Contrary to the reputation of journalists as heartless vultures, all of them care deeply about the people on whom they report, and in some cases are still haunted by things they have seen. Beyond that, their views about how to find and tell stories are as varied as their personalities and life experiences.

With this book, my message to journalists is: here are some people who know a lot, have proven track records, and want to share with you what they have learned through experience. To general readers, I say: if you embrace clarity, brevity and honesty, and develop your skills as a listener and observer, you will become a better communicator, regardless of who you are and what you do. You will tell stories that make people listen.

News Reporting

News reporting is the foundation stone of many journalism careers, and covering general news is often an entry-level job. That should not be confused with it being an easy job. The role allows a reporter to sample all kinds of stories: hard news, soft features, politics, sport, court cases, natural disasters. From one day to the next you don't know what story will be assigned, where it will take place, or how much time will be available to work on it. Covering breaking news involves filing at least a line of copy for social media within seconds, and something considerably longer online within minutes.

Some journalists spend their entire careers reporting daily news because they either thrive on the adrenalin, have a knack for breaking stories, or relish the art of conveying a large volume of information in as few words as possible. It is a job for people who work well under pressure and love the challenge of writing quickly and succinctly. The best television news reporters write with elegant brevity and can covey a great deal in a few seconds of script. Radio news journalists may have as little as seven or eight minutes in which to write, record and file a story in order to make key bulletins at the top of an hour. A print or online reporter will have barely filed one story before their editor asks them for their next angle. News reporting is relentless and not for the faint-hearted.

While many reporters branch into other kinds of journalism, such as investigative journalism, feature writing or anchoring, every media organisation ultimately lives or dies on the strength of its frontline news coverage. It is the material from which almost all other media content is then built.

Chris Reason

The Seven network's Chris Reason is one of Australia's most accomplished and dogged television news journalists. His experience covering breaking news and disasters is close to unparalleled. He has reported innumerable major international stories, including 9/11, the Boxing Day tsunami, the deaths of Nelson Mandela and Princess Diana, East Timor's independence, the 7/7 London terrorist bombings, and the war in Ukraine. Closer to home, he has covered the Beaconsfield mine disaster, the Thredbo landslide, and multiple elections. In 2015, he was awarded the Graham Perkin Australian Journalist of the Year Award for his work on the Lindt Cafe siege. He also has multiple Walkley awards and two Logies for news reporting.

Reaso, whenever I lecture journalism students, I tell them about a time when you and I were covering the same story. It was 2007 and accused terrorist David Hicks was returning to Australia from Guantanamo Bay, to be held in a local prison. Day one of the story was no problem: good pictures, told itself. Day two, absolutely nothing – no vision, and a press conference with a bloke from Corrective Services who was the most boring talent imaginable. He didn't give us a single useful grab. He stood there and said, 'At 0600, Mr Hicks got out of bed. At 0630, he ate a bowl of cornflakes. At 0700, he was taken to the shower.' I filed something very dull – phoned it in because I thought there was nothing interesting in it – and then, since I was heading out to meet you for a drink, I thought, 'I'd better just check what Reaso has filed.' I switched on *7 News* and you had started with great archival vision of prisoners in orange jumpsuits at Guantanamo, shackled together, shot on a long lens, very dramatic, and your voiceover was something like, 'After years of the utmost secrecy, now we're getting every last detail,' and then you cut to the Corrective Services guy reciting his list: 'At 0630, Mr Hicks ate his cornflakes . . .' I kicked myself because it was such a lesson to work creatively with what you've got.

That's a great story. I remember it well. It was fantastic because we had known so little about him and all of a sudden we got this stream of information that was ridiculously detailed.

When you're a television journalist, you've got to make the best of what you have. You know you have this much file vision, this much new vision, so it's all about working with what's there, especially if you're restricted and you know you can't get any more. I mean, the subject here was locked away – and was going to be for some time – so you're dealing with the sources and pictures that are before you. Sometimes, as slim as that can be, looking at it sideways can create something – as it did, luckily, that day.

I like trying to push myself and do my absolute best every time I'm on a story, however mundane it may be. I just refuse to write it off: I think that's a slippery slope, and a dangerous path, for a journalist to take. Firstly, it's important to get it right for the people who are in the story, but also for the people watching. But then beyond that, if you want your career to progress, you always have to be aware that someone is going to be there trying to beat you – hopefully a young journo trying to make mincemeat of me – with something up their sleeve that I need to be aware of. I'm always conscious of what the competition could have, whether it's a better picture, angle, frame of information, interview, exclusive, or even just something as straightforward and simple as having presented and told the story better. I feel that pressure all the time. I want to keep myself competitive and as close to the top of the game as I possibly can.

What were the core skills you picked up at the start of your career that have held you in good stead throughout your career?

I started on a small suburban newspaper, *The Redland Times*, which was a great way to begin because I got to report on everything in the community – from the greyhound races to the strawberry festival, local council, courts, police. I built a good grounding in general news skills. You see what makes a community tick.

Obviously the fundamentals are critical – accuracy, balance, telling both sides of the story. And being a local paper, people were quick to walk straight in and shout at you from reception if you got something wrong! I learned quickly that people cared, whether it was a cricket score or the spelling of their pet's name.

I remember my first defamation case so clearly. A local hotel was slammed in a council meeting for being a fire deathtrap. The hotel was furious with our front-page coverage and legal letters were flying, but I'd reported it accurately and the hotel caved. I'll never forget that first feeling of pride in our journalism, that we'd done something useful. In an old-fashioned way, I still consider journalism a public service. It's an extremely important part of democracy and how the community functions.

I went from there to a tabloid; I was crime reporter on *The Daily Sun* in Brisbane. That taught me so much – how to cultivate and keep contacts, how to chase a story and write to a tight deadline, how to make complex things simple, how to make dull things entertaining. There has to be a touch of the salesman about a good journo, to be able to talk their way into something, to get someone to open the front door, or open up about themselves.

Give me an example of how you find your way into a story.

Think laterally. Is the pack running this way? Then you run that way. Try and always do something different, look at an alternative way of getting in. The Thai caves was a big one, with the kids trapped. That was an extraordinary story that had world attention. We were running on fumes. Three days that rescue went on, plus the weeks in the lead-up to that rescue. There would have been five, six hundred world media in the town at the time, and we'd been pushed further and further back from the caves, hadn't been able to get anywhere near them while the rescue operation was going on.

We staggered over the line, the last kid's out, the last live cross has been done, and I said to my cameraman, 'You're exhausted, I betcha the cops and the army are exhausted, I betcha they've all gone home. And I bet they're not guarding the perimeter around the cave anymore. Let's go and have a look.' The cameraman wasn't very happy, he just wanted to collapse like we all did.

But we jumped in the car and we drove up past the first perimeter. The roadblock: empty, abandoned, no cops. We go past the second perimeter, 500 metres down the road from the caves, there's a soldier there, his head's on the desk and he's asleep. We just continued driving past. We pulled up at the mouth of the cave, the epicentre of this story that had transfixed the world for the last two weeks, and no one was there. And I said, 'Let's go!' We jumped out of the car and we briskly walked into this cave. There were some soldiers still there, some rescue workers packing up for the day, and I said, 'Let's just start rolling, mate.' We were there inside the caves, down where the kids had gone. It was a good scoop – only four journalists got into those caves out of the hundreds that were there.

Again, a little bit of lateral thinking. Where's everyone else going? They're all going to bed. Let's go the other way.

What constitutes good writing for television news?

You have simple sentences of eight words, ten words maximum sometimes, to describe each issue or point or picture. Choosing words carefully is extremely important. I find most of my script-writing comes from sound. I tend to do all of my shot-listing first, and I choose the sound I want to use. Once I have the sound in order, then I write in and out of the grabs and the sound on tape [upsots]. Foolishly, I always start at the top of the story, with the opening line, which can sometimes be the reason I'm spending one, two, three hours too long writing the story.

What a lot of young reporters don't do – or take a long time to learn – is use their voice. A pause can be so powerful, lingering on a word. I always admire Mark Burrows from Channel 9. He lingers on one word – it might be just a fraction of a second longer than the normal person saying that word, but the listener will go, 'Oh, yeah. It *is* troubled,' you know? 'It *is* dark,' or whatever the word was that he lingered on.

What's the harder story, a major disaster or the Royal Easter Show?

I'd much rather cover the Boxing Day tsunami or Fukushima than have to do a Royal Easter Show, not because colour stories are less significant, but because they are so much harder to write. I'm not gonna take anything away from important disasters, but at the end of the day, they're something quite simple. This happened. This was the effect. This was the cause. And this is what's going to be done about it. There's a very repeated, obvious structure to a disaster story. And I've done so many of them.

Colour stories really challenge me. I tend to go towards them, I want more of them because they're something I feel I can't do very well and it's always fun to challenge yourself.

When people talk about 'writing to pictures', what do they mean?

Look, television is all about pictures. It's the most important and dominant element of a television story. You get a series of pictures on a story, particularly incidents like car crashes or natural disasters. You look through a feed of pictures – big stories will have dozens and dozens of feeds – and you look for the pictures that impact you. You develop, over years, a gut instinct for what pictures will work on television, and what pictures instantly tell a story.

That shot-listing process – which I'm forensic about, I take very detailed shot-lists – you're using a series of stars and high-lights to work out which ones are best, and then weeding that down and going from there. Once you have those pictures, you might not have to write to them. With a good picture, you can let it sit and let the sound underneath it speak.

8

When you work with a camera operator, what kind of briefing do you give them on the way to a job?

Summary of the story so they know what we're talking about. Sometimes there's assumed knowledge on a running story. Sometimes you'll need [to give] a detailed briefing. You'll say, 'Look, we're going to this situation, and they might be reluctant to talk. So, we'll keep the camera in the car and I'll give you the nod when I think it's comfortable to bring it out.'

The camera operator is the most important part of the crew. I mean, the editors are extremely important, the producer's extremely important, but out there on the frontline of the news-gathering process, it's you and your camo. The great relationships produce great journalism. If they can read your mind, you can read their body language, vice versa, you can create wonderful moments and make the job so much easier.

You've covered so many massive stories that it's hard to know where to start, but could you tell me your recollections of the Thredbo landslide? [The 1997 disaster at the popular ski resort that killed eighteen Australians.]

That was really traumatic. I haven't had – yet – a diagnosis of PTSD, but something happened to me on that story. It was a very difficult one to cover. We were there day after day reporting the tragedy, and then Stuart Diver [the sole survivor] was found and suddenly it turned around to a story of hope and survival. Disaster stories are easier overseas because you fly in as a complete stranger and you have no attachments to the locals. But when you're in your own backyard and a disaster happens, you're tiptoeing through the sensibilities and sensitivities of the local community.

We tried too hard in that story. Locals were angry about our coverage there. It was one of the very first times Australia did rolling coverage of a disaster. We just weren't very good at it. Every Australian was praying and hoping and wishing that everyone would get through and everything would be alright, so it was with the best intentions that the media were there. But it ended in a fight — a very public, ugly, physical fistfight brawl, the only one I've ever been involved with in all my years of journalism. It was at the local pub, journalists on one side, locals on the other, a whole bunch of police force members from all around the country in the middle, and suddenly someone started swinging. It was so ugly, Leigh. It was awful.

A year later, I was in Papua New Guinea covering a tsunami on the northern coast, death everywhere, all sorts of awful scenes. I remember waking up in the middle of night sweating and crying about Thredbo, really powerful imagery coming back into my mind.

The sheer volume of trauma that you've covered is hard to fathom. Have you tried to process those experiences?

I don't think I have processed it. There's probably going to be a time of reckoning for me. But I compartmentalise and have very strict borders in my mind. I've always gone to work on those assignments believing journalism is important, that it's critical, and that somebody has to be there to record these events. We can't just leave it to authorities and cops and emergency workers to record what happened in their official reports. Someone has to be there to be the independent eyes and ears of the community and let people know what happened. It's not being a vulture, it's a very fundamental role in society, to help us grieve together or rejoice together or get angry and demand change together. Yes, that is sometimes a very difficult and emotionally exhausting role for a journalist to have to do, especially in times of disaster. My father was a policeman, and I don't want to put myself anywhere near the importance of the role of first responders, but I feel that journalists are important, and that we have a job to do. And in the same way policemen and paramedics have to put their personal feelings and fears aside, so do we.

In the late 1990s, you were diagnosed with cancer and it recurred in 2002. Did that experience affect the way that you approach being a journalist?

It did. It gave me a great insight into life's difficulties and traumas and tragedies. I had fresh eyes. I could have gone back to *The Redland Times*, started again and enjoyed it all over again with great relish and enthusiasm. You just have an appreciation for all the opportunities you've been given. The danger for me now, twenty years on, is forgetting that and falling back into old habits.

There's no job like journalism. There's no job that gives you the passport to get to the sorts of places, incidents, moments in our community and our history that journalism provides. And whether it's that young guy back at the *Redland Times*, just having the fun of seeing a community tick, or whether it's the foreign correspondent who's off to the latest disaster or war zone, to have the privilege and honour of being there to watch these things happen, and to interact with the people who are making those things happen, is just amazing. You pinch yourself.

Samantha Maiden

Samantha Maiden is the Political Editor of news.com.au. In 2022, she won Australian journalism's highest honour, the Gold Walkley, and in 2021 she won the Graham Perkin Australian Journalist of the Year Award, the Kennedy Prize for Journalist of the Year, and Press Gallery Journalist of the Year for her coverage of the case of Brittany Higgins, the young Liberal staffer who alleged she had been raped at Parliament House. The story had enormous political and social ramifications. Samantha started her career as a general TV news reporter for Seven and then moved to the ABC. She has spent twenty years with News Corporation covering federal politics.

Sam, you arguably break more news than anyone in the country. Tell me some of the ways you go about finding stories.

There's a link between breaking stories and not trying to be across absolutely everything. Being across everything is great and, depending on your job, useful, but I just don't have enough space in my brain to focus intensely. Just hyper-focus on the things you're super-interested in.

There is an element of needing to be a bit obsessive. Too many journalists write for other journalists, or want other journalists to think they're great. You've got to have no shame in being like, 'I'm going to stay on the story, I'm going to keep filing on this story, if no one else is filing it I don't care, I'm just going to keep going.'

Something about political journalism that I think is worthy of reflection is that there are two different models, and I'm not saying either of them is right or wrong. But there is a model of political journalism that I haven't ever subscribed to, which is that you become incredibly close to the government of the day. You become a bit of a cipher for them; your power is based in the idea that you have a hotline to these people. Now, I obviously did not have a hotline to Scott Morrison. I always thought we had a professional relationship but I didn't get invited to Kirribilli to eat steak and watch the NRL. And I never thought that was a problem because I prefer to be more of an outsider. People can become beholden to that incredible access but maybe they're always being told things they're not allowed to report. I would just rather break stories.

I'll give you an example: anyone could have broken that Hawaii story about Scott Morrison. [In December 2019, the Prime Minister was secretly on holidays in Hawaii while Australia was experiencing catastrophic bushfires.] In fact, I later discovered there was so much more knowledge in the press gallery than what had been reported. Scott Morrison had done this weird thing where his office had called in some of the mastheads – which I blessedly wasn't involved in – and basically said to them, 'The PM's going on holidays. You need to keep this secret cos this is for his family.' Didn't say where, didn't say he was going overseas.

It's that classic access thing, right? I didn't know anything about it. Basically, I just started noticing. I was like, 'Where the hell is he? Is Michael McCormack the Acting Prime Minister? What's going on?' And then there were these rumours he was in Hawaii. His office was just so disparaging and rude to me. They were like, 'No one cares about this. You're the only person who's interested in it, you're being a weirdo.' It wasn't quite that explicit, but that was the flavour.

And then I just got the shits. Some of my best stories come out of getting the shits. When I get annoyed, I'm like, 'Right, let's go.' I just become obsessive. Do I know anyone who works at the airports? Do I know anyone who works in something related to the airports? What about unions? Had anyone seen him at the airport? I started calling people who worked in airports, and eventually I found this person that reckoned Morrison had gotten on this flight on this day. I suppose I could have been a bit more cautious and tried to get more confirmation . . . but just the fact that he was overseas, his office wasn't saying where he was, they hadn't called me back – not responding was almost like a yes.

There was a bit of a moment of Thelma and Louise going over the cliff with that story, where I was like, 'Alright, I'm just gonna report that this person has sighted him going to Hawaii.' But there was still a moment of me thinking, 'God, what if he's landed in Hawaii and he's flying on to somewhere else.' I was just scared. But I thought, 'No, I think this is what's happening. This person's seen him getting on the plane. I'm strapping on my seatbelt, and we're driving off the cliff.' Obviously, that could have ended painfully. But it didn't.

Then a similar thing happened the day after, when late at night, I noticed on Facebook that people were sharing this photo of him in Hawaii. I sent it to the PMO going, 'Is this him?' I was thinking, 'My God, he's been in Hawaii before. What if this has been mocked up?' Again, we ran it and we sourced where it was from – and it went from there.

How often do people come to you with a story versus you following an instinct like that?

Both happen. I do get anonymous tip-offs. Often I'll have this reaction of, 'Oh, that sounds like rubbish . . . but I better check it out.' Then you find out that it's not rubbish and you're like, 'Oh my God!' A good example of that is, after the 2022 federal election, I got an anonymous tip-off that the Governor-General had appeared in these ads for a building company. [The person] sent me an encrypted email. I read it and thought, 'That sounds like baloney.' I went and looked at it and it did happen. I emailed the person back and they had other suggestions of things I could chase up.

If you break enough stories, it becomes a bit of a self-saucing pudding, because people seek you out.

With Brittany Higgins, I had gone on *Insiders* and had a discussion about the employment conditions inside the Canberra bubble. Someone had said, 'Oh, staffers can go to the Department of Finance.' [To supposedly make a workplace complaint.] And I had said, 'Well, no, they can't.'

Political staff don't have the same access to unfair dismissal claims as other workers, they're at the whim and favour of MPs. All an MP needs to say is 'I've lost confidence in you' and you could be out the door. And so, because I had demonstrated an understanding of the working conditions and how fragile they can be, Brittany Higgins decided I was the person to write her story. She also felt that I would not be cowed by the government; she was very concerned about how the government would react so she wanted someone who was going to be fearless and not intimidated easily.

The day the Higgins story was published, I was contacted by an anonymous person who said, 'You need to look into the fact that the Department of Finance ordered the room to be cleaned the weekend after she'd been found.' Now, this was a classic example where I just read it and thought, 'Well, that can't possibly be true.' I put all these questions to the Department of Parliamentary Services, and they came back saying that there wasn't anything nefarious in the room being cleaned. From their perspective, it was more about two people being in there after hours. The thing that I found gobsmacking was that the department revealed to me that not only had it been cleaned, but the decision to clean it had been the subject of a secret police investigation. The AFP had investigated whether it represented tampering with a crime scene, and had concluded that it didn't because they [the department] didn't know there was an allegation when the cleaning occurred.

You're talking about things that are top secret – the cleaning of a minister's office, an AFP investigation. When you start hearing rumours or you receive anonymous tip-offs, how do you then dig further and find out whether it's true?

I think it's just basic 101 journalism. In the case of that anonymous tip-off, I put questions to the AFP and the Department of Parliamentary Services. I'd like to say that there was some sort of magic, but it was standard journalism.

Next year will be twenty-five years that I have worked at Parliament House, so obviously there's a lot of people I know.

And there's a lot of people you can tap – current and former politicians; some of them will help you, some of them won't.

Brittany Higgins was obviously a massive story, and maybe it is the most important story I will ever write . . . [Samantha starts to cry.]

Are you right? Should we keep going or do you want to stop?

Yeah, it's okay, I just find it very hard to talk about without getting emotional. I don't have any complaints, but it's dominated my life for nearly two years. All the court case stuff has been really stressful. [At the time of writing, there has been an abandoned criminal case and a separate, ongoing defamation matter.] I'm completely okay with the way I conducted myself but there's always going to be an element in these cases of journalism being on trial. Mainly I'm just worried for Brittany, right?

With a sensitive story like this, that you know is going to be big, how do you think about your duty of care to the human beings in your stories versus the readers and the public interest?

Oh, look, it's huge. It's very traumatic for people who come forward, whether they're whistleblowers or making an accusation of sexual assault, and I think that's very poorly understood. I've really wrestled with the idea of what that unleashed for Brittany Higgins, and it's something that still concerns me. I think she has found the media attention very traumatic. It's a real double-edged sword because, yes, she's someone that wanted to campaign for change, and the campaign that Brittany Higgins has waged has changed laws. It's led to this huge national debate that's been applauded by thousands of women around the country. But it's

17

been deeply, deeply traumatic for her, and it's changed her life. Certainly for the first six or eight months, I was in contact with [Brittany] just an incredible amount. You have an ongoing duty of care for these people. You don't do the story and just walk off, you're tied to them in one form or another for the rest of your life.

When you're reporting on an unfolding story like that, do you ever deliberately hold information in reserve so you'll have more stories to file in subsequent days?

Yes and no. I would never do it in a way that was manipulative or misleading. When I first put all the stuff together with Brittany Higgins, I remember thinking, 'There's too much here for one story, it's too confusing.' This is another thing I've learnt over the years: sometimes, particularly when I was at *The Australian*, I would put too much detail in the story. I would read stories other people had written and be like, 'Wow, you've stripped out quite a bit of detail there, and the story actually makes a lot more sense.' There's a real balancing act to it.

But in the case of Brittany Higgins, I thought, 'Okay, number one, we have an allegation of a sexual assault in a minister's office.' That's pretty explosive, right?

But you then had the allegation that she had been brought back to the room in which she said the incident had occurred for this employment meeting with Linda Reynolds [Minister for Defence Industry]. In digital, you've got more flexibility [than in print or TV] so initially I thought, 'Maybe we put up the allegation first, then move in the afternoon to that next thing.' But it didn't work out that way because when we got all the responses back on the Sunday for publication on the Monday, Senator Reynolds said that she didn't know the full story, and had she known, she wouldn't have met Brittany in that same room. So for reasons of fairness, that response had to run in the first story. I thought, 'I can't have that waiting.'

Then there were other aspects of what Brittany Higgins had told me. For example, there was this voicemail message of her then-employer, Workplace Minister Michaelia Cash, saying, 'Sleep tight, everything's under control.' Now Senator Cash would later say that she didn't know there was an allegation of sexual assault, just that there'd been an after-hours incident. That wasn't something I put away thinking, 'Oh, I'll ferret that away and roll it out later.' But I didn't deal with it first thing, there was just too much happening. If you're trying to roll out a narrative, there are times where it's too confusing to drop everything out in one story.

What do you think is the difference between off-the-record and background? And how do you use them?

This is a very difficult question. On one level, it's straight-forward – if something is off the record, it can't be used in any way. But, for a lot of politicians, they're telling you things off the record not because they don't want them to be used – they want you to report them – they just don't want it to be linked to them. A lot of tricky areas come up in political reporting because it's not the same as a public servant who's blowing the whistle on malfeasance. A lot of the time politicians are using you to mount proxy attacks on their enemies.

Now, obviously, if a politician tells me, 'I'm going to chal-lenge for the leadership,' or their supporters tell me, they want that reported. They are using you, so you have to be a little bit cautious in what you're doing. At the end of the day, you have the responsibility to tell your readers what's going on. So obviously, if I think the Prime Minister of the day is going to be dumped, that is newsworthy. I want to report that. But you also need to be careful about checking the information they're giving you. A lot of the time, they're trying to manipulate you to put out stuff they don't want their fingerprints on.

If supporters of Team Red are pushing something about Team Blue, you should say, 'Team Red is saying this about Team Blue.' You're not identifying the person but you are providing some context about where that information is coming from.

Do you believe in objectivity in journalism?

How would you define objectivity?

Setting aside your own biases and opinions in your reporting.

Yes and no. In general, yes. But should I set aside my view that I think homophobia is wrong? Or that racism is wrong? I don't have particular views about the Labor Party or the Liberal Party. I don't want to say I don't care who the government is but I don't sit there thinking, 'Oh, I really want that mob to win.' But I do believe that abortion should be legal and affordable and available. Equally, I'm genuinely interested in the alternative views, so I'm respectful of them.

Switching from reporting to writing, what do you think constitutes good writing for a print news story?

More than anything, it needs to make sense and be clean and clear. This is a terrible thing to admit: I don't think I'm a particularly good writer. I'm good at breaking stories. I'm good at angles. I'm no wordsmith, but that's okay, because some people who are, are not good at what I'm good at.

How did you learn how to be a news breaker?

I have controversial views on this. I don't like journalism courses, I'm very sceptical of them. I'm not saying there's not a place for them, but I'm horrified at the idea of thousands of young people being pumped through journalism schools, being taught by people who hate journalism, when there are not enough jobs for them. Some [teachers] have had great careers and run fantastic courses, but there are a lot of other places that are staffed by people who hate the media, didn't like where they worked, have all these problems with the industry, but also just weren't very successful.

I really wanted to be a print journalist. I'd done a degree in politics and I edited the student paper at uni, which was a fantastic experience. But when I got out of uni, it was the recession, and it was really hard to get a job. I was doing volunteer work at 5AA radio station and they suggested there was a cadetship going at Channel 7. I was just a scruffy university student, I didn't want to be a TV reporter. But I was like, 'I really need a job, so I'll go and talk to these people.' Anyway, funnily enough, the guy that hired me decided to hire me over all these journalism graduates – he was like, 'I think you can break stories.'

So I was a cadet, but my job was just to come up with endless ideas for yarns for the other journalists. I was basically a producer. Right from the start, I worked in an environment where breaking stories was valued.

The other thing that that guy did – which I fully support – is he wouldn't let me on air for about a year. He was like, 'The minute you get on air, you're gonna get obsessed and self-conscious about how you look.' And it's true, you do. I quite like going on TV to have a bit of a rant and rave and chat but I think the key to being good on television is to be yourself. There's nothing more ridiculous than watching someone drone on, lower their voice by an octave and TALK LIKE THIS.

I really feel like I didn't actually start learning to be a proper journalist until about 2002 – which was about eight years after I started – and it was because I sat next to this guy from *The Courier-Mail* called Michael McKenna. He was such a madman – he'd go, 'Feed the beast or the beast will feed on you!' He was joking, but he was like, 'C'mon, I need stories, I need ideas.' I'd listen to him on the phone, just the way he'd talk to people and extract information. The other thing that I learnt from him, which was terrifyingly good, was that there was this book called the Coalition Directory, that doesn't exist anymore. It was a hardcopy book of every politician's name in the Liberal Party and all their staff. Can you imagine?

He would keep this magical book in his top drawer. Sometimes you'd ask him if you could use it and he'd pull it out like he was giving you heroin.

Eventually I worked out that I needed someone to leak me that book myself. Once I got it, I was off and flying. You'd ring these people and they'd be like, 'How did you get this number?' and you'd be like, 'Mmm, don't you worry about that. Anyway, I've got a question for you.' And it was because I had this fucking book with all of their fucking numbers in it, which I learnt off Mike McKenna. You learn from observing other journalists.

Nas Campanella

Nas Campanella is the ABC's Disability Affairs Reporter, filing for television, radio and online. She has extensive experience across all aspects of general news and current affairs, from courts to regional affairs. Her voice is one of the ABC's most recognisable, from her years reading news on triple J and other ABC radio stations. She has also undertaken work for ABC International, offering journalism training for people living with disability across the Pacific.

Nas, in broadcast news, you have to be good at reporting and writing, but ultimately, if people can't understand what you're saying, then it's all for nothing. Voice is so important. What constitutes good vocal delivery?

A voice that's warm, friendly, easy to understand, and talks to you as though it's a friend. Every time I go into the studio, I think, 'Okay, let's picture someone who I just want to sit down and have a coffee with.'

Also, the crux of news reporting in a voice is authority. I breathe real deep down into my belly to try and get that deeper, more authoritative voice, as opposed to high and pitchy. When I listen back to voice reports that I did twelve years ago, they're so high-pitched. Over time, and with maturity and confidence in your reporting, you feel like, 'Okay, I've got this, I know what I'm doing,' and it's reflected in your voice.

I also used to pronounce every single vowel and consonant so strongly. It sounded so forced that it was not natural. So while you want to sound very well-spoken and clear, you also need to pull back just slightly, so that you still sound like you're talking to someone at the pub.

When you started, did you think about which words in a script were the important ones to hit?

Definitely. I did a voiceover course when I was in high school, and at NIDA. They taught us to underline the words that were the most important. Obviously, I couldn't underline cos I wasn't visually looking at a script – when I was 'looking at' a script, I was listening to it using my screen-reading technology. But I would go through the sentences and think in my mind, 'What is the key point in this sentence?' and that's what I would try and remember when I was reading the script aloud.

For people who aren't familiar with you or your work, can you elaborate on what you mean when you say you couldn't underline?

I'm totally blind. I can't see a single thing. I use a program called JAWS, screen-reading technology, which is a little robotic voice that reads out what I've typed. I input the script into a PC, then I listen and repeat what I hear. I can put punctuation into a script – and I can even underline – but I've got to be careful to have the settings correct, because it may read out that underline and punctuation. So, 'Leigh Sales comma lives in comma.' That's why it was easier for me not to underline the key points and just remember what they were.

Obviously, a very important skill in journalism is listening. Do you think relying on your hearing so heavily gives you any advantage?

Sometimes, yeah. Inherently, I listen not only to what people are saying, but also their tone. Sometimes I can get a sense of, 'Is that person really sure of themselves?' and I can then ask further questions based on their tone.

Maybe it's because I don't look at people. Maybe it is because I rely so heavily on my hearing that I do hear these other bits and pieces, where I go, 'Mmm, okay. I reckon they've got something else to share on that point.'

One thing people often say is, 'You're a good journo if you're a good listener.' You have to actively listen. Really listen, because you never know what you might miss.

One of the barriers to active listening is thinking about what you're going to ask next. That's very difficult to not think about in an interview.

This is something I struggled with in the transition between radio and TV, when I found myself continually interrupting people because they were pausing. I thought they had finished what they were saying, but they were just stopping for a moment before continuing. And just as they were about to start talking again – and usually it's the bloody best grab – I go and interrupt. I've had to also not be afraid of silence.

How important is the quality of your writing to your ability to deliver a script in a way that connects with the listener?

It's everything. I think that's what makes a good voiceover. For so long, I was thinking the writing needs to be sophisticated and not the way that I often speak, which can be slightly bogan.

People want to listen to a voice telling them a story in a way they can understand, in a way that makes sense to them. And they want to be told that story by someone they feel is a mate. When you do write the way you speak, it's easier to read and it comes out more naturally. It flows better.

How do you get your copy on paper to sound like you speak?

Sometimes I actually sit and go, 'Right, what am I trying to say here?' particularly with intros. I find intros to radio and TV packages really tricky. I don't just want to say, 'The government's announced blah, blah, blah,' I want to say something like, 'You've been hearing a lot about XYZ,' and get into it in more of a casual way.

Words like 'grant', 'government', 'regulation', 'reform' – they're not very hooky words. But if you hear something about someone's actual life or experience, something that a human being relates to, it hooks you into the story more.

That's the thing. One of the last stories I did was about funding to move younger people with disability out of nursing homes and into their own homes. I could have just started off with, 'There's X-million dollars being spent on this.' Instead, I started with something along the lines of, 'Imagine being a young person in a nursing home, not being able to pick what you eat, when you eat.' That really hits people, because they start to picture themselves in that situation.

Unless you have direct experience of something – having a child with autism, being a farmer, living through a drought, and so on – other people's worlds can be invisible, and you may not even be aware they exist until someone explains it. One of our jobs as journalists is to make people understand so they can have empathy, right?

It's true. Covid really brought to the fore some of the issues that the disability community had been experiencing. For loads of people, coming out of a five-month lockdown meant going to have beers at the pub and getting back to normal. For loads of the people in my community, the disability community, it was an extended lockdown. They weren't coming out now that Covid was being allowed to float around in the community. They had underlying health conditions that meant they were still terrified.

It was about describing that to people so they could see themselves in someone else's shoes. I find that's what I do a lot in my job, actually, because people often can't imagine or picture themselves in that situation or haven't even met people with disability.

The one thing I've found during my career is that human beings are endlessly interesting. Everyone you meet has a different story and a different history that's got them to where they are, and it's interesting to be able to ask people about that, learn about it and then write about it.

That's what I loved most about getting into journalism. My first internship was at the local *Penrith Star* newspaper, not far from Mum and Dad's place. I got to talk to these incredible people who had so much life experience and so many stories to share. It really reaffirmed for me that this was the industry I wanted to be in.

I think a lot of people haven't actually been asked their story. As a junior journo, I remember being scared to approach people to talk, but a lot of the time people do want to talk, particularly if you ask your questions sensitively and are genuinely interested.

That's definitely true if you show genuine interest, ask questions in a respectful way and explain a bit about yourself and who you are.

[It's particularly true] with my job now, interviewing people with disability, who have never been asked for their opinion or personal story. It's special when you approach people and show that you are genuinely interested in them and what they've experienced. For me, I am in that unique position where I also have lived experience, so I can say to them, 'I have this experience – at school I was bullied, I get it. I get it. I'm a safe space for you.' That's important.

Other than giving that reassurance, do you rely on anything else to put interviewees at ease? It can be a stressful experience for them.

28

Especially if they haven't been interviewed before, or, if they've had bad experiences, which is so often the experience with my job. Many people [in the disability community] have been burnt. Their story has been twisted into some sort of inspiration-porn thing, and it wasn't what they wanted or expected. So, it's talking them through the process, from who's going to turn up – camera operators right through to photographers – where they'll be in the house, what their role is. Sometimes, I go back and tell them which parts of the interviews I'll use because they are so nervous. It's just being transparent – going back and forth, letting them ask any questions. For my first *7.30* story, I had several Zoom conversations with a mother and her daughter to make them feel at ease about filming. It was important for them because they needed to put a face to the voice, and the mother wanted to ask me a whole bunch of questions about anything and everything.

If somebody says to you, 'I'm actually not comfortable with you using that grab,' how do you approach that?

I haven't had too many of those situations. You don't want it to happen – if people say things on the record, they say them on the record. In order to avoid that, it's about being very transparent and honest about the story from the beginning – 'This is my job, this is the story.'

I will ask, 'What do you want to get out of this?' but I often know because they've approached me about a problem they have, or I've identified an issue and then found the talent to match that story. I will often say, 'Is there anywhere that we shouldn't go?', particularly if it is a traumatic experience they've had.

For radio news, sometimes you have a very short window of time in which to file a story. If you're covering a court case or an inquiry, for example, you might be filing every hour for a news bulletin. In that circumstance, what's your process?

I literally work backwards and figure it out. I'll go, 'Okay, twelve o'clock is the bulletin, but the news desk will have to look at it, that'll take a minute. It'll take me thirty to forty seconds to record, and so on . . .' Generally, I would start scripting at quarter-to, put the voice down by latest ten-to, giving it enough time to be popped in the system. Out in the field I record on my phone, top and tail it and send it in via email. So, you've got to allow for fingers hitting the wrong buttons and for it to actually hit the system. It is a real juggling act.

For me, particularly when I was covering courts on my own, I also had to factor in 'Where am I going to sit?' Make sure I'm near the door, make sure I can quickly get out, make sure I can shove my laptop under one arm, phone and cane under the other. Beforehand, I would always scope out a spot where I could quickly run to, usually in a corner crouched on the floor.

For a radio news or current affairs story, you could have audio of an interview, but you might want to also use what's called atmosphere or natural sound. What is that and how do you use it?

Oh, I love natsot, I use it a lot in my stories. I don't get the luxury of enjoying the pictures, so for me, it is about the audio. Natsot's important in my stories. Basically, it's taking the listener to where you are. Letting them in on the location, letting them really hear what the person is doing. For example, for a story we did on braille Lego being launched, I had natsot of the kids actually playing with the Lego. It provides an interesting point of reference, as opposed to just voice–grab–voice–grab, which can become quite monotonous.

In the field, you also have to actively think about natsot because you can't get it later. It's not like an interview, you can't ring back.

Exactly. And you don't want it to sound forced either. As a general rule, I know that I will want atmos. So I'll always think about the atmos that's possible to gather and ask the camera operators or record it myself.

We did this beautiful story about a couple who both live with Down syndrome. They'd done long-distance for a year because of the pandemic. It was an online story just because of how beautiful the pictures were. But then I wanted to do a radio current affairs piece, because [in the interview] they talked a lot about music and film and how that had kept them together.

They were celebrating ten years and going to get married once they could finally [be together]. They talked a lot about their favourite songs and what they wanted to dance together to, what movies they would talk about on the phone during their separation, which made me think, 'Actually, this could be a really beautiful radio current affairs piece.' It sounded gorgeous, and it invoked a real sense of emotion, I think, for the listener.

That's an incredibly good point, the emotion that audio can deliver. Pictures are very powerful obviously, but good audio can spark your imagination.

Totally. Particularly for me. With that story I just mentioned, it had very little of me and my voiceover in it – it was just these two beautiful people talking about their relationship, with music and films that they loved woven within it.

You cover disability affairs for the ABC. How do you work that round?

I've had a lot of contacts for my whole life, really, because I have lived experience and have been in and out of groups and Facebook pages and all those things. But then when the role became public, and people started seeing me on TV . . . I mean, the stories are endless. My inbox is flooded each week. Hundreds of emails – that's no exaggeration. People who, all of a sudden, saw they had someone they could talk to, that they could share their story with, and often their problems. I'm never short of stories. In fact, I've always got too many.

That's a lot of pressure on you, because you can't do everything.

I felt that very acutely, I won't lie. It's a huge amount of pressure. Up until recently, there's only been me across the country in my unique role. It is an enormous responsibility. I feel that, but I also love journalism and love my job, so it's about picking and choosing what I can do. I've gotten better at not taking on too much. And delegating – I don't have to be the only person that does these stories. It's taken a long time to figure out how to say no, and to realise that you can't be and do everything all the time for people. So, for me, part of the process has been realising that.

You recently had a baby. I bet that makes filing a radio news story on the hour every hour feel like a walk in the park.

It's funny, the other day, someone said to me, 'Oh my gosh, the sleep deprivation is horrendous, isn't it?' And I thought, 'Look it's bad, I am exhausted constantly, but I've also been a shift worker for so long. I know what sleep deprivation is.'

Mark Burrows

The Nine Network's Mark Burrows has headed both Nine's US and London bureaux. Mark has covered many of the biggest stories of the past thirty years, including the Romanian Revolution, the Oklahoma bombing, the death of Princess Diana, and the Iraq war. He is a repeat winner of Walkley and Logie awards for his journalism.

Let's say you're assigned Remembrance Day, a story you might be given annually. How do you go about finding a unique story for that year?

You really have to be open to exactly what happens on the day, don't get wound up ahead of it. If it rains, that's probably part of it. If there are big crowds, that's part of it; if there's a demonstration. You have to be super-relaxed and open yourself to what's happening on *that* day. You can't approach it like, 'We do this every year, it's the same old . . .' You have to go in with an open mind, use your eyes. There are a bunch of people to talk to and they are fantastic people to talk to. Just make that the story.

You just start chatting to people who are around you?

The cameraman is getting shots and I trust him to do his job. I stay close. He's looking down the lens, so he's worried about pictures. I have a sense of people conversing, I'll chat a bit, not too much. I might see somebody: if it's a good face, I can tell it's going to be a good character and I will tap the cameraman. You know what it's like, Leigh, you have an innate sense that this person could have a good story.

It doesn't always work. You get the ones where you go, 'Okay, that's great, have a nice day,' but often you get someone who's good. You let the talent drive the narrative rather than you bellowing too much flowery IT WAS ON THE ELEVENTH DAY . . . Yeah, okay, we've done all that, we know that. You concentrate on what's before you in that very moment in time.

Hearing you talk about the clichéd, thunderous way of TV scripting reminds me of something I saw this week which made me rip my hair out. The reporter's script was, 'Angry and frustrated, striking teachers flooded Macquarie Street . . .' It was the sentence structure that annoyed me because nobody talks like that. How much attention do you pay in your writing to getting it conversational?

If you looked at one of my scripts, you'd probably go, 'Oh my god,' because I tend to write in very short phrases. I did a story last night about the Russians bombing a plant in Mariupol. The opening words were 'In there, somewhere . . .' and then it went on. I never write a sentence with three ideas, let alone two ideas. Sometimes I will use only six words.

I've become acutely mindful of what the audience is looking at. I love a good pause and I love a bit of sound. Whatever sound I hear, I will incorporate it: the sound of a tank, an excavator – which was what was in the story last night – I will use it because you're trying to frame the picture the audience is looking at. Fewer words make it easier for them to understand. The effect of the pauses and sound-ups gives people a split second to catch up with what you've just said. Then you can give them a little bit more, not too much, a bit of interview, a bit of sound again. The big mistake a lot of reporters make is they've got *all* this information and they're going to give it to you.

'In there, somewhere . . .' is an excellent way to open a story, because firstly it's not going to repeat what the newsreader just said in the introduction, and secondly, even as you said it just now, that set of words gave me a visceral feeling of dread.

Yes. I was looking at the pictures, and the pictures showed this carpet bombing of a steel factory. I was struck by the fact that there were children and civilians and Ukrainian soldiers there just getting completely blitzed. That was it. The immediate imagery. It's not about the bombing, it's about the people who are in there.

Everything you're talking about, whether it's being in the moment at Remembrance Day, using the sound, limiting the script, using pause, all seems to be built towards giving people the sense of what it's actually like to be there.

That's what you're trying to do. When you fail at that, the story is never as good. I was in Kiev, I went to a few missile strikes, and it was incumbent on me to give you a sense of what I saw and felt. You take people in there are much as you can.

When you're interviewing somebody for a package for television news, what are you listening for when they're speaking?

I'm looking for an uncomplicated expression. I'm looking for something that's authentic. I will drive myself away from a clichéd response. News interviews, as you know, are always quite short. If it's something on the run, something on the move, I will start talking to somebody and say, 'What happened here?' or 'Did you see it?' and you have to listen to what they're saying. I don't go in with a list of questions. I'm in the moment. I listen to the person and they will give me the pointer to where it's going to go. I let the interviews drive themselves a lot of the time.

A young reporter asked me this week what to do if the interviewee is just bombarding you with data and you don't have the numbers at your fingertips to fact-check them.

Sometimes politicians, all they want to do is bombard you. They know you're not going to run a grab that says, 'This is a 4 per cent increase in GDP, divided by the last twelve months with a factor of seven, that just shows you how well we're doing.' You will run a grab: 'This will save people.' They are clever enough to know what you're going to run.

I will sometimes let them go. Let them get the numbers off their chest. Then I know I can just spool through the first two minutes. I will often wait towards the end of a press conference. I will get the best grab almost as the last thing because they will relax. Politicians show up to something because they have something to say – 'I want to make this point, and that point, and then this one' – they want to get these things out. Let them get that out. You don't have to use it. It's the follow-up stuff. You might get a better grab that way. You have to think on your feet.

Do you ever run your own questions from press conferences in news packages?

Yes. It depends. I did it quite a few times during covid, [using questions] to the Premier and the Chief Health Officer. The use of the question is another way of introducing sound into a story that might be so-so. You've got upsots, you've got pauses, you've got the actual grabs, and the question is just another technique that breaks up the audio stream of the story. You might go to a question that takes the story off on another tangent. Rather than having to use your voiceover, you can use the question to do that hard work. You might have a nice to-and-fro in a press conference where the camera darts to the reporter. That's a nice technique.

Adds a bit of visual interest too when the camera does a quick whip pan from the talent to the journalist.

That's everything. With a story, it's not just telling a story, you are trying to grab people by the scruff, and say, 'Hey just give me 1.40 here and I'll tell you a good story.' You have to do it with words, pictures, you've got to give them a bit of drama.

Leigh, I love what I do, and it sounds a bit funny but I've always thought of a news story as like a little scaled-down movie. It'll have a start, I'm going to take you here, I'm going to bring you back; in the end, I will finish with something. It sounds ridiculous but I really try to do that. I like a good opening line and I like to round it off. When it's over, I want people to go, 'Gee, whew.' That would be a good reaction to me.

There's sometimes a snobbery that exists around long-form TV journalism, such as documentaries being superior, but I believe there is a genuine art to television news reporting and telling a story in a concise way.

There's no doubt about it. I've known a lot of people over the years who do long-form and nothing but, who've looked at stuff I've done and said, 'I don't know how you did it.' I have to clip really tight, it has to be a very pruned story. I can take a story that's ten or twelve minutes long and turn it into a two-minute package and sometimes it can be just as good. Just because it's long doesn't make it better.

I think you learn what the heart of the story is and where the core emotion is coming from and then you ruthlessly excise the rest.

It's like cooking a good pasta sauce. Let it simmer, reduce, reduce, reduce, taste, you've got it.

What do you think makes a productive relationship between a journalist and a camera operator?

It's a very special relationship. I started [as a journalist] in Hobart in 1980. Three great cameramen I started with. Journalists must have a good appreciation of what news cameramen are trying to do. They're looking through a viewfinder. You might see something that they don't see. You've got to be tactful: 'Those guys over there look interesting.' In a dangerous situation, I stick close. I'm the eyes; they can't see stuff coming behind them. You are such a team. I've worked with people where it hasn't worked, no doubt about it. But when it works, it's so great. It's the old cliché - they are trying to make you look good. If you don't appreciate that, and give something back, you're wasting your time. If you're not going to appreciate what the camera operator does for you, lugging the gear, getting the shots, and giving you the pictures for you to write to, if you don't appreciate that, get out of the industry.

A piece to camera is when the reporter breaks the fourth wall and directly speaks to the audience. What is the purpose of it?

It shows the audience who the storyteller is. Also, when you don't have pictures for something, you can paint one with your words to the camera. So if you've arrived at the plane crash and you don't have the plane crashing, you can say, 'I've spoken to people and they believe the plane came over the hill, it dipped and then dived suddenly before it hit the ground.' It makes sense, because you're standing in front of the wreckage. When there's a lot of action going on behind you, if there's a tank or soldiers, it can have the effect of putting the reporter quickly into that scene. It can help the people watching identify with what's going on. That's also done via the words you choose.

When you're in the field, how do you judge 'Okay we have enough now, I can go back and start writing'?

It depends what time it is. It depends how much material I have. I hate having too much material because I have no intention of trawling through two hours of it. I'm very clinical about what's been shot. It's experience that tells you you've got the story. I'll turn to the cameraman and say, 'We've got it.'

I can knock off a story in one hour. Other reporters will stay there for three hours and the story is not better for it. Just because you're casting a bigger net and catching more fish doesn't necessarily make it better. I find it easier to write when I have less stuff.

You use pauses a lot in your vocal delivery. Do you have any other advice about how to deliver a television news story?

I would never use a line or a word that makes people go, 'What did he say?' You can't have people in the lounge room going, 'What's that mean?' It might impress your friends at dinner but you're going to kill your audience.

The worst thing that anybody could ever say to me is, 'I didn't understand when you said . . .' That, to me, is death. That is complete failure on my part. I try to make it absolutely clear.

In 1999, you won a Walkley for your coverage of the Interlaken Canyon disaster. What was that story about?

That was a group of Australians who were in a canyon in Switzerland, and due to flooding and some other reasons, a huge wave of water came down and a number of them died. Others clung to the side of the wall and ropes and eventually got out. I went to the canyon and the water had subsided. But I had found out there was a chalet where there were Australians. I went up there without the cameraman and I spoke to somebody and introduced myself. I said, 'I wonder if anybody here can give me a comment about the canyon, if they heard from anyone?' And he looked at me and said, 'Not right now, but you just have to wait.' I went outside with the cameraman and we sat in the car. The competition showed up and then left.

After a good wait, three hours or so – I had nothing else going, there was no point going back to the canyon – a group of about five people came out. I got out of the car and said hi. They said, 'Are you the guy who wants to talk?' I said, yes, I just wanted to know had they heard about the canyon. And the cameraman picked up the camera and I said, 'Is it okay if we roll?' and they said yes. I said, 'There was an accident in the canyon and lots of Australians have been killed, what do you know about it?' And they started talking: 'The water came down the canyon really fast, it was like a wave, and nobody could get out of the way.' You can hear on the tape, I've gone, 'Sorry? Were you in the canyon?' And they said, 'Yes, we were with the people who died.'

I hadn't realised it. My brain was going a million miles an hour. I was able to quickly go, okay, right, and got a great interview as they described what had happened. It doesn't sound much now but it was a huge story when it happened, as nobody had heard a thing.

You said that when you first went into the chalet, you didn't take the cameraman in with you. Why not?

In a situation like that, when people have died, walking in with a camera rolling is an excellent way to destroy any chance you have of getting an interview. That's from experience. Done it, it doesn't work. You can walk in and you might get people saying, 'Go away, we don't want to talk to you!' And some journalists will run that grab. But that's a very short play. I go in and try to be as respectful as I can. Interlaken was a case of that working. You walk in, softly spoken, you say, 'I wonder if anyone here might be able to tell me what happened, people back home in Australia would like to know.' Then they're likely to say, 'That guy outside from Channel 9, he seems reasonable.'

A lot of reporters don't like doing death knocks and of course they can be difficult, but I have found sometimes that people really do want to talk.

No doubt about it. I remember an old police reporter saying to me, when you do a death knock only two things will happen. One is they will tell you to get off their property right now, and you will get off the property immediately. Or they will invite you in and tell you where to plug in the lights. And it's true. It's exactly what happens. Some people do want to talk and it's incumbent on you to be respectful and not milk it for the wrong reasons. The secret is not to push it. When it's obvious somebody is not going to talk to you, go away.

Rounds and Foreign Correspondence

Once a journalist has some experience covering general news, they will often shift to reporting a round – a specific topic, such as sport, business, the arts or politics. A similar mid-career step is to become a foreign correspondent. A rounds reporter and a correspondent perform similar roles, in that each is assigned a beat: one subject-based and the other geographic.

The benefit of covering a round or a defined region is that a journalist has a chance to cultivate deeper contacts, build broader knowledge, and offer greater context and history in their reporting. The risk is that once a reporter becomes an expert in a particular field, they will assume too much knowledge on the part of the audience and litter their stories with jargon. There can also be a danger that the reporter will pull their punches in order to avoid alienating contacts they must deal with week after week, a tendency that must be resisted.

Lisa Millar

Lisa Millar began her career in newspapers at The Gympie Times *and Brisbane's* Sun. *In her early years as a journalist, she worked political rounds in both the Queensland and federal press galleries. In the latter part of her career, she became one of the ABC's most experienced foreign correspondents, with multiple postings in the US and the UK. She now co-anchors the ABC's* News Breakfast *program. She also spent a decade on the board of the Dart Center for Journalism and Trauma, and has written about her adventures in journalism in her memoir,* Daring to Fly.

You started in journalism in the 1980s on a regional newspaper in Queensland. What kinds of things did you do?

I started as a cadet, the bottom rank. I did the horoscope for the newspaper and I would make up my own when I got bored! One of the most valuable things – this is in the first six months – was that I looked after the letters to the editor. People hand-delivered written letters, which meant that you were always in very close contact with people in the community. Then I did local council rounds around Gympie, so I would drive to whatever town and spend the whole day doing the council meeting. I'd do Magistrates Court – we looked for any well-known local business people who had been picked up drink driving or whatever. I also did police rounds, which involved ringing about ten stations around Gympie.

What do you feel are the lessons from that early grounding that you've carried with you through your career?

Accuracy, because you're in a small community and if you get something wrong, then the person down the street is going to tell you about it. To not be intimidated by people in authority, even though you might have close connections with them. You may be seeing the mayor at your tennis fixtures on the weekend but you still need to report as firmly and aggressively and proactively as you would on any other situation. And also I learned, I think, that you weren't just there to be writing the bad news, you were actually there to help foster a community as well.

What do you think are the basic skills that a good journalist should try to cultivate?

Curiosity is number one. If I'm out anywhere with another journalist socially and something's going on at the end of the street and they're not interested in finding out what's going on, then I just think they're in the wrong industry.

If you're out and about and you see something, what do you do?

I did it just yesterday. I saw police cars gathered down on the beach where I live, and I thought there had either been an accident in the water or a shark sighting. I took my phone down there, getting ready to record some video because I thought it might be useful. I always think it's better to inquire and get the information and get the video in the can, to ask the question and then discover you don't need to use it, than to regret that you didn't ask the questions or film an event. You don't check in and out of your journalism job. That should be something that's with you all the time.

You went to Brisbane, after Gympie, and you worked on *The Sun* newspaper on police rounds. How do you start a round?

When I was appointed, I was given a list of numbers of all the police stations in Queensland. I was given the media person for the police in Brisbane, and I was told what the basics of the job were. You've got this top layer of basic numbers and information, and then you have to work out who's underneath that layer. There will be an area commander for police and you want the name of that person so you can ask for them by name when you ring. Also, come up with something to ask better than 'Has anything been happening?' If you say that to a police officer, they will say no. It's just what they consider their job. It's like you asking me, 'Did anything happen on breakfast television this morning?' I would say, 'Nah, it was fine,' because I'm used to it, it's my job. But actually, I did three hours of live television, we did a live cross to Glasgow, you know. . . things happened, stuff mucked up. You've got to find a way to form your questions to elicit information that is not just going to be a no or a yes.

How do you do that?

The questions I would start asking were, 'Did you get much of a break through the night?' and they would then say, 'Oh yeah, we were at Maccas for an hour,' or, 'Oh God, we didn't get a break at all.' 'Oh, how come you didn't get a break?' 'Oh, we were at the car crash on the highway.' And so on.

What I would also do, back in the day, it doesn't matter if it's on paper or on a phone, is that every single person I came into contact with, I would take their number. Whether it was a victim of crime, whether it was a young constable. I do it to this day. If I meet people, the owner of a cafe down the road, I take their number. You never know when, as a journalist, you might need that particular number. You cannot start too early in developing a contact book. And the danger is to think that the only people who go into your contact book should be important people. If there's an earthquake on the street where that cafe was, well, that person is now the important person.

On police rounds, did you have to do many death knocks?

Yes, I did, almost every second day or so.

What's your advice about how to handle one?

I do think there are times where people want to talk after a trauma. As a journalist, you're often approaching them quite soon afterwards. If you get a no, then that is a no, you can't push someone. You certainly can't badger them. You can't threaten them with bad publicity if they don't give you the story or they talk to somebody else. Unfortunately, I know that there are reporters who operate that way, and I would encourage people reading this to know that you can successfully elicit incredible stories from people while acting empathetically, compassionately, intelligently.

My advice is to try and approach through a relative. Explain to them very clearly what you're offering. Don't fib. Don't tell them that you can give them a 1500-word feature about their loved one if you can't.

Spelling people's names incorrectly . . . people who've gone through trauma, to have errors and inaccuracies, I think is just one of the worst sins, because you're adding to the pain. They've lost someone in their lives and then you as a journalist couldn't even bother to get the spelling right of that person's name. Basic stuff like that is so important.

You've got to empower people who have been disempowered by grief and trauma, give them options that make them feel like they are in control of the situation. Don't say to someone, 'Stand right here, we're going to do it here because the light's right.' It's like, 'Where would you like to do this? Would you feel more comfortable in your garden? Would you feel more comfortable in your home?' And also say to them before you're rolling or recording, 'What is the message that you would like to get through here? So I can be sure, in this interview, that I am caring for the reason you have done this.'

The other thing is, it is okay as a journalist to have empathy and to feel someone's grief and to feel that pain, but don't ever try to tell them that you understand it, or you know just how they feel. They're the wrong words to use.

With a round, you don't simply cover a story and move on, you're dealing with the same people all the time. How do you repair relations after you've covered a story that one of your contacts might not like?

If you're a journalist who adheres to accurate reporting and fairness, then even if someone does not like a story, they are going to have to accept that it was right. How do you repair relations? You never apologise for what you've done. If you're reporting accurately, it's not a sense of having to say, 'Oh, look, sorry, I had to do that, the boss made me.' It's that, you know, this was fair and accurate. I think anyone who is in a position, whether it's in the police or politics, will know that there will be stories that are going to make them look bad. People will profess irritation and anger, but it generally passes. If you wait long enough, they'll get over it.

In 2001, you went on your first foreign posting to Washington, DC, and you've done two more since, one to Washington and one to London. When you are sent to cover a major international disaster, what do you take?

Well, it depends what country it's in. Power adaptors, extra batteries for everything. You want to pack as little clothing as possible, though, because you're going to have camera gear if you're working with a camera operator. You never know what might happen.

For example, the Italian earthquake that I covered, the cameraman and I turned up at Rome airport and the only car they had to give us was a Fiat Panda. It was tiny and we needed to get all our gear in there. Now if I had packed a different jacket for every day that I was there, we wouldn't have been able to fit into that car, we would not have been able to get to that emergency.

It's good to have the Google Translate app on your phone so you can be ready to hit the ground running.

What else do you take? Notepads, pens, plenty of identification. Depending if you're going into a natural disaster, you take baby wipes, hand sanitiser, masks, because we needed masks well before covid for dust and disease. Your most comfortable shoes.

You do not try to be a glamorous TV presenter when you're going to an unfolding disaster.

Sticking with the Italian earthquake, how does it work logistically when you arrive in a country where you don't speak the language and you don't know a single person?

We tried to hire a fixer, but she had already been booked by Channel 7.

What's a fixer?

A fixer is a local who you employ on a per-day basis to travel with you. You pay their accommodation and food and fee, and use them for however long you need. They speak the language and they have contacts that help you get the stories you need. They translate for you. They get you through police roadblocks. They read the local papers every morning to see if you're missing something because you don't speak that language.

One other thing I should mention: when you turn up at events like this, you find out the agencies who you might be doing your live crosses with – AP, Reuters, EU – and your foreign desk may have booked you a time slot with those agencies. The advent of the liveU [a portable transmission device] has meant that we don't need to use those agencies as much as we did in the past, but sometimes, the liveU signal may not be good and you don't want to miss your slot if you're the lead story, so you will go to the satellite truck and book a time with them. Those people are invaluable. You form a relationship with them because these are the people who can save your arse. You rock up and find out where they are, and even if you haven't booked any time with them to do live crosses, you say g'day, you find out who the staff is, ask them if you can go and get them anything, because they may have been chained to a camera for twelve hours. They might remember that and help you later.

And then you also rely on the foreign desk in Sydney to alert you to messages about press conferences or other things you may not be aware of because you're deep in the story on the ground.

What is the foreign desk?

The foreign desk is a group of people at head office coordinating the overseas news bureaux. They will be across stories that are being assigned. If emergencies happen, and stories break, they will decide how they're going to be covered. And they also keep across the wires and the information coming in, whether it's on Twitter or other social media, and feed that information back to you. They also are there to make sure that you're staying safe. So you make arrangements to connect with them, especially if you're in an area that's dangerous, to let them know you're okay.

How do you manage your fear and anxiety when you're sent on a dangerous assignment? I'm thinking of the London Bridge terrorist attacks.

There is nothing wrong with admitting that you're nervous or slightly scared about a situation. When I arrived on the scene I was by myself, we couldn't get the cameraman to join me initially, and they still believed there were terrorists loose. And so the police were very agitated. You have to box it up, because you can't let fear take over. I went straight to the cordoned-off area, spoke to a police officer: 'Can I get beyond this point?' No, he said. 'What's down there to the right?' I asked. 'Where is the police search?' You just get as much information as you can and then process how you're going to use it. The first thing you've got to think about is 'How do I get something on air? How do I get this news information back?'

Now, I was just a reporter who had been at a party and all I had was a mobile phone. On that occasion, people were coming out of the cordoned-off area because they'd been at restaurants and cafes and they were terrified. They had silver blankets around them to keep them warm, some of them were bloodied because they had either tried to protect someone who'd been stabbed or they'd been injured themselves. And I would go up to them, I would say to them, 'Are you okay?' Some of them wanted to know how to get a taxi, how to get home. And because it was my local area, I was able to help them with that. But I would say, 'Before you go, can I talk to you? Can I interview you?' I had my phone, and I always keep my phone fully charged, so I would take a photo of someone, tweet the photo with what they had told me – with their permission, of course – and then I would pass the phone over to them and say, 'Are you happy to speak live on television to Australia?' and they would then speak. That was how I managed to get content out. You're thinking, 'How can I do this? How can I keep myself safe?' And so I stayed at that cordoned-off area and got people coming out that way.

Last question. You are now studio-bound as the anchor of the ABC's *News Breakfast* program. What do you miss about being an on-the-road reporter?

The adrenaline of not knowing what any day might bring. It's addictive and I loved it. I love the fact that I could just indulge my inherent curiosity . . . like I would have a glass of gin in London and think, 'What is the story with gin and Britain?' And you know what I did? I found a gin tour for people who wanted to build their own distilleries. I did a four-minute radio report on it.

You've found a way to get paid to be a sticky beak.

I have nailed it!

Robert Penfold AM

The sign-off 'Robert Penfold, National Nine News' is one of the most recognised in Australian journalism. Robert was a foreign correspondent for close to forty years, based in London and Los Angeles. He covered many of the biggest international stories of our lifetimes, including the fall of the Berlin Wall, the Challenger space shuttle disaster, Nelson Mandela's prison release, the Balkans conflict, the 9/11 terrorist attacks, and Hurricane Katrina, for which he won a 2006 Walkley Award. He began his career at the Macarthur Advertiser *in Western Sydney before moving to television. Robert retired in 2019 and in 2020 he was awarded an Order of Australia for his services to the media and broadcast journalism.*

Some journalists really like investigations, some love working in the regions – what appealed to you about being a foreign correspondent?

What I loved about it was that I was already a big traveller. I met my wife Shar and she wanted to travel as well, so when I was about twenty-four I resigned from television news in Australia and – as Aussies do – went and lived in London. I had that adventurous spirit. When I was offered the opportunity to become foreign correspondent, I jumped at it straightaway. I thought, 'This is an opportunity for me to see the world at [Nine Network owner] Kerry Packer's expense, it's going to be terrific.'

One of the key challenges for a foreign correspondent is that you can be covering the biggest tragedy in the world but you might be pushed out of the news bulletin by local events at home. Local news always trumps foreign. How challenging is that when you're in the field?

It's heartbreaking. Having done the job for forty-odd years, I came to know that was always going to be the case.

In 2011, we went to Haiti one year after the earthquake. The government had estimated that 300,000 people had died in that quake. When we were there in 2010, we'd covered this quite exciting rescue of this young girl out of the rubble so we were going back to find her a year later and do this story. We go back, we gather the whole thing, get it all up and get the story out. I phoned through: 'We've got this great story.' 'Well, don't worry about filing it, maybe file it tomorrow.' I said, 'Why?' They said, 'It's flooding in Brisbane.'

All of Brisbane went under. 'Sorry, it's not getting a run.' From memory, I don't think we got a single story up from Haiti during the four or five days we were there. Eventually we were told to come home.

In that sort of scenario, would you argue the toss or accept it?

I suggested, 'Can't you run it on *Today*?', other ideas. They said, 'Send the story down and we'll see if we can get it in.' I said to the cameraman, 'There's no way [it's getting a run], the way they're talking about it.' We moved on, it's just one of those things. Sometimes it's tougher for the cameraman. It doesn't break my heart any more, it is what it is.

Did knowing that local news would always trump foreign news influence how much danger you were willing to put yourself in?

Never. I never thought of it that way. People are saying to me at the moment, 'Boy, I bet you wish you were in Ukraine now.' And I go, 'Do you know – I don't. I'm older and I'm probably more sensible. I am not sad that I'm not there at all, because it's danger-ous and I know reporters are gonna get shot.' Whereas back in the day, even though I had Shar and our young family, I went barrelling into those places. We got some terrific stuff, whether it be in Northern Ireland, Iraq, Soweto, or around Yugoslavia and Slovenia. Interestingly, I didn't worry too much about the danger of it. I did always ask the cameraman, 'Do you want to come or not?' I was always pretty careful – I wasn't the first one down the dirt track, I went later.

The things I saw around Europe, particularly, were some nasty situations. I remember once we were in a Belfast cemetery where the IRA were being buried. The British army made the unusual decision to stay away from the cemetery and let them do a traditional IRA funeral. But a Protestant got into the middle of it and threw hand grenades and started shooting – killed three people and wounded another fifty. And it was all happening around us.

Something a foreign correspondent has to get used to is this weird rollercoaster where one day you can be covering a tragedy like that, and the next week you're expected to cover the Academy Awards – and you can't be precious!

Yeah, you do the lot. I loved that, though. People ask, 'Who was the most fascinating person you ever interviewed?' Well, to me, it was [comedian] Robin Williams, who was just a great character. I used to go to the Oscars and watch all the colour go through. I loved doing the Oscars and I did every one of them until the day I left.

In these roles, you meet a lot of famous people, but every now and again, I'd meet someone so famous – say, a Hillary Clinton level of fame – and get this weird sense of, 'Oh my god, they're actually a real human being.'

Yeah, that's right. We'd go in and do those terrible junket interviews, where you go to a hotel, sit outside the door and, you know, Russell Crowe is sitting in the room. One reporter after the other goes in, and you've got three minutes to sit down opposite the person and get something. The nice thing about it was everybody loves Australians. It was a very handy thing. I would play up the Aussie thing very quickly. It would work in Italy, Greece, because they all have relatives in Leichhardt and Melbourne. England would put on that 'Bit better than you Australians', and then they'd have a joke and we'd talk cricket. South Africa was the same, even out in Soweto. And India, the minute we said we're Australian and you drop the name Shane Warne, there was an immediate connection.

Creating that instant rapport is very helpful.

Very much so, you have to use leverage. As an experienced journalist, you know you've got to keep that conversation going. You have to find something very quickly that you've got in common with that person before they walk away, or they don't want to know about you. It's making the connection. And that's a real talent in itself – being able to walk up to somebody cold, warm them up, then ask, 'By the way, would you mind standing there and doing a TV interview? Here's the cameraman, here's the sound recorder, here's the microphone, here's the lights.' It takes a bit of skill to be able to convince somebody to say yes.

That's hard enough in an English-speaking country, but when you're a foreign correspondent, you have to try to connect with people when you don't speak their language. Did you have any strategies you would deploy in that circumstance?

I'd always insist on an interpreter. That was a rule – I would always pay the money and just tell Sydney later. I learnt that very early on in the piece. I was roaming around Africa somewhere without an interpreter. It was just a mess, hopeless.

Often we would work through Reuters and so I would ask them, 'Hey, have you got any young uni students who might like to come out and earn $300 a day?' They very quickly would find their neighbour or their nephew or somebody. More often than not, that was the technique I used. When I went to Cuba, we got these young students and they made more money in a day than they would have in a month. I was so happy. They were terrific and they spoke beautiful English.

When you've been a foreign correspondent for a long time, how do you continue to bring fresh, outsider eyes to the country in which you're living and reporting?

It's to do with your inquisitiveness. I'm always interested to know a little bit more, ask a few more questions. When I go somewhere, it's always quite new to me – even if I go to Washington again. I'll always look for a new angle or try to find something different.

You know, an Australian prime minister visiting the White House is super-routine. He turns up, goes in, sits in the chair, the president's in the other chair, all of that. But I always look at it and say, 'Wow, this is a great experience and this is perhaps the first time somebody has seen this back in Australia.' You can never be blasé about an experience like that. If you just want to get a few pictures and go home again, that shows in your story.

When you've been living abroad for a long time, how do you keep in touch with the audience at home to get a sense of what issues they might care about?

Yeah, that's a very important thing for foreign correspondents – you can't get disconnected from home. As a result of that, I still to this day bring up *The Sydney Morning Herald* and have a peek at *The Age* or *The Herald Sun* or the Nine website every day. You talk to friends and family back home. You must keep in touch with what's happening.

Talk us through a disaster assignment. You see a breaking-news alert flash up on CNN, there's been a major gun massacre. What happens next?

Let's look at what happened, two years ago now, in Las Vegas, where a gunman got into a hotel, up on I think the fifteenth floor, broke the window and started shooting people at a country-music concert across the way. I was in the newsroom, it was early evening, and these reports started coming through. At that point it was obvious to me that it was more than five or ten people dead. It was Las Vegas and it was a big crowd. I got on the phone and said, 'There's a big shooting going on in Vegas. I don't think we even should muck around trying to fly there, we should go there *now*, alright? We'll set off, it's going to be a five-hour drive, but I can still be there before you get on air tonight. It'll be tight, but we'll still be there in time for the six o'clock news.' The second reporter we had here, I got her to stay in the studio at Nine in Los Angeles and she covered us from there while I was driving with the cameramen, full pelt.

If you're anywhere within five hours of where [the disaster is], you drive. You don't try to catch a plane. You're going to spend an hour and a half at the airport, another hour on the tarmac, one hour in the air, blah, blah, blah. Better to just bite the bullet and drive.

We made it in time for the evening news. Sadly now, there are other times when there are mass shootings and it's a toss-up whether to even go because there have been so many mass shootings here – a shocking thing to say. People are very wary about going to what isn't a 'major' catastrophe, as far as a shooting is concerned. The Australian and the world audience has become so used to seeing this here, when it's one or two or three people dead, that sadly, it drops down the bulletin very quickly. It shouldn't be the case, but it does.

Do you have any tips for dealing with extreme sleep deprivation?

You just have to push on. Have a Coke or a coffee and stay up. Somehow you always make it through. Then you crash for a while and you put on the alarm for three hours later.

What's the relationship like between the foreign correspondent and the desk back home?

That has to be fantastic. I say to every young reporter who's here, 'Don't spit the dummy, don't fight and scream at them, because they've already made their decision. There are twenty-seven of them in the newsroom and they're all nodding their head saying, "This is what we're going to do," you know? And you're the kid kicking the toys around upstairs, throwing a hissy fit, while you're out here at the expense of the company having a lovely time living in America. So shut up.'

Is there anything else you want to say about the art of foreign correspondence?

Yeah, probably one of the most important things is having a very understanding partner and not taking it for granted. I've been extraordinarily lucky with Shar, who loves travelling around the world and has loved the experience. But in London, we had three children under five and I was travelling pretty much endlessly. You can imagine what it was like – absolutely full-on. A young mum who's got all three children, trying to deal with all that and then me going into dangerous situations. The irony was that often her mother or my mother would call her and say, 'Boy, I don't know what Robert's thinking.' Shar would say, 'I don't know anything. I don't see the news here, I'm probably better off not knowing.'

There have been several situations – without getting too personal – where reporters have come on a posting with their partners. I know one person who went home one night and found the keys to the car on top of the television set and the apartment empty. He said, 'Boy, I was really surprised,' and all of us thought, 'Well, you shouldn't have been surprised.' When you come over with a family or partner, more often than not they've got nothing to do other than just stay home while you're galivanting around the place. It's not an easy time. It was a few years before I realised how much torment I probably put my poor partner through, and that she'd just put up with it, put on a brave face and pushed through.

Other than being conscious of how much strain the job can put on a family, is there anything a correspondent can do to help make life easier for their loved ones?

I didn't do this, but this is what I would do: you have to be strong enough to tell the boss before you go, 'I'm taking a family with me, and I hope you'll understand that there may be times where you'll want me to do [a story] but I'm going to ask the other reporter to go on that job because we've got a birthday party for my three-year-old.' These are terrible things to miss in your family. I would advise any person who's getting a foreign correspondent's job to lay out exactly to the head of news, who's sending you there, what your family situation is. Be very honest.

Do you think editors and news directors are sufficiently under-standing of those pressures?

I've found that they are, once you actually talk to them about it. But the young reporters who come over here don't want to even bring the subject up with them.

I certainly know the feeling that you cannot say no because you've been given this big job, or it's such a big story. But I've also learnt over the years that nobody at the other end is going to set the boundaries for you. The demand for news is insatiable, it's around the clock. If you don't set your own limits, nobody will do it for you.

That's exactly it. Back in Sydney, it's this: 'Well, he didn't complain. His wife's having a nervous breakdown, but he didn't say anything about it. I would've allowed him to go and do whatever he needed to fix it.'

When I was talking to the foreign desk, I got to know them. And you were saying earlier how important that relationship is – my relationship was very much to let them know about the family as well. 'We've got the birthday party this weekend.' So that they've always got in mind: 'He has a family thing, he's not the person I can call to stand there at three o'clock in the morning for a live cross.'

It might also make the difference with a story that's lineball. If they go, 'Oh actually, it's Rob's daughter's tenth birthday,' that might be the thing that makes them decide they don't need the story after all.

I think so. [If you're] doing an overseas posting, make it clear that you're taking a family with you and that they're a priority. It's so important.

Bridget Brennan

Bridget Brennan is the ABC's Indigenous Affairs Editor. She was previously the network's Europe Correspondent and has also worked in the US and in Hong Kong for CNN. In 2016, she was the Andrew Olle Scholar, an award granted annually to a mid-career journalist viewed as likely to become one of the ABC's top talents. It provides a year-long opportunity to work on the ABC's major programs alongside highly experienced journalists. In 2023, Bridget was one of the recipients of the Golden Quill award from the Melbourne Press Club for a Four Corners *report into violence against First Nations women. Bridget is a Dja Dja Wurrung and Yorta Yorta woman.*

When you're assigned a round, where do you start?

I always begin with the big national organisations. It can be advocacy organisations, non-profits. In my round, Indigenous affairs, they support so many people. If you have those relationships sorted, that can be a bedrock for your round. In Indigenous affairs, these organisations have been around for forty, fifty years: since the start of black activism, really, in the sixties and seventies, around childcare, health and education. If there's a big breaking story, they're often the organisations you need quickly.

I always find background chats with their policy people super-helpful. They're often willing to give you an hour to talk: 'These are the big issues we think the government should be focused on.'

From there, you can go to state organisations, community groups. People you've interviewed before, I go back to them all the time. They may be influential, powerful people or they can be totally unheard-of people, like elders who live in Wagga Wagga who just bring a great perspective.

How many stories do you self-generate and how many are assigned?

These days they're all self-generated unless there's a huge breaking story. Sometimes I get a call from the desk at 8 a.m. to say, 'There's a big national story, we need you on it.'

That's the way I like to work, I don't like to be too reactive. My sense of pride comes from stories I've generated or owned.

How do you generate your ideas?

Once you get your name out there, people tend to call you. There was a story I did about New South Wales south-coast fishing rights where a lot of people had been prosecuted under the Fisheries Act, but they were hunting on their own land. It was a big debate and turned into a national story. That came about because an elder contacted me after seeing my work and said, 'Why don't you come down and do this story with us?'

A lot of advocacy organisations want to give you a story as an exclusive and then give it to other media outlets the next day. That happens a lot with human rights and legal organisations who are doing a lot of pro bono work for Indigenous communities. They will be quite organised and say, 'These are the dates you can go to community, these are people you can talk to.'

They might give you material but then you might want to explore broader angles, perhaps talk to people with an opposing view. How do you manage those tensions and protect your independence?

You be upfront. You tell them if you're taking it on that it's your story and they don't own any part of it. 'We'll take your pitch, we think it's potentially an interesting story,' but we make it clear that we don't necessarily think it's valid, that it's the right perspective, or that we're championing a particular point of view or perspective. We're not cheerleaders for a cause. It's about being upfront from the get-go. It's saying, 'If I take this story on, you're going to have no control over the direction in which it goes.'

Usually, I think people get that. I've had one or two instances where I've had to have pretty strong words with organisations, where they are very proscriptive about how they want a story done, or they want to see parts of a story, which I never do.

Do you have to do any work managing expectations? Sometimes I've done stories where people have come to the media as a last resort, or they're telling their story because they want something to change. Sometimes media coverage causes change but often it doesn't.

You can never promise there will be an outcome from a story. In my round, we are giving a voice to people who have not typically been given much air space at all. It's like disability in the mainstream media. They [the interviewees] can be distrustful, rightfully so, because unfortunately a lot of journalists have done the wrong thing, or we haven't paid attention to these issues.

So I'm upfront that we can tell a story but we can't control the outcome. I don't know whether the prime minister is going to comment or whether it's going to change a law. We can only tell someone's story. If you're upfront about that from the beginning, it makes things much easier.

The advantage of covering a round is that you get to know the subject well and you build a bank of contacts. But what are the challenges of being on a round as opposed to covering general news?

The biggest challenge is that you do become quite known in your field. There are lots of different vested interests or points of view in the community, so when things get heated or passionate, you can sometimes cop a bit of flak. You sometimes have to do some tough reporting. That can be difficult.

It can also be difficult because you start getting a huge volume of story pitches. People go, 'There's a specialist, they'll want to cover this.' Literally 90 per cent of the pitches I get, I have to say, 'Sorry, we don't have time to do this.' That can be hard because you feel like you're letting people down. The reality is you have to turn down a lot of things even when you're working very hard.

Even though I enjoyed self-generating stories, every now and again when I was on a round, I would think it would be such

a relief to be back on general news and just walk in and be assigned something every day by the chief of staff.

Oh, absolutely! I can be quite jealous of journalists who get do quick turnaround stories.

Or the political reporters who are up the top of every program.

They get the lead every day! That's another challenge, I guess; you do have to sell your niche topic sometimes to the executive producers or network bosses. You have to be creative. Sometimes stories can be quite procedural, or they may only appeal to a small audience, so you need to be quite creative with your pitches about how it's going to sell to a large audience. I hate that word 'sell', but that's what we're talking about.

I guess if it's not something appealing in and of itself, because it's tough subject matter, it's persuading them why it's important to do it anyway.

For a long time Indigenous affairs was done badly and in a really boring manner. So we very much looked at our analytics and our data to see what stories would do well with audiences, and we started to think about who was going to be at the heart of our stories. Who would be the central characters, how they would relate to a large audience. That became the focus of our work and we started to get so much more traction.

Do you have any tips for deadline management?

I got a great tip from a colleague, which was to focus on only one story at a time. He was really good at going, 'Okay, I've got five stories I'm committed to but I'm going to park those for now, not make any calls, I'm going to go hell for leather on this one story and get it done, and get it done well.' On a round, you might be juggling quite a few stories at once and it's not a great way to work.

Also, when you're a foreign correspondent, in a matter of hours you might be filing a digital piece, radio news, current affairs, television news, and getting ready for your live crosses as well. There's probably more stuff I've forgotten! If you can go, 'Okay, who is going to be clamouring for a script first?' get that done first. Also, the piece of work you can't stand doing: get it done. I can pump out a TV news story very easily and I like writing them, but I hate [writing] radio news! Even though it's only thirty seconds, I can sit there for ages playing with it. So I would force myself to do that first and get it out of the way.

If you're a roundsperson or a foreign correspondent, you can also never be certain when major news might break, and then all your half-done stories get derailed.

Absolutely. Sometimes for months I cannot get to a story and I have to call contacts and say sorry. I think I'm getting a bit better at being realistic and saying to people, 'Look, I won't get to this until October.' Things take so much longer than you think they will. Something that you think will take fifteen minutes will take an hour.

Also, it's good to remember you can put your hand up for help. If you're in a newsroom and there are other people around, very rarely will people say they can't help. If you're really under the pump and drowning under work, it's so much better to put your hand up early. It can be hard when you're young because you think you have to do it all yourself. But we're all in it together, and someone will be able to send your grab off for you or call the network desk.

Do you prefer collaborative stories, such as the one you did for *Four Corners* on domestic violence, or do you prefer flying solo?

Most of the time I prefer to be in a collaboration because the stress is spread across more people! On your own, you can very much get into your own head and get fixated on certain ways of doing things. When you're on a team, you can be really creative and it's fantastic to have people who disagree with you. It's those moments where you've got somebody going, 'Mmm, I'm not sure about that . . .' or, 'I think we should go down this other road,' that's really useful for you.

There's so much pride in putting something out as a team. When you make a mistake as a team as well, you're owning it perhaps between two, three, four people. Maybe you all missed something and that can be easier than when you're on your own and you've fucked up. That can be really hard and you can beat yourself over the head for a long time.

How important do you think it is to the craft of journalism to be open to disagreement, to step outside your own views, not just on how stories can be done, but on issues you're covering?

So, so important. Especially for my round. There is a misguided view that Aboriginal people have the same view on political issues, for example. A lot of Aboriginal people have common life trajectories and we've faced a lot of the same traumatic things in our lives, but if you go out and talk to a wide range of Aboriginal and Torres Strait Islander people, there are some really divergent views. That's where I think Indigenous affairs journalism hasn't been done very well, because if you're not capturing that diversity of views and diversity of experience, it ends up reinforcing a really limited view of Aboriginal people to a non-Indigenous audience.

The referendum campaign for the Voice to Parliament is going to be a perfect example of that. There are going to be so many different views on this proposal in the Aboriginal community and the views are going to be so multilayered and nuanced. Sometimes when I talk to non-Indigenous people, they're quite taken aback to learn that not all Indigenous people think constitutional change is the right thing for them. I think that's because we've failed in journalism to present the hundreds and thousands of different views there are in the community.

You did a cadetship at the ABC. How did you actually learn what to do? Was it people teaching you, just watching others, all of the above?

It was all of the above. I was in the Sydney newsroom and it was pretty intimidating. I did feel like a sock in a tumble dryer most of the time! There was a lot of crying in the toilets.

We had great training as cadets. A lot of people say you have to learn on the job but I'm actually a big one for what we can learn at university and what we can learn in our newsroom training. I think it's really important. That's definitely how I learned to write news. I would also watch the news every night. Even if I wasn't assigned a story – which happens for weeks and weeks when you're a cadet – I'd watch the news each night and study some of my favourite journalists and the way they wrote.

Also, a supportive boss can be a godsend. I went to Darwin and I had two managers who would throw me in at the deep end and put me on a mining story or a politics story when I didn't feel ready. They really trusted me. That was the most nurturing environment and I learned heaps there.

I was lucky with that too. Bosses would give me a shot at doing things when I didn't have the experience on paper. The best thing was that they not only said, 'You can do it,' they said, 'I will help you do it.'

That's the best. 'You can do it, I will help you do it' is the best thing you can hear as a young journalist.

What would be your main tip for somebody starting out in journalism, for that person crying in the toilet every second day because it's overwhelming?

One of the things I say to young journalists is, 'You're going to have some really tough days. Someone is going tear your script to shreds and you will feel really deflated. You just need to remind yourself that somebody upstairs at *Four Corners* is having their script torn to shreds as well.' I think that can be one of the most difficult things in journalism. We have a lot of extra pairs of eyes on our work and a lot of opinions. We work in a really fast-paced environment, so sometimes the feedback can come across as quite cutting and tear your confidence down. But each time, if you can learn something about how to improve, then you're going to be so much better in a year's time, then in five years' time.

What I wish I had also done earlier was get an area of expertise. You will love journalism ten times more when you find an area that you're really passionate about. That's not to say general-news journalists aren't passionate – they're passionate about the daily news cycle and breaking stories. But for me, there's just so much joy in becoming a subject-area expert. It's like unravelling all these threads. You go to this person, the next person, the next person. You feel like you're in a community and you're bringing stories that nobody else has.

Investigative Reporting

Regular journalism plus persistence plus time equals investigative journalism. There is a romance around investigative journalism, probably thanks to *All the President's Men* and the notion of reporters such as Bob Woodward and Carl Bernstein meeting Deep Throat contacts. But in real life it's less glamour than hard slog. (For my money, the most realistic film I've seen about the process of investigative journalism is the 2015 movie *Spotlight*, about *The Boston Globe*'s painstakingly slow and difficult investigation into the systemic cover-up of child sexual abuse by the Catholic Church. It perfectly captures the laborious and, at times, frustrating nature of this kind of reporting.)

Quality investigations can make the names of media organisations and reporters, and, of course, destroy the reputations of their subjects. Australian history is full of astounding investigative journalism that has undone political leaders, business bosses and union heavyweights, and achieved justice for everyday people who would have otherwise remained powerless. One of the most satisfying outcomes a journalist can experience is when their work causes positive change. Many reporters are drawn to investigations for this reason. The reality, though, is that this form of journalism can be exhausting, fruitless, and dangerous.

Kate McClymont AM

Kate McClymont is Chief Investigative Reporter at The Sydney Morning Herald. *Her investigations have exposed corruption in politics, unions and sport. She has won many awards, including the 2002 Gold Walkley for revealing that top rugby league team the Canterbury Bulldogs was breaching its salary cap, a story with enormous ramifications in sport, business and politics. Kate's journalism has resulted in several investigations by the New South Wales Independent Commission Against Corruption, most notably into Labor politician Eddie Obeid. She has co-authored two books,* He Who Must Be Obeid: The Untold Story *and* Dead Man Walking: The Murky World of Michael McGurk and Ron Medich. *In 2020 Kate McClymont was awarded an Order of Australia.*

Does an investigative reporter need different personality traits and skills to a general news reporter?

Yes and no. I think the skills are the same, it's more the amount of time it takes and being willing to do it that relates to personality.

For example, I don't mind making thirty-five calls and only one of those comes up. But if you're a daily news reporter, you don't have the time to do that. It can skew the way news is reported. Think about yourself: what if Leigh Sales was kidnapped and the journo got your school yearbook. They spoke to the third person on the left, the only person they could find, who said, 'Leigh Sales was a dreadful person.' That goes into the story. They haven't rung ten people to get a more comprehensive view because they just don't have time. But you do with investigative journalism. It relies on persistence, patience and doggedness.

You can start to file a story when you have only pieces of a puzzle, you don't need to have solved it. How do you decide when to start publishing?

Sometimes it's frustration. You know there's more out there but sometimes you just say to yourself, 'Right, I've got enough to write a story.' This is the beauty of newspapers: you can do a story – it can be little or big – and more information usually comes once people know you're looking. Sometimes you're inundated but you can also do a story and think, 'I've really nailed this, more people will come forward' – dead silence. You never know. It's funny, I've also had calls from people overseas, even years later, to say, 'I looked up criminal A and saw you've done stories on that person in the past.' It can be a really long process.

I presume if you file a story and no info comes in, that's a moment to think, 'Well, do we keep going or not?'

It depends how worthwhile you think the story is. You usually have a good idea about whether it's a big story or not and you move on. You get a feel for that. Sometimes you actually don't have any idea that you're on a big story. Once I was on something and I didn't even know that it was a good story until I went round to the sports editor and said, 'Hey, I'm looking at [allegations relating to the Oasis Stadium], but I've been given information that the Canterbury Bulldogs Rugby League team is a million dollars over the salary cap. Is that something you'd be interested in?' The story wins a Gold Walkley. Did I or Anne Davies [the co-reporter] have any idea we were onto a big thing? No, we did not.

You were working on something else?

Yes, I was following the money. You can't overemphasise how important that is – that old saying of 'follow the money' is still so true today. I was looking at the Oasis Stadium, this $900 million development – it had a basketball arena, water park, residential units. It was a partnership between the Liverpool Council, the Bulldogs and Macquarie Bank. We were following the fallout from a breakdown in relationships between the key players when we discovered that some of the money the council had put in was secretly being used to pay the footy players.

One thing that's interesting is when you do get information, it's often motivated by revenge or hubris. As a journalist, you have to keep in mind that nearly always you are being used. It doesn't mean that you can't do the story or that the information isn't correct, but you do have to keep on your guard. There are probably other things that you're not being told about the other person's role in whatever the story is. Fallings out between business partners – or divorces – are always the most opportune time for journalists.

You're also cognisant of the [need for the] person you are investigating not being tipped off too early. I've done stories in the past where word has got to the person very quickly, and they start threatening those who they think might talk. Sometimes it's actually played to my advantage, because the [threatened] person has been so angry that they've rung up to say, 'Are you looking at something? Because I've been warned off.'

Sometimes other people learn that you're doing the story and they volunteer information. Every call I make, I try to get two or three other names to follow up. Even if that person knows nothing, it's always worth saying, 'Who would you suggest I talk to? Can you advise where else I should look?' It's tilling the field as widely as you can.

Many times you have to cold-call strangers. Do you find that difficult?

Oh, it's always difficult. Trying to ring people and say, 'Look, I believe that you've been involved in some wrongdoing with X, Y or Z' – it's never pleasant. But I always try to talk to people in the least threatening way possible, to make people feel valued and appreciated: that you have lesser skills, they have the knowledge, and 'I'm just wondering if you might be able to help me with this.'

If you ring somebody and their initial reaction is no, they don't want to talk to you, what do you do?

Sometimes I email or text them saying, 'Look, I know you're reluctant to speak to me but these are the areas where you might be able to help.' Or you can try to go around the back door and get another friend of theirs to call them. Sometimes you know that the door has closed but it doesn't stop you from trying again. That's what's good about text messages and emails – even if they won't speak to you, you can get a message to them saying, 'Please have a think about it,' or, 'Why don't you just meet me for coffee and see for yourself?' Try those things.

I know speaking on the telephone is convenient and quick, but meeting someone face to face, you get so much more out of them. You have the time to chat, maybe show them photos or documents – it might prompt them. I often say, 'Look, here's my notepad, draw me a diagram of the key people,' or, 'Show me what you're trying to explain to me,' just to give them some investment in the process. I try to keep people involved in the outcome. I ring them and say, 'Thank you so much for that piece of information, that was really helpful.' People are very sceptical about journalists and feel that we just use and abuse them. If you try to make people feel as though you value and appreciate even the smallest thing they have done for you, it helps.

What about when you've got somebody who's really putting themselves on the line by giving you information – maybe they're trying to do so anonymously, or they're blowing the whistle on some form of corruption – and they want your assurance that they're going to be okay. How do you deal with that?

If you give your word that you are going to look after somebody, you absolutely must do that. You would have to go to jail rather than give them up. The basic tenet of journalism is trust. You would never burn a source or give a guarantee that you have no intention of keeping – you can't do that. If it comes to the crunch, and that person has said to you, 'I will never give evidence for you, I can never appear in any documents,' you have to consider whether you can go ahead and do the story. It's as simple as that. You can't think that your story is more important than the word that you've given to them. And if it means not doing the story, so be it.

Someone might come to you and say, 'This, this and this has happened,' and you go, 'Look, that's great, but I will have to go to that person and they'll possibly make allegations against you. I have to do both sides of the story, and you must be aware that this will happen.'

It's not fair to tell people that it's all going to be roses. Sometimes it's dreadful when you have to ring people up and say, 'Look, I've actually found out that you stole this or you did this.' But your obligation is always to your reader first. If someone comes to you with a story, and you give them a promise of anonymity, you have to keep that. But it doesn't mean that there aren't two sides to a story.

You mentioned earlier that divorces and business partnerships can be rich sources of stories. How else do you find stories?

In the most extraordinary ways. A lot of it is simple observation. One of my favourite ones was, a parent at a private school rang up to tell me about another parent at the school. He said, 'This guy's name is Michael Williamson.' I said, 'I don't know who that is.' He said, 'He's the head of the Health Services Union.' I said, 'Right . . .?' And he said, 'He's also National President of the Labor Party . . .' 'Yeah . . .?' He said, 'Well, he's got five children at private schools, and my understanding is that union bosses are on an income commensurate with their highest paid union member.' I said, 'Look, I don't know that, but I'll have a look at it.' He said, 'He and his wife, who doesn't work, both drive a top-of-the-range Mercedes-Benz, they've got five kids at private schools, they fly first-class.' But the thing that really angered him the most was that Michael Williamson constantly outbid them at the school charity auction.

I thought it was as good a reason as any to have a look at something. The first thing you do is ASIC searches. You see whether people have mortgages, what property they own. It took me about half an hour to find that he had a company, say it's called IT Solutions. I'm going through the annual report of the Health Services Union, and I see that IT Solutions is getting a million dollars a year to provide consultancy to the union. I went to the third-party declarations and, funnily enough, there was no declaration that the head of the union owned the company that was getting the million-dollar payment. I then went to the council records, see who's building their house, and I find the union architect has done the renovations on the home and that he's built the holiday home too. That's enough reason to start doing a story. In the end, he went to jail for five years. He'd stolen something like $20 million.

ASIC searches, council records, annual reports: how did you know where to look?

It was working with other journalists who helped me, like Marian Wilkinson and Colleen Ryan. Someone taking the time to say, 'Right, this is what you can do, this is what's available for you to use.'

But it's really expensive. ASIC searches aren't cheap. I could never do my job as a freelancer. Sometimes you'll do fifteen in a day, and they're about thirty dollars each. So you need the backing of a big organisation – for legal threats as well.

You're no stranger to legal threats, and even death threats. How do you deal with the fear of pissing people off?

You're gonna piss people off. If you didn't piss people off, you wouldn't be doing your job. You can't worry about that.

It's funny, sometimes people come up to me in the office and say, 'Perhaps you could look at this story? I don't have the stomach for it.' It might be a bikie gang or something. And I say, 'Why not?' and they say, 'The fear and terror is just too much for me and I don't want to do it.' I go, 'Right, pass it over.' I'm just an innately optimistic person. I think people might want you to stop what you're doing but they don't actually want to kill you. Well, that's something I cling to!

With these big investigations, you can collect an enormous amount of material. Do you have any particular method by which you organise that material?

Yes. I think one of the most useful tools is a timeline. It helps you organise in your mind what happened when. So often, as you're doing a timeline, you realise that events are connected – 'Oh my god, that email arrived at 2.20. At three o'clock, that person is seen on CCTV driving to X's house', or, 'Ian Macdonald has just been to see his departmental chiefs about a mine, and within half an hour, he's meeting Eddie Obeid.' It takes a bit of time but it's a simple method of keeping things organised in your own head.

Say you're sitting at your computer, it's a blank page in front of you, and you're thinking about your opening paragraph: what thoughts are going through your head?

What's the most crucial point of this story? What is the crucial news element? Okay, is it more important that he lied to a judge or that he stole the money? Or that he tried to threaten his colleagues? It's trying to not get too many things in the opening paragraph, so which one of those has more news value? Or more interest to people? Is that better in the second paragraph? It's those kinds of judgements you're making.

As you're writing, are you thinking stuff like, 'Use the active voice, cut the adjectives'?

Yes. And also trying not to have your voice – a judgmental voice – in there. You have to let the facts speak for themselves. If you want your reader to feel outrage, you must have the person in your story doing things that cause outrage.

You don't write, 'In an outrageous move, Mr Smith did blah, blah, blah.'

Exactly.

Is there anything you feel I haven't asked about that you think is useful knowledge?

Look, it's the treatment of other people. Even if the story's gone to air or print, it's so important to send a text or a note saying, 'Thank you so much for your help.' It's amazing how, later, they might tell somebody else.

Also, treat everyone equally – even the criminals. Treat them with respect. Everyone has a story to tell and it's up to us to listen, to be polite, to not be too judgey when they're telling you they've murdered somebody. Just try to be a decent human being and not give journalism a bad name.

It's that person's story and it's important to them. They're trusting you, putting it into the hands of an outsider. That does deserve respect.

It's amazing how many people have got out of jail and asked if we could meet. I initially think, 'Oh my god! No! They *do* wanna kill me!' I always ask them to come into the work canteen because I think they're not gonna kill me there. And it's surprising how many people say, 'Look, fair cop, guv. You treated me decently, but now can you look at my enemy? This is what you should be looking at.'

Hedley Thomas

Hedley Thomas is arguably the most accomplished investigative reporter in the history of Australian journalism, with seven Walkley awards to his name, including two Golds. He has spent his career with News Limited, mostly at The Courier-Mail *and* The Australian, *and his stories have prompted many major inquiries and exposed serious corruption and criminality. One of those led to his book* Sick to Death: A Manipulative Surgeon and a Health System in Crisis – a Disaster Waiting to Happen. *In 2018, he made a podcast for* The Australian *called 'The Teacher's Pet', which resulted in the conviction of Chris Dawson for murder almost forty years after the disappearance of his wife, Lynette. The podcast went to number one around the world, and at the time of writing has attracted some seventy million downloads, a groundbreaking feat for an Australian media organisation.*

Hedley, how did you learn to do journalism?

I started as a copy boy at *The Gold Coast Bulletin* in 1984, at the end of Year 12. The offer I got was to be this sort of jack-of-all-trades, lowest-rung errand boy. The advice from the editor was, 'You'll learn from journalists, photographers, compositors and page designers and then you'll have a cadetship.' It was a really important way for me at such a tender age to be immersed in every part of the paper, because I began to appreciate how the dynamics come together. There's a really symbiotic relationship as well between advertising and editorial.

It was the last year that typewriters were being used in newsrooms, so the copy was on paper. I would take that from wire baskets beside the journalists' typewriters to the subeditors and they would then work on it with pens.

Did you pay attention to what was in the copy that you collected and dropped off? And how it had been amended by the subeditors?

Yeah, I would study that, and sometimes take photocopies of what the journalists had written and just work out how the editors were changing it.

It's funny hearing you talk about the 'old days' of journalism, because now you're working in very cutting-edge technology and podcasting, which is a fairly new way to do investigative reporting.

I love podcast storytelling because I can go really deep and wide into a story. My wife says it's cos I love the sound of my own voice! I still have to satisfy people I'm interviewing that I understand what I'm talking about, and win their confidence; I have to satisfy the listenership that they'll get something interesting and informative; I have to satisfy the editors that there will be a story that could break new ground, that could be successful editorially, and hopefully also successful commercially.

Leigh, I was wondering about what makes the difference between a journalist who intuitively understands the essence or angles of a potentially complex issue and the journalist who just reports it once over lightly. I reckon one of the most valuable things for young journalists is exposure at an early stage to courtroom scenes involving really skilled barristers, who are experienced questioners, and [also involving] sometimes evasive witnesses. I've spoken to lots of people involved with university journalism courses and I say, 'Why the hell don't you get out of the lecture hall and take the students to a commission of inquiry? A Royal Commission? A Supreme Court cross-examination?' All these potential, free venues where they will see very sharp-witted lawyers refusing to take the deflection and evasion from the witness, maintaining focus, listening to what they're being told by the witness – who's an interviewee – and then developing a narrative to make their case. I had that experience at an early age and stage of my career and it really helped me a lot.

I find myself getting so frustrated listening to interviewers when it's obvious they're not actually listening to the last answer they got; they've usually got their pre-scripted questions. So often, they'll get a fantastic answer, or an answer that's crying out for a follow-up question, but they just move on, because that's not on their list.

Listening is such a core skill, and often a lot of the good follow-up questions are very basic, such as, 'Why?' or 'Can you tell me more about that?'

One hundred per cent. There's nothing worse than the questioner who's determined to almost orate an essay as part of the question.

Or the question becomes wrapped up in a couple of other questions so that it's convoluted and the interviewee is completely confused.

I felt that your podcast series 'The Teacher's Pet' should be a teaching tool for university journalism courses. The way you reported that highlighted so much about how to do top-notch journalism: the way you approached people, your manner in the interviews, the way you ran out of angles and had to think laterally about where to take the story next.

I'm really, really proud of what we achieved with 'The Teacher's Pet'. It was such a highwire act because we were producing an episode a week – from scratch, after the first five or six had been recorded. New material was then coming in. It was exhausting, but we got there.

For people unfamiliar with it, what is that series about and where did the idea to do it come from?

It came from an idea I had in 2001 because of a chance reading of a newspaper story in *The Daily Telegraph*, about the inquest into the disappearance of a woman called Lyn Dawson. The story recounted that there was this famous footballer, her husband, and he had been a schoolteacher who had this unusual relationship with a student. She was babysitting in the house and then the wife disappeared.

That teacher ended up leaving Sydney and he began teaching at Keebra Park State High in 1985, which was my school on the Gold Coast. I had left Keebra Park at the end of 1984, so we had no overlap, but I had the connection to the school. I just thought it was interesting – there's a local school and a Queensland angle.

As a features writer at *The Courier-Mail*, I thought this could be a remarkable weekend feature piece.

I got the go-ahead and went to Sydney for a few days and met Lyn Dawson's sister. And then I went to the Dee Why police station and read the brief of evidence that the coroner had seen. I sat there for the best part of a day, just taking notes. I was completely amazed by this story and I wrote a lengthy feature called 'Looking for Lyn'. It was a story I was personally quite moved by because of the circumstances: she had two daughters, who grew up believing their mother had left them. The allegation was that she'd been cold-bloodedly murdered so their father could be with his teenage girlfriend. It was so compelling, tragic, unresolved, and crying out for a broader treatment.

My father died in 2017, and after he died I wasn't sure whether I wanted to continue doing what I was doing in journalism – I went through a flat spot. If I stayed in journalism, I wanted to find something that would really motivate me. And I had toyed for a while with the idea of a podcast. I was grappling with 'What story do I already know relatively well that would be a great candidate for this kind of treatment? Of course – Lyn Dawson's story.'

Why were you keen on a podcast?

People were talking a lot about podcasts. I thought, 'Well what's going to be the longest form of journalism I can imagine? That has to be a podcast.' They weren't going to run 170,000 words of my writing on Lyn Dawson, but if I wrote that much over week-by-week episodes, [my editor] might not realise what was going on and I'd get away with it.

I also had this great belief that this case was capable of being solved, that it was an outrage that it hadn't led to proper action.

I felt that if I gave it a really good shake, and was able to find or reveal new evidence, there could be a positive outcome.

How did you begin investigating afresh all those years later?

I'm a bit of a stickler for not wanting to do any writing until I have scoured every archive, every source, looking for snippets of the story. It could be a big read or a documentary done years ago; it might be an obscure court file relating to one of the parties, completely unconnected to the core material. I want to have a really big starting folder of documents because that gives me confidence that I know as much as possible about what's going on. I had the luxury of time, and then the luxury of being able to receive, from Lyn's family, the police brief of evidence that went to the coroner. That gave me names, so I could start finding witnesses, and then find people who were mentioned in the statements who hadn't been interviewed. I just started to build from there.

It starts for me with just spending a month, two months, making dozens and dozens of calls and downloading, printing, photocopying everything I can possibly get. You read it and read it again. There's nothing worse than starting with all these random strands. It feels like a bowl of spaghetti – how do you untangle it?

I'm still stunned that people want to share as much as they do about their very personal lives with a complete stranger. When you've won people's trust, when they're persuaded that you're genuinely interested – it's not just a quick grab and then we move on – that's when I often get the best results.

I also find that when the interviewee reaches the end of their sentence, the normal thing most interviewers do is say something. Our brains are wired to do that. But a lot of the time I don't. I just shut up. There's this slightly awkward silence for a while and then the interviewee often, to kill that silence, speaks fluently and spontaneously and authentically about something they might not have been intending to say. They just roll, they fill the gap. It's often brilliant material that I can then develop and use.

I actually noticed this listening to 'The Teacher's Pet'. A few times I thought 'Oh god, this awkward silence that Hedley is just letting run.' I noticed it because I know myself how difficult it is to do. But then you heard the pay-off.

You know, I used to be terrified of doing these sorts of interviews. When I was at *The Courier-Mail*, back in the late eighties, early nineties, one of the things we used to do on the Sunday afternoon shift was ring up the then premier, Joh Bjelke-Petersen. It would usually be a follow-up from what was in *The Sunday Mail* that day – he might have announced something in relation to poker machines or a new grant, whatever.

And I just found myself frozen, or almost stammering in those interviews. My heart rate must have been through the roof. It wasn't because I didn't understand the issue, it was just confidence. I don't think you can teach confidence. I think it just comes over time with experience and realising that you can do justice to a story. Now, I don't get really nervous. My voice doesn't change, because I'm fifty-five. When I was twenty-four, that was happening quite a bit!

'The Teacher's Pet' won your second Gold Walkley. Your first was in 2007 for exposing the Australian Federal Police's pursuit

of a man called Dr Mohamed Haneef. Can you explain who Dr Haneef was and how he came to police attention?

He was an unassuming, overseas-trained doctor working at Gold Coast Hospital. He was accused of being involved in terrorism after his distant second cousin was involved in a really serious terror event in Glasgow. I was watching the story unfold and seeing the prejudice against Haneef.

It was 2007, an election year. [Prime Minister] John Howard had been promising crackdowns on terrorism. Suddenly, there was this sexy story on the Gold Coast about a Muslim doctor who, at least to the journalists writing it up, was leading a terrorist cell or planning something in Australia. He became public enemy number one.

I thought some of the coverage of him was very thin and I was fortunate that one of my contacts – a really good legal contact I'd known for years – said, 'I think this is complete bullshit.' I said, 'Yeah, it just doesn't feel like there's much substance there,' and he encouraged me to talk to one of Haneef's lawyers. He was just stunned at the misinformation that was clearly being leaked by authorities to journalists at Fairfax papers. My colleague Cameron Stewart [another senior reporter at *The Australian*], who I love, was also getting these lines from the AFP that were the complete opposite of the story that I understood to be the case. I thought there were serious questions and answers that were being completely ignored. It must have been tough for Chris Mitchell [then editor of *The Australian*], because he's got two senior reporters who he trusts and we've both got completely different takes on this one story. I remember my dad, who had a strong influence on my career, saying, 'You've really gone a long way out on a limb with this one. I support you but I hope you're right, cos there's no way back.'

Again, it comes back to a fundamental principle of journalism: checking whether the information being spouted by people in authority, from which they have something to benefit, is accurate.

Leigh, I don't often trust the people who make self-serving statements about our national security, or the operations of our infrastructure or our courts or DNA laboratories. This partly goes back to the training I had, without realising I was being trained, in commissions of inquiry in courtrooms, and watching people with well-rehearsed patters being absolutely torn apart because they just roll with those patters while the facts say otherwise. I was challenging the government with factual material – Mohamed's witness statement to the police. It wasn't subjective, it was incontrovertible, whereas what was coming out of [Minister] Kevin Andrews' mouth and John Howard's mouth was just rubbish. It was very disappointing to see journalists going along with it. It showed me how group media campaigning, an agenda, can really corrupt and distort the truth in journalism.

I don't care about making lots of friends in journalism. If I upset people with something I write, I don't care. Like, Twitter? Twatter. I'm not on it, it doesn't bother me. Too many journalists have become hostages to what they think is the perception of them by ugly, agenda-driven apparatchiks, and others on social media platforms.

If you pull your punches because you fear you might get people offside and be the subject of a pile-on, that's a big problem. The nature of the job means you must ask uncomfortable questions of people in power on all sides. Some of the Haneef coverage also demonstrated one of the risks you face if you're covering a round: dealing with the same contacts and being dependent on your access to them. They can mislead you.

That's true. If you're the national security writer, or the police rounds person, you're not going to – to use a crude term – shit in your nest. Good editors have journalists who are just free-ranging, not tied to a beat. But if you're a rounds person, you still have to be as rigorous as possible. You should be able to expose serious and damaging problems in that round.

Even if people don't like what you're reporting, when you're covering something long-term, you depend on your contacts and the audience respecting your integrity, your fairness, your commitment to accuracy and truth. My experience is mostly in federal politics, and while not every politician likes every inter-view I do, one would hope that they respect that I approach the job the same way regardless of who is in power.

Absolutely.

You spent a couple of years outside journalism, working for a resources company, and then you came back to journalism. Did that time away change how you approached the job when you returned to it?

A little bit. I left partly because I thought, 'Right, I've just won a Gold Walkley, I'm never gonna get any better than this.' I thought there was this weight of expectation – what's he gonna do next? I just thought, 'I'll do something else, I've peaked.'

I worked with Queensland Gas, and later BG Group, for a while as one of their senior comms people. It did make me realise that a lot of journalists, at least in the resources sector, could get much better stories if they were more rigorous. It made me a little bit disappointed that there weren't more journalists with an investigative eye. I never told any lies in investor relations, but it's what you leave out that's waiting to be extracted. It taught me that every communications manager, every spin doctor, is holding back. They know there are skeletons and they don't want you to find them. Going back to journalism and knowing that – cos I'd practised it – made me more confident and more determined.

Marian Wilkinson

Marian Wilkinson has been a trailblazer in the Australian media, part of a group of journalists who spearheaded a resurgence of investigative journalism in Australia in the 1980s. She was the first female Executive Producer of ABC TV's flagship Four Corners *program. She has also been a Deputy Editor and Washington correspondent for* The Sydney Morning Herald. *She is the author of three books:* The Fixer: The Untold Story of Graham Richardson; Dark Victory, *co-written with David Marr; and* The Carbon Club. *She has two Walkley awards for journalism, along with many other accolades. In 2018, she was inducted into Melbourne Press Club's Australian Media Hall of Fame.*

What's the first really big story you remember breaking?

The one I probably learned the most from was in 1981. I had been reporting on crime and corruption for *The National Times*, which was a weekly newspaper, quite famous for those kinds of stories. The story concerned the New South Wales Assistant

Commissioner of Police, Bill Allen. He was interesting because he'd been hand-picked by the Premier, Neville Wran. There were a lot of rumours about him that he may have had links to organised crime figures. I got a tip-off that the federal police were investigating him. That was a pretty bloody big story.

I didn't run it straightaway and that was the most interesting part, and what really had an impact on me. I had got a call from a very senior federal police officer who said, 'You're right, this is happening, but can you not run the story, because you're going to blow our investigation.' I was in my twenties at the time. I used to have very combative relations with police and the government over corruption issues. I discussed it with my editors and we held it, because it was the most responsible way to go. We did eventually run it and Allen ended up before a police tribunal and the premier was embarrassed.

It taught me for the first time that on these big corruption stories, pretty much everyone from the premier to the prime minister knows what's going on. If you're covering these kinds of stories, you have to deal with that big league and you have to deal with it in a way that you can live with personally and as a journalist. That was a big moment for me, when I matured as a journalist.

How difficult is it to publish something when you're certain it's right but nonetheless you know that when you publish, it's going to have a massive impact?

It's always difficult. I talked to Kate McClymont about this not long ago and she said to me that before she runs a big story, she always has a knot in her stomach, feels physically sick. I feel the same, because you know the person who's the subject of the story will come back at you. Once in a blue moon, you get somebody who goes, 'You got me guv, I'm resigning, goodbye.' But powerful people almost always fight – a lawsuit, defamation threats, it goes on and on – and often quite viciously, dropping stories about you to other media, going to your bosses. I certainly had cases when I was at *The National Times* when Sir Peter Abeles, a very powerful businessman at the time, went to one of the Fairfaxes [the owners] to try to get my story stopped.

What kind of things do you tell yourself, or do, to give yourself the emotional energy to withstand that kind of pressure?

It took me, Leigh, a long time to learn that. I found it very difficult in my twenties. I was incredibly lucky because I had strong journalism mentors around me: Brian Toohey, Evan Whitton, Paul Kelly and David Marr as my editors and colleagues. They were really tough, and they taught me to be really tough in journalism. I think they taught me to behave a lot tougher than I actually was.

You were the Executive Producer of *Four Corners* from 1990 to 1992, the first female in the role. You had to manage a team of mostly male reporters who were all very strong people: Chris Masters, Paul Barry, Tony Jones, and so on. How was it doing that job in that era as a woman?

Really tough. The job, anyway. I specifically said I only wanted to do it for a short amount of time. In my heart, I was always a reporter, not a manager, but I did have a passion for the stories. I think it's fair to say that not only because I was a woman, but also because I was young, there was a lot of pushback. Also because I had come out of print and not television. But I learnt a lot from it.

People draw a distinction between a journalist and an investigative journalist. What do you think the difference is?

A lot of it is to do with time, but also whether you want to be one or the other. I have gone between the two because it is very hard to be an investigative journalist if you want to do daily reporting. Impossible, actually. For an investigative journalist, you need a very strong editor or manager who you're reporting to and you must be given time. You then have to do this painstaking, often frustrating work. Sometimes you pull it off, but many times you don't. It's a very difficult road to hoe. I've been a daily journalist for periods and I think it makes you a much better investigative journalist, because you understand how the daily flow of news and information works.

Why do you think that helps?

You get to learn how government structures work. You would know, Leigh, because you've done some really big rounds: you get to know how a politician's office works, how the bureaucracy works, because you're trying to pull together information on a daily basis on all sorts of different stories. You learn how a department interacts with the minister's office. You learn how business is involved with government, and which consultancy is producing a report that the government will release. It's all those things that are a real education in how power works.

A journalist with a round has the advantage that they get familiar with a beat, they have contacts. An investigative reporter is often dropped onto a story with none of that, but with the expectation that they will uncover new information. What's the first thing you do in that situation?

Depending on the story, I would usually talk to my colleagues who cover the issue as a daily round. If you're lucky enough to work in a collaborative news organisation, say if you're on *Four Corners*, you can speak to ABC News reporters. They can be very generous in getting you to first base.

Then the most important thing is to research, research, research, but hone it. Don't go too wide or you'll get lost down a rabbit hole. Work out what you're actually trying to find out. Then before you contact people, either the subject of your investigation or the person you want to woo as your whistleblower, find out as much as you can about them and who they know. The more you understand about them, the more you are going to be able to pull them across the line.

How do you pull somebody across the line?

It's really hard sometimes. You often get an instinct from the beginning about whether they do want to tell you their story. With a lot of people, particularly someone who's at the centre of the story, you can tell from the outset if, for example, they've done a confidentiality agreement for a bucketload of money and they're never going to talk.

I got a big insight into this from a senior public relations person in Sydney. She said to me that the majority of journalists who contact her clients clearly know bugger all about the stories they're chasing and she would have no difficulty flicking them off. So the key is to know a lot before you get in contact with an interviewee.

A little device that really helps is to try to find out something they don't know but that may intrigue them about the story. That's a really good way to keep them on the phone.

If it's a whistleblower, sometimes they're taking a considerable risk, sometimes with their job, sometimes legally. How do you juggle the balance between getting them to talk and protecting their interests?

That's one of the biggest issues in investigative journalism, because we don't have good whistleblower protection in this country. I feel I haven't always done it that well. I think about that a lot now when I talk to people and I try to lay out the consequences for them. If it's a really important story, it's probably going to fuck up their life in a big way. The journalist has to be honest with them about that. There's also a limited amount of emotional support you can offer them. It's important to tell them that at the outset.

You did a story in the late 1980s that was very famous and won a Walkley Award, in which you got a whole lot of Liberal coup leaders to spill the beans about how they deposed John Howard as Opposition Leader in favour of Andrew Peacock. Why did they all talk and did they regret it later?

Last part first: yes, they certainly did regret it later, very much! I worked on that with Monica Attard; she was a researcher at *Four Corners* and I was a reporter. The story of the coup was quite well known in terms of who was involved. The players had been named. It was a matter of how we could do this on television.

Monica knew a lot about the story and had followed it closely. Both of us did initial off-the-record interviews with some of the players. It was then about persuading a couple of them over the line. We knew that if we got one, we would get at least two. It was basically a case of saying, 'This was your work, it has produced this "brilliant" outcome, we would like to tell your story on television.' Maybe it was the effect of two young women on men who were high on the adrenalin of their achievement, I don't know. What did help was, when we started the on-camera conversations, I had all the details of what had happened at my fingertips. The more I could elevate the conversation to an insider conversation, to the minutiae of what they had done, the more they opened up. That on-camera part of it really came alive because I tried to talk to them almost like I was another Liberal Party operative.

How common a device is that in journalism, trying to be in some way relatable to the person you're interviewing, trying to fit into their culture?

Critical. If somebody thinks you're talking their language, they're much more willing to open up. I've found it with business people, politicians in particular, backroom operators; it's a device I've tried to use ever since that Howard/Peacock story. I don't think it's at all duplicitous. I think what you're trying to do is get them off-script, off their talking points – where they will stay as long as they can – and into another kind of conversation.

How do you come up with your story ideas?

I'm one of those annoying journalists that every time I pick up a newspaper – I read three of them online first, *The Australian*, *The Australian Financial Review* and *The Sydney Morning Herald*, and then the hard copies too – I go through everything from the front page to the gossip pages to the real estate column. I think, 'Oh, that's interesting! Why was he sitting with her at the tennis?' I have a mind that loves piecing things together. I do it in the context of power structures, whether it's government, business, the public service. I love seeing how those things interact. A lot of ideas come out of that reading.

A story you reported for *Four Corners* in 2011 was titled 'The Inside Man'. Who was the inside man?

The inside man was a famous investigator in the New South Wales Crime Commission called Mark Standen. He was legendary, both in the New South Wales police but also nationally, in the government and among lawyers in town, because he was considered the state's top investigator into organised crime. He was one of those characters who had old-school instincts about how to track organised crime, but he also had this vast apparatus in New South Wales behind him. He had the power, he had the reputation, and he turned out to be a criminal himself. He was busted, he went on trial, and I just thought, 'This is a fabulous story,' and I wanted to tell the story of that trial and his downfall.

The first step in journalism is the identification of a story, but with this particular story the events were in the past; the trial, being inside a courtroom, provided no pictures; and Mark Standen was in custody, so not going to be giving an interview. What made you think, 'Here's what I'd love to do: make forty-five minutes of television on something that has no pictures and no available talent'?

[*laughs*] People would say that's why I'm a print journalist who's never really made the transition to television! The Executive Producer, Sue Spencer, was both intrigued and horrified for the reasons you mention.

The first time I thought it could make a TV story was when I found out there were hours of audio tape and there was some video surveillance of Standen and his partner in crime. One of the first things I did was set up conversations with the barrister prosecuting the case and the defence barrister and the court officials. What I said to all of them was, 'This is an amazing story whatever happens, whether he's acquitted or convicted. What you do in the courtroom will have huge ramifications for New South Wales and also around the country. What I want to do is get as much of the exhibit material on the record and available to *Four Corners* as we can.' They were all very open to that because they wanted it to be an open trial, so that helped enormously.

We worked out what we had in video and what we had only in audio. It was all the crims talking to each other; it was like an episode of *Underbelly*. We then worked out what bits we could best reconstruct. There was an amazing scene in a car park where Mark Standen was busted by federal police. There were scenes around the city, where he had been meeting with his criminal partner and having these really dodgy conversations. There were incriminating phone calls in a car. Janine Cohen, the producer, ran through all these actors' pictures and we found this man who looked exactly like Standen, and that really helped us with the reconstructions. We approached it almost like a docudrama.

The use of reconstructions in television journalism can be controversial. When do you think they're appropriate?

My feeling was that this was a classic case where they could be used because we had the tapes, the transcripts, and we had the context of the trial. We knew at which stage of the conspiracy these events occurred, so we had the correct timeline. Where reconstructions get dodgy is when the reporter is trying to put words in the mouth of people, or they're trying to make it a lot more dramatic than it was. You have to be incredibly careful, because you think somebody is just acting out words but *how* they say words really matters. Luckily, we had tapes of the real people speaking, so we knew what they were emphasising and what they weren't.

Do you start writing before you've gathered all the material?

Yes. I always write a shooting script, a structure. It's partly to keep me, the researcher and the producer on track, so we aren't going down rabbit holes. That's not to say we may not have to change tack and start again, but by and large, once you've done the research, you should know where you're going.

What's in a shooting script?

For something like *Four Corners* or *7.30*, it should be based around the talent who are going to come on, and the sequences that will tell the visual story. For example, if you're interviewing a farmer, you want that farmer to be doing something on the farm. It gets much trickier when it's a story with a lot of complex material. You have to think then how to illustrate it. The shooting script allows you to put that together and you very quickly see where the gaps are. You might say, 'I've got all this complex material and nobody to explain it. Is there a commentator we can get in to explain it to the audience in simple language? Or is there a graphic that can do this much better than some video?'

You're now freelancing, and the first thing you did after leaving *Four Corners* was write a book about climate change called *The Carbon Club*. What drove that decision?

I decided I had to focus on something that really mattered to me. Freelance work is not very profitable and it usually takes a lot more time than you think, but right now it works for me. I had done the environment round for *The Sydney Morning Herald* in the 2000s, covering climate change. Climate change is a bloody hard topic for the general public. They know it's important but it's a bit like, 'Enough already, I know what it's about, just get on with it.' But I strongly believe today it's more critically important than ever to cover. The transition that the world has to go through in the next two decades is going to massively disrupt our lives, our business structures and our politics, and I think it's really important to get on top of that. For me, as a reporter, climate change is unfinished business.

Features and Books

Some journalists thrive on the adrenalin of daily news and the discipline required to convey information with brevity; others are far more interested in the latitude and depth afforded by long-form journalism, such as feature articles, documentaries or books.

Every journalist who makes a career in long-form has their own unique way of going about such a complex endeavour, learned through experience and often from the pain of trial and error. Sometimes they borrow narrative techniques from fiction and TV drama, but the biggest difference between these forms is the inability in journalism to resort to invention. No matter how inconvenient, the journalist is constrained by the facts, and more often than not they will be writing about something of which they have an incomplete picture.

Features and Books

Trent Dalton

Trent Dalton is a feature writer for The Weekend Australian Maga-zine *and previously worked at* The Courier-Mail. *He is a two-time Walkley Award winner for excellence in journalism, and a four-time winner of the national News Awards Features Journalist of the Year. He is also a bestselling novelist: his* Boy Swallows Universe *is the fastest-selling Australian debut novel ever and has won many major literary prizes. Trent is also the author of* All Our Shimmering Skies *and the nonfiction collection* Love Stories.

Trent, one of the things that strikes me every time I write non-fiction is that I can only work with what's in front of me. If a person doesn't remember something, if they're not cooperative, if they aren't good talent, that's all you have and you have to adapt.

That's it. I've had great lessons from early editors who've said just that. I'm like, 'Oh my god, he didn't say much,' and they're like, 'Well, that's not good enough. It's your job to get more.' That's powerful stuff to remember. Like, maybe there's somebody else I can call, maybe I won't stop picking the phone up until I do get more insights.

That is inhibiting sometimes but it's so expansive as well. You're in someone's living room and your job is to listen and get all the quotes. I have my recorder and my notepad. I let the recorder get the words and the notepad is documenting the pictures in the photo frames, the tattoos on the person's shoulder, the grazes festering on the kneecap. That's the cool stuff. Fiction, you have to make all that stuff up – nonfiction, it's there!

Do you show up for a story with a list of questions? Or do you just go with the flow of the conversation?

I sometimes have really well-researched questions. But then I don't refer to them unless I'm totally desperate. I always read over my questions, know exactly where I want to go, and have a million questions up my sleeve that I can go to the minute the conversation dies down a touch.

The key is this idea that the subject will open a window and it's our job to open it further. It's those moments that I missed when I was a twenty-one-year-old novice because I was always referring back to my questions. Like, 'Oh, that's when Mark died, but don't worry about that. That's another story.' It's our job to go, 'I'm sorry, but you just said that thing about Mark. I'd really love you to unpack that for me, if you don't mind.' And invariably, they won't mind at all. Maybe someone hasn't asked about Mark in frickin five years, and they really appreciate you doing so. So that's where, over the years, I've started to realise it's really about that human-nature stuff more than what's on your little question page.

Oftentimes, it's that moment when you have been a bit rude. This isn't a normal conversation, this is a feature article you're trying to piece together. In my waking life, I'd never interrupt someone's thoughts to ask something invasive. But when you're in that mode, you've gotta be awkward.

You can pretty much ask anything if you preface it by saying, 'I hope I don't seem insensitive, and you don't have to answer this if you don't want to, but blah, blah, blah.' If people have opened the door themselves, they will almost always go through it.

Oh, Leigh, that is powerful. I phrase that sentence in so many different ways. Sometimes I'll say that like, 'Mate, please tell me to fuck off . . .', or, 'Listen, I know this is so hard to talk about. But if you don't mind, I think we might be able to go places that mean a lot to people.' And you're more than okay if they do tell you to eff off. It's just you being honest and not being devious in the chat. Towards the back end of my feature writing in the past ten years, that's been so much more powerful than me trying to weave my way and trick people into giving me something through elaborate questioning. It's been so good just to be open and go, 'Hey, here's the elephant in the room. Let's go there together.'

Do you ever show people in the story what you've written before it's published?

Great question. I interviewed Natalie Joyce, Barnaby's [the then Deputy Prime Minister's] wife, around the time when it was all really intense with their relationship. It was a case where I didn't want to make things even harder for her [their marriage was breaking down in public and Mr Joyce's lover was pregnant]. She was like, 'Trent, I don't want to dictate how this story's gonna sound, but this is really personal stuff. Can you please just let me make sure I can own my comments in the way I want to own them?' And I was like, 'Well, hell yeah.' What the hell's wrong with that? Whereas at uni, I was always told, 'Don't you dare ever show anyone your quotes or story.' But I just wrote a nonfiction, feature-writing storytelling book called *Love Stories*, and it was so wonderful to show the people their story before it got published and get them on board. It was really relieving for me.

Ultimately, I've realised my sleep is important to me, and I mean that in a sense of my guilt. When I was young and ambitious – trying to make a name for myself, whatever you want to call it – I think I did things the wrong way. And I lost sleep over it. I'd write a feature piece and people would go, 'Oh wow, you're really spiky there. I love how you really got in there and you were a bit of a smartass.' It's such a cowardly thing because you've got all the power – you're the one frickin writing the story. They don't have the chance to do their witty retort back to you. In my mid-twenties I remember doing it quite a bit. Thinking I was funny where it was just hurtful to people.

I was also taught to never show people the story. The logic behind that goes that people will then want to pull their punches. But when I wrote *Any Ordinary Day*, every person in that book had been profoundly traumatised and I could not have lived with myself if I had added in any way to their troubles. Also, I knew that because of my profile, my book would be *the* record of their story. I felt an obligation to show those people my writing about them before it went to print. Interestingly, only one person asked me to take out a minor detail.

They will honour you for doing it. They don't want to stifle you. It changes everything sometimes. Like they will go, 'Wow, because you did that, I'm gonna tell you the thing that I was holding back.' It's quite remarkable, the act of trust on both sides.

You spoke about being a young journo and the mistakes you made in going a little hard. Another mistake journos can make when they're starting out is thinking that nuance is going to weaken a story. The idea that if somebody has done something wrong and you show they're actually a decent person, it excuses what they've done. Or if they're a good person and you show that they're complex, it undermines their decency. But actually, I think the opposite is true.

Oh, hell yeah. Slim Halliday, a convicted killer who escaped Boggo Road twice, became a family friend who did odd jobs around our house, and looked after my brothers and me when my parents were away. My old man has demons – the man I first loved went away to Boggo for ten years – so I've built my life around finding nuance in flawed human beings. I absolutely love bringing that to journalism. I've done countless stories where you're interviewing a killer, or someone who has done the most horrendous things, but you're trying to piece together the story because life is so frickin' grey.

Man, I remember going to interview Alex Milat, Ivan Milat's brother. It was a frickin' brilliant day for a feature writer. Alex was a very interesting man, he's as gruff and as scary as Ivan no doubt was. I remember going to his place in the backwoods of the Sunshine Coast. It was 2 p.m., one of those eerie sort of days where no one felt alive on the whole entire planet except Alex and me. I go into his living room and I see on top of his television a

framed photograph of his brother Ivan, one of the most notori-
ous killers in Australian history – it was almost a shrine to Ivan.
I was like, 'Oh, of course. He loves him.' Like, life is so frickin
complex.

I remember Alex saying something like, 'Our dad raised us
to believe that killing a human is just like cutting the head off a
snake. It's one and the same.' I remember even in the moment
going, 'I've gotta pull him up here.' I was just like, 'I'm sorry,
Alex, I just gotta say, mate, it's not the same. It's just not the
same.' And he got really angry.

That led to this hilarious moment where he goes, 'Come
downstairs, go down there into that room.' He prompts me to
go down the bottom of the stairs, and there's this little basement
area that you had to duck down to get under, basically under
Alex's house. He's still pissed off from my comment that killing
a snake and killing a human isn't the same. He goes, 'I want to
show you something.'

It looks like the basement of every crime film you've ever seen.
There's rusted, medieval machinery, things I've never seen before.
And I remember seeing this hammer placed on the corner of this
workbench, and I was like, 'Why would you have a hammer placed
just like that?' He comes into the basement after me so there's
no getting out. It's just Alex, me and the machinery. Of course,
I'm bringing all my frickin lack of nuance. I'm treating this guy
unfairly. And I'm building up all these scenarios in my head. He
goes, 'Go to the end, go to the end.' And he goes to this machine
that's got this big lever on it. He comes up, pulls this lever – *clunk,
clunk, clunk*. Then he goes, 'Hold your hand out,' and I hold my
hand out and he pulls the thing that he's just built out of this lever
system. He pops in my hand a bullet and says, 'That's for you.'
It was a bullet-making machine. Turns out he's a rifle enthusiast

and he loves shooting. He was almost saying, 'Here's your souvenir from your experience with Alex Milat.'

The lesson is: go with the story, man. When Alex Milat says go down to the basement, I'm sorry, you've got to go. When the lead singer from Kiss says he wants to drink some red wine, drink the red wine. When Renée Zellweger wants a shot of tequila, shoot the shot. Do it because it'll be so great for the story. You got to just go, 'I think the reader wants me to go down into Alex Milat's basement.'

Do you try to establish boundaries with people in your stories? For example, do you make it clear to them that you are not their friend?

Oh, that's such a great question. I'm not as good at that as you are. I watch you every night and they keep coming back to you. I think that is because you establish those boundaries. Everyone knows where you're at. I get to that front door and I am the most charming mofo you could ever come across. I'm all out and all open. I'm not saying I want to be their friend but I'm trying to express to them, 'You will never be listened to for two hours of your life the way I'm going to listen to you. You will never feel more heard, more seen, or that your story has ever been more valued.' And if that makes them feel like I'm their friend, I can't control that. But the fact is, I'm just trying to get through that door. And what comes from that is this sense of friendship. I've become friends so many times with people.

I'm not as good as a political journo setting those boundaries, like, 'Mate, I'm not your friend, I'm here to serve the public.' Feature writers find that really difficult because you want to establish a connection, and a lengthy one. It's a very fine line.

I've had so many of those horrendous Saturday morning phone calls, it makes me sick even thinking about it. That feeling on Friday night and you know it's all coming out on Saturday, where you're just waiting for that person you've spent a week with to either call you the biggest cunt or the greatest saint. It's just horrendous waiting to hear what they think of you. I'm not good at brushing that aside. That's my greatest flaw as a journo – or as a human being – caring so much about what people think of me. If you're a journo and you have that, you're doomed. It's been really interesting trying to navigate that. By the time I got into the world of fiction, it was so liberating. I was like, 'I'm not hurting anyone.' I don't have to get any Saturday morning phone calls.

Some people get into journalism because they want to change the world, some want to see the world, some want to understand the world – what attracted you to it?

I wanted to understand my past, to be honest. I think part of my motivation was to get paid to go into people's living rooms, sit for sometimes hours or sometimes three days, and hear them talk about aspects of their life so I could work out the shit that was in the back of my own mind. I'm trying to work out the motivations of people, what's good about human nature, so I can understand the decisions that people I love the most in my life made, and, dare I say, love them even more. As a twelve-year-old, I was just trying to work people out. You know, why is that person doing that? As an adult, I found a wonderful home in journalism because every day I get to go out and ask questions and try to understand people.

Pamela Williams

Pamela Williams is one of Australia's most decorated journalists, with six Walkley awards, including the Gold for a 1998 series on a major waterfront industrial dispute. She began her career in 1985, writing for The Bulletin, Pacific Computer Weekly *and* Business Review Weekly, *before moving to* The Australian Financial Review, *where she held various positions including Editor-at-Large. She is the author of two books,* Killing Fairfax: Packer, Murdoch and the Ultimate Revenge *and* The Victory, *an account of the coalition's return to federal power in Australia, widely considered one of the best political books ever produced in this country.*

You specialise in business and politics, and readers particularly look out for your forensic long-form articles about election campaigns. You filed a major feature after every election for twenty-five years. What kind of preparation do you do in the lead-up to a campaign?

These campaign stories are incredibly long. I want access on lots of levels, and ideally to the campaign war room. They all say no.

I get in touch with contacts I've had a long time. I chase pollsters, key people behind the scenes; they all say no. I'll make more calls over the coming weeks. 'If I just keep calling and calling in the campaign will you give me five minutes, or even two minutes, on the phone so I can check things?' At that point, one or two people might conditionally agree. That's the door open. If they all say no, you proceed anyway. That's where I get to. I try to build from there. You have to take what you can get and then run with it.

What case do you make when you're trying to talk people into cooperating?

I make a case that it will be an early draft of history. I say if they don't talk to me, I'm going to be covering the election in any case. Me covering it is not negotiable. What I propose always is that nothing any source tells me, not one single word, will be published until after the election is over. I give an absolute ironclad commitment I won't discuss anything I see or hear during my reporting – not to the news desk, to my editor-in-chief, nothing, no one. My fundamental commitment is if I get help, and I'm privy to what's going on contemporaneously, the deal is nobody will know until it's all over. It means they're not taking a risk during the campaign if I see or hear something [they don't want me to]. I would never phone the office to pass it on. That's the key to the kind of access I need.

But people still say no. In 1996, John Howard wrote me a polite letter that said no access under any circumstances. I did later manage to write a book on that campaign. In 2016, twenty years later, the Libs absolutely barred me from the war room, but some operatives smuggled me in at one point and hid me in a storeroom with the door ajar so I could hear some speeches. The campaign director was so annoyed when I texted him later to confirm he was wearing a green T-shirt on the day, and he tried to find who'd leaked. I'd spotted him through the crack in the door. I had to be smuggled out again later. I've still got photos inside that room full of mops and brooms.

Given that access is limited, and they are scared to let people in even with the assurances you give, how do you find out what's really going on?

I travel back and forth between the travelling roadshow of the PM, the travelling roadshow of the opposition leader, and the two campaign headquarters. I only do the two main political parties in that intense way. Getting anyone in headquarters to talk is a nightmare and you spend hours sitting on park benches or in hotels, waiting.

After the first week, I go on the road. The prime minister and leader of the opposition travel constantly, so if I want to see it, I have to be there. I'll be on the media bus, and that's very helpful because I can set up talks with senior political staff who travel too. When you get to where the PM or the opposition leader are going – the side of a riverbank in Tasmania, or somewhere in the far north – the key advisors are always with them and those are the people I need. Maybe they might check something in their diary or maybe they're going to tell me something that's occurred that I really want to know more about. I criss-cross the country, but to be honest, you can't be everywhere and so at the start of the campaign, I really need to figure out which side I'm going to mostly travel with.

And how do you figure that out?

Usually it's whichever side interests me more in terms of what kind of horror will befall them if they lose.

You think that's the more interesting story, the losing side?

Not always; it might be the side that's going to win. It's about which side will fight harder and be more dark and desperate. The main thing I think I can bring to the readers is the campaign war rooms, as in what happened behind the scenes.

So you want to find out *who* decided we should go to the riverbank in Tasmania today, why they decided that and what they're hoping to get out of it?

It may be that I'm trying to think through: if there's been a catastrophe or crisis, are they trying for a reset? Has there been some polling on something, have they switched to announcing something different to what they had planned? Are they trying to change the headlines? So I'm really going to the riverbank so I can get in the ear of the PM's advisors, to arrange to talk to them later. And I'll definitely be looking for a lot of colour that will enliven these scenes.

When a reporter says they want 'colour', what does that mean?

For me it means small details that enhance the political or business picture I'm working on. It may be that the kind of shoes Malcolm Turnbull is wearing indicates his minders somehow forgot to tell him to be one of the gang. So he looks elite. It may be that Anthony Albanese, for all of his makeover, his new glasses and linen shirts, maybe by the time he's in a pub in North Queensland, somebody might ask him about all his fancy stuff and want to know, 'Are you still one of us?' At that point, if I'm there, I'll take some photos for myself so I can remind myself of the colour in the moment later, when I'm writing.

But it has to be relevant. Colour writing otherwise is just pointless. If Morrison is having a meal in a pub, I might note the look on his face, or whether he's ordered the schnitzel or steak. It will matter to me whether he puts tomato sauce or mustard on it. But you can't just overwhelm readers with those descriptive elements. It might be that's the moment his polls crashed and he's trying to look normal. Or let's say Morrison is having his schnitzel, and a guy bursts in dressed in an elephant suit and he's protesting about climate change. Then I can add this little discordant note that just as Morrison was reaching for the tomato sauce, this elephant started jumping around the room.

When you're reporting a big story like an election campaign in such incredible detail, how do you organise your material and keep track of what you've got?

I take longhand notes. My mother wouldn't let me learn short-hand because she thought I'd become a secretary. Each set of notes, whether it's observations or whether it's meeting somebody for an interview, on the top of the notes – and I think this is critical – I write down the date, the time, their full name and their phone number. And where I am, physically. At the top of the first page of every set of notes. These are my secret notes. No one else sees them. At the end of each day, I rip my pages out of the notebook, staple them together and put them in a safe place.

I can't afford to lose a notebook because that's my whole coverage in there, my gold stash. That's why I rip out the pages every day. So then I have a chronological set of notes. Some of those are from before the start of the campaign, when I talk to them about setting up the headquarters.

At the end, I have to deliver sixteen thousand words, to run usually over four parts. These are big pieces, mostly starting on the Tuesday after the election. You have to write it really quickly at the end of the campaign – and you have to know where things are.

In a campaign, things roll so fast, and there's so much information, it's hard for even the operatives to keep track of when things happened. So if somebody says, 'We had to restart the ad campaign because we could see we were sinking in the polls, but we were running out of money,' you've got to say to them, 'What day was it?' 'Oh it was yesterday.' 'But are you sure it was yesterday?' 'Oh I think it was.' 'Can you please check your diary,' I say, and they say, 'Oh just write that it was yesterday.' And I say, 'But if I write it was yesterday and it wasn't yesterday, turns out it was the night before, well then I am the one who is wrong.'

For me, to be wrong means everything because it means I'm misleading readers and every word in the story then is subject to dispute: what other facts didn't I check? 'Oh I don't have my diary, it's in my other phone,' so then I'm saying, 'Can I ring you later to check?'

When I ring them later, eight times out of ten they'll say, 'Oh lucky I checked this, it was the day before at 6 p.m.' Every time, you must check everything.

Do you record audio of your interviews?

No, never.

You write it longhand as you go?

Everything is in longhand. I know everybody records these days, but for me, the pace and the timing in which I'm writing these enormous pieces, I can't handle going to find audio in a phone and figure out what came where and then listen to it and take notes of bits of it; it would crater the entire exercise. I have to be able to flick-flick-flick through notes, because I can visualise in ten seconds where something is in them.

At what point do you start the writing?

I start on the Friday, the last day of the campaign. I have a massive pile of stapled notes. I basically decide to kill myself instead of doing it. Because that will be the easy way out. I look at the notes, I look at the whole exercise, and I think about my poor hands from all the typing ahead and I think I should just bail and resign immediately. Then about ten minutes later, I open the notes and I start.

I read all my notes the Friday morning, while still keeping an eye on everything going on, because often there's a bomb thrown on the Friday. I have a huge pile of yellow stick-its and I put markers in my notes, and if I can I'll start a bit of writing. If I find something I think might make the top of the story, I note it. My brain has been thinking the whole way along about structure, but you can't really [finalise] structure until you know what you've got, because the intro might come on the last day. In the federal election in 2019, the intro did indeed come at 1 a.m. at the end of election night, which was Bill Shorten standing devastated in an airport hotel in Melbourne making the speech that everything was lost. For me, in the end, that was the most emotional thing and it was far more interesting to me than Morrison's victory, because it was the denouement of six years of Shorten's dream, smashed to pieces.

I write what's in my notes onto the screen. It's a big block, usually in four separate documents split into the four stories I will file. I keep vomiting everything out all day Saturday. There's no real 'writing', it's just getting words on the screen. And by the time I finish that, we are more or less through to 6 p.m. on election night. Then I have to go back and work out what the intro is. Once I have the four documents on screen with all my material in them, with big asterisks to remind myself of key moments, and important things written in capital letters, I have to keep coming back to the intro. I cannot proceed one step further until I've got the intro dead right.

And that has to wait until you know the election result?

It does. And what I base it on is what, to me, has been the most interesting thing of the entire campaign.

Okay, you've got your intro set, you've got this big block of unpublishable text with reminders to yourself written in every-where. You wake up Sunday morning, you've got the bones of an intro, you've got an absolute mess after that: what do you then do to transform it into an actual story?

I will have tried on the Saturday to get some kind of organising principle of the three or four parts. At this point, I'm going to not just be writing, but also fact-checking on the phone. I will have already done so much fact-checking as it's gone along – because every time I've found out about a meeting, I've gone to other people who might have been in that meeting. I won't say, 'Oh, I heard you had a meeting to swing the advertising strategy,' I'll say, 'How's the advertising strategy going, have you done anything else?' I'll try to lead them to tell me.

On the Sunday I always get up at 4 a.m. I rework yet again the intro. I'm so fussy about the intro, it sets the scene and the pace. At 4 a.m., I will start mucking around: where is the comma and where is the next comma. I might start with a hundred-word paragraph and I'll pare that back and back. This for me acts as a kind of discipline for my writing.

For example, in 1996, I started with two paragraphs of John Howard's chief of staff Grahame Morris writing in his little blue plastic-covered diary his view of how they'd gone in a debate. And how he scored the debate and how in his mind this was the decisive moment where they went from underdog to in with a real chance. Once I had that, I knew I was set.

So your frame then was 'The underdog is in with a chance.' In 2019, your frame was Shorten and this bitter, unexpected defeat. I presume that helps dictate, among all the mass of material, what's in and what's out?

It does, although when you've got such a lot of space and you're writing four thousand words a day, you can use a lot of material – but it has to be interesting all the way through. If you bore the readers, they're going to stop halfway through the first paragraph.

On that point, after an election, everybody knows the outcome – what are you counting on that will motivate people to read the piece?

It has to be that it is absolutely studded through with raisins of material that they didn't know: backroom politics, the hidden campaign operation, who said what to whom, was there any fighting, what did the pollsters think. I'm always much more interested in the machine politics than the show on the road, which you've already seen on TV and in the daily reporting. The readers know all of that, so I'm as much as I can devoting my reporting to things they don't know. You must have something that really hooks people.

How did you become a journalist?

It was very sudden. I was thirty. My nine-year-old daughter had just died from cancer after years of fighting to save her. And I had to find a way to survive. It was a very bad time. I had joined this group called Australian Skeptics trying to bust faith healers who preyed on the sick. Through that, somebody told me about something happening in relation to a Victorian trade union. I thought, 'Oh that's something I could write a story about,' so almost overnight I decided I would become a freelance journalist. I know it sounds crazy. I made some phone calls and told people I was a freelance journalist. I rang up the editor-in-chief of *The Bulletin* magazine and asked would he like a feature on this union thing. He said that sounds great. I wrote ten thousand words and they rang me back and said, 'What's this ten thousand words? We don't publish ten thousand words!' So I cut it right back and they ran it in January 1985, and so from that moment I was in fact a freelance journalist! About a year later I got a job at *Business Review Weekly*.

So I was self-taught. I discovered I could write but I looked around and thought, 'Okay, who are the best people?' I would advise any young reporter to do this. Go read every word by someone else who's great. Try to unpick it, figure out who they talked to, and how they made it interesting.

I very strongly feel there should always be a place for bringing in people with street smarts and who have an aggressive perseverance. In journalism, that will get you a very long way. We should never underestimate life skills and experience. Lots of people come into journalism sideways like me.

Benjamin Law

Writer and broadcaster Benjamin Law is the author of The Family Law, Gaysia: Adventures in the Queer East *and 'Moral Panic 101'* (Quarterly Essay), *and the editor of* Growing Up Queer in Australia. *He writes a weekly column for* Good Weekend *for which he interviews public figures, and he hosts an ABC Radio National pop-culture program called* Stop Everything. *His feature writing has appeared in more than fifty publications, including* The Monthly, frankie, The Guardian, Monocle *and* The Australian Financial Review. *Ben is also an accomplished screenwriter and playwright.*

Ben, I've had to revert to a plan B because of a technology issue, and I'm now putting my iPhone on speaker next to my iPad, which will record via voice memo. There's a lesson here for journalists – things don't always work out as you plan and you have to adapt!

Completely. I mainly work in print, so when it comes to recording interviews, you're always going to encounter something that fucks up. In the early days of doing interviews with artists for street press – which felt very high-stakes, usually paid in CDs – I had that thing you stick on the back of a landline that you bought from Dick Smith. That's so old that I refer to Dick Smith and landlines, two things that barely exist anymore. Then I also had a technically illegal phone tap that I bought from Hong Kong: you stuck your phone line in one end and then it had a microphone output. I was like, 'Am I doing something for which I'll be arrested?'

You were the first person to get me onto automated transcription of interviews.

Do you use Otter?

Yes, I do.

Otter's such a lifesaver. But do you know what I'm doing now? Outsourcing my transcribing to a human transcriber. It's great.

Do you get all your interviews transcribed in full?

Look, I used to do more long-form interviews for much bigger feature stories. The interviews that I do nowadays, for Radio National or *Good Weekend*, are usually thirty minutes and done. So I'm outsourcing the transcribing and my transcriber transcribes it in full. But way back when I used to interview people over hours, or a series of days, I would have my little Moleskine reporter notebook. I would have all my questions written down, I'd be writing notes as I went, paying attention to how people were saying things, surrounding sounds, or anything that I wanted to follow up. But because I knew the horrors of transcribing, as I was going I was making marks like 'ten minutes to 11:20 – boring, do not transcribe.' That's what I call active listening.

In long-form feature work, whether it's articles or books, keeping track of your material, knowing what you've got and where it is, is critical. How do you manage that?

It's so hard. I actually changed how I work because of that. I used to keep folders for every project or story I was writing. All my audio and transcripts would go in there. But then – this sounds like daytime TV – I changed to another software platform, which you'll love, Leigh. I started using Scrivener, which a lot of novelists use. It's designed by writers, for writers, and it encourages you to write in discrete chunks rather than one long scroll. It can put all of your audio and all of your notes and scribbles in one document.

The other point I feel our conversation illustrates is that when you're interviewing, sometimes you have to follow where circumstances lead. Because so far, I've not asked you a single thing on my list . . .

And I just want to derail and undermine you, so I'm glad it's working! For me, it always depends on the purpose and context. When I'm interviewing someone like Matthew McConaughey, I'm like, 'God, this guy's time is going to be tight.' Or I interviewed Michelle Yeoh and they only gave me twenty minutes when they promised me thirty So you just have to go in there like a cruise missile.

But if I'm doing something quite complicated and sensitive, if you have the luxury of time, you really do have to hold space for the person you're talking to. Years ago, I did a cover story for *Good Weekend* about survivors of childhood sexual abuse where the perpetrator was their sibling. Apparently that's one of the most common forms of childhood sexual abuse and it's very rarely talked about. In a way, you need them to lead the conversation because the way in which they've remembered and then subsequently processed the incident is not something that's within my realm of understanding.

You have a weekly column in *Good Weekend* called 'Dicey Topics', where you ask public figures to discuss normally taboo topics by having them roll dice – they might land on sex, money, death, life, politics or bodies. Given the limited number of topics, how do you ensure that every one of those chats feels different to the others?

I've got a master list of questions that I find generally interesting for each of those topics. So when it comes to death, I'm interested in knowing what someone's first encounter with grief was, what helps with grief. When it comes to money, I'm asking the poorest and richest they've ever been, or what their plan B might be. Those general questions. Then what I overlay on top of that is, of course, all the specific stuff. Just before I spoke to you, I was interviewing [novelist] Geraldine Brooks and we landed on death. Her husband, Tony Horwitz, a Pulitzer Prize-winning journalist, died three years ago. They'd been married since the mid-1980s. Of course, when she lands on death, we're gonna have a much more specific conversation about Tony.

I wasn't as confident when I started doing that column. Nowadays, I find that even if I do replicate a lot of the questions – and I do tend to – everyone's story is so bloody different that they're going to give me something completely specific and interesting and not at all like the previous interviewee.

What is the difference between a discussion over the phone or Zoom versus an in-person interview?

It's always best practice to interview someone in person. I used to do all of my interviewing in person where possible. But when the pandemic hit, everything became exclusively Zoom or phone. The pros of that are access and efficiency. There's something about scheduling a Zoom meeting where it's like, 'Okay, we're getting straight into it. No simple talk, no buffering. It's an appointment in your diary.' The benefit of face-to-face interaction, of course, is there's trust and intimacy that is built, which is difficult to replicate over Zoom. You notice more about body language and that does affect the way you might question someone.

Plus, for a book or feature, you need colour to fill it out. You need the non-verbals that explain a person's life to you – what their kitchen is like, and so on.

I don't think I can do that over Zoom. Good nonfiction writing uses all the tools that fiction writing uses – character, space, description – and your toolkit is suddenly limited if you're just having a virtual interface.

In this book, only a few people I'm interviewing aren't from a traditional newsroom/journalistic background. You're one of them. Do you feel that not being a traditional journalist gives you any advantage in approaching writing about real-life events and issues?

I can totally list the disadvantages, Leigh: mostly it's that I don't know what the fuck I'm doing. I mean, I did a creative writing degree at QUT [Queensland University of Technology]. And because it was so bare bones at the time, I was borrowing a lot of journalism subjects, which I bloody loved because I wanted to write creative nonfiction and it was still a genre where people were figuring out what the conventions were. Joan Didion, Hunter S. Thompson and Tom Wolfe had done it for years and years. They called it the 'new journalism'. My point is, I learnt about the inverted pyramid, I learnt how to do interviews, but when it came to other things, like media law and how to professionally conduct yourself within this space, I'm like, 'Whoa, I really wish I learnt that stuff.' Like, when sources get angry at you, how to manage that. I'd call my editor and say, 'This source is angry at me,' and they'd be like, 'And that's okay, Ben. You held them to account, this is what's going to happen.'

Because I don't come into a story from a hard news background, one of the advantages I have is I use my instincts. When I'm doing a death knock as part of a crowd that's been knocking on someone's door all week, I've had to rely on my judgement: 'If I was that interviewee, how would I want to be approached?' That's when I use my creative writing instincts. Maybe one of the advantages is that I'm more amenable to changing my mind or approach as things go along, and don't just relying on a toolkit that's been handed down to me.

How do you judge how many words a story is worth? For example, whether something is a feature article or a book?

This reminds me of when I was a bookseller. So many books, especially nonfiction, would come in, and you'd just hold it up to your fellow colleagues like, 'This could have been a feature article.' And then sometimes you read features where it's like, 'Oh my god, don't stop there. Give me more!'

I think part of it is being a reader. When I make those judgements as a reader, you want to transpose that onto being a writer as well. 'As a reader, do I want a book about the history of disposable pens?'

As a freelancer, you're constantly pitching for your life, right? Every pitch is the only access you have to work. Often what I'm doing in those pitches is comparing a story to other stories that I've written for that publication, or stories I've published elsewhere. It helps the editor's understanding – 'Okay, so it's like that story about the bear hunt in Iceland, but you're going to be doing a giant fish hunt in Fiji. That was roughly three thousand words, so this is going to be roughly three thousand words with that same style.'

You plucked an idea about disposable pens out of the air because one was in your hand. It makes me wonder how you come up with your ideas.

I used to run masterclasses for people who wanted to get into freelancing and creative nonfiction. The exercise I would make them do is actually one I do myself. In the back of my brain, I'm always asking, 'What am I really interested in? What do I have expertise in?' And that might be from my personal background or my personal interest. That's always an advantage because you come into the story bringing that interest, and curiosity, and hopefully a sense of authority in terms of what you're talking about. And then I think, 'What are the things I've been interested in but still don't know much about?' Questions that you feel can't be answered at dinner parties or book clubs, you know?

When I find myself in a conversation and I'm stuck, I think other people might feel discomfort but I feel excited.

I remember way back, before I even had the language for anti-vaxxers, I found myself in a dinner-party conversation with tertiary-educated people working in the arts and media. One said, 'Well, I do think there are too many vaccinations for the following reasons, don't you?' And I'm like, 'Oh, I'm not sure I do believe that. But it's really interesting coming from you, because I thought the anti-vaxxer movement was quite niche and "over there". So where's this coming from?' I couldn't quite figure it out, and that became a big story for *Good Weekend*.

Then there are things you hear about on the radio or television. I'm not a daily news journalist, but sometimes I'll hear a daily news report that fires my interest.

Then, I think the other thing is just being a shameless busybody, Leigh.

I keep a notebook in which I write down ideas and thoughts and observations, many of which I might never use. Do you?

You've actually tapped into a secret shame or vulnerable spot with me, because I have always felt like an imposter for not keeping a proper notebook in the way that you, Helen Garner, David Sedaris, Joan Didion – actual writers – do.

Thank you for using my name in that sentence.

Any time I started writing a diary in January, I'd end in March, because I just can't be fucked. But I do send emails to myself. If it's the middle of the night and I get an idea or something connects, or if I'm walking down the street or even doing laps at the pool – I'll hop out of the pool. If I put it down some-where, then it's somewhat cemented in my brain. Sometimes I'll even take a whiteboard marker to my window and it just hangs around like vandalism.

You wrote a big nonfiction piece for *Quarterly Essay*, called 'Moral Panic 101'. What was it about and where did that idea come from?

That was about the media reporting and the moral panic that ensued once the Safe Schools program – which started as a state program in Victoria then expanded into a federal program – was being attacked and painted as a bogeyman in the press. Specifically, the News Corp press, and more specifically, *The Australian*. The essay came about because I was following the story closely. I felt invested as a reader, as a gay man and as a queer person, and I felt so angry about a story that I thought I understood. I forget what I was reading, but I realised my preconceptions about this program were actually wrong. It's not a school-based delivery program, it's about getting principals to sign a pledge that they will protect some of the most vulnerable demographics at school. It was actually so light-on in terms of what was required for a school to be a safe school. These new resources teachers were equipped with – that people were in a huff about – hadn't even been officially used in classrooms by that time. And they definitely weren't mandatory. I just lost the plot.

Long story short, sometimes I write to make sense of a mess. That mess might be in my mind, or a story that needs clarifi-cation. As I started writing that essay, I thought it was gonna be a feature – I realised it wasn't gonna be a book – and then

I thought, 'Actually, the perfect format would be a twenty-something-thousand-word essay.'

Even though you started that essay from a position of personal investment, to me as a reader, it read as a very clinical piece of investigative work, where you were saying, 'This is what the media is claiming, and this is what the facts are.'

It's a really good point, Leigh. I knew coming into it that it was clear what my inherent biases and passions were. I wasn't hiding them. I have a stake in this conversation. It is personal for me. But, knowing that I could compromise the story if I got too emotionally invested, my instincts were to remove some of the emotion. When you lay out the stats, there is no argument against them. When you lay out the timeline, there is no argument against the chronology.

I remember when I signed on to do the essay, I started reading David Marr's *Quarterly* essays and his other work. What I cracked was that so much of his work is just laying out the chronology of a complicated story. You start seeing how the dots connect. As much as these stories are wrestled with and reported in a daily news cycle, our memories are short, and our capacity to understand the way that this story from two days ago connects to this story today is limited.

As you say, if you know you're writing something controversial, part of the key is having the facts, the timeline, absolutely locked down. I'm keeping a timeline at the moment about a sexual assault case I'm following closely with the possibility of doing a book. The other day I noticed, 'Hang on! That date! Those two people went to the police on the same day. Were

they colluding? What was going on here?' Just laying it out in a methodical way can be such a useful investigative tool.

Completely agree. And I learnt that from working as an associate producer on a documentary. Part of that job was doing the research. It was about gay-hate killings in Sydney that climaxed in the 1980s and mid-1990s. It was basically a sport to go so-called 'poofta bashing'. It's an incredibly complex story that takes place over decades and it was so intimidating to even know where to start. The most handy thing was, 'Let's just go through it day by day and let's start seeing where these pieces actually start aligning.' And then you realise – similar to what you're talking about with the sexual assault case – 'Those two things happened around the same time, similar accusations were made. What contact do we need to get to clarify how these two stories might connect?' You wouldn't have seen it if you hadn't laid it out chronologically.

Very few people are able to straddle as many different genres as you. You do radio, print, books, journalism, plays, TV, fiction, nonfiction. Did you sell your soul to Satan to get all this talent?

You calling me a genre slut, Leigh? Is that what you're saying? Sometimes I think I have something wrong with me. I can't pay attention to things, or maybe it's that I get excited a little bit too easily. Which sounds terrible, like a dog that's about to hump your leg or something. But, you know, I'm a deep, omnivorous reader; I like going to plays; I like seeing movies; I like watching TV; I like reading nonfiction. And I'm excited by the possibilities of each of those forms.

Interviewing

Interviewing is at the heart of all journalism, whether it's a quick grab from a witness to a disaster or a lengthy conversation for a podcast. It is one of the most complex skills in journalism because there are as many ways of conducting an interview as there are people on the planet. Each person has their own story – sometimes two witnesses will even have a unique take on the same event. That means the role of the interviewer is to listen with great care and to alter their technique as necessary, in the same way a musician listens to others in an orchestra and adapts their timing or pitch.

In every interview, the mission is to find the truth: the facts of an event, a celebrity's true personality, a politician's motive. Interviews can be aggressive and confrontational when a journalist is questioning a person in power on behalf of those less powerful. They can be gently probing when the subject has suffered great trauma. They can be witty and expansive, reflective and quiet, or awkward and hard to watch. But every great interview, whatever the subject, will hold an audience rapt.

One of the things for which I'm most known in journalism is interviewing. Even though I've not included my own tips on the matter in this book, you will learn a huge amount about my approach if you pay close attention to the way I question people in these pages. You might notice how each conversation differs significantly from the next. That's because I'm not reading down a list of pre-prepared questions, I'm carefully listening to what each person says and responding. Listening is *the* most essential skill for any interviewer.

Laurie Oakes

For decades, Laurie Oakes was one of the most respected and best-known political journalists in Australia. His weekly interviews with politicians on the Nine Network's Sunday *program were compulsory viewing, as were his evening reports for National Nine News, along with his political columns for* The Daily Telegraph. *Laurie worked in the federal press gallery from 1967 to 2017, having started in newspapers and eventually becoming Nine's Political Editor. He has won innumerable awards, including a Gold Walkley and the Graham Perkin Australian Journalist of the Year Award.*

Laurie, the first step in the interview process is the choice of who to invite. When you were doing a weekly political interview, what were your considerations?

I'm a news person so the newsworthiness of the subject was always what counted with me: who was in the news, who was likely to make news, who could provide genuine, interesting background on the news.

Once you had a guest locked in, what was your preparation like?

Intense. The kinds of interviews I did, I used to spend hours preparing. My clipboard became a bit of a trademark and people assumed that I had prepared questions on there. I did have possible questions, but I also would have written down a whole lot of things: answers I might get, or was most likely to get, and how I could follow those up most productively. I had ideas about how to get around the kind of defence mechanisms a particular politician might use or how to divert them away from talking points. I had information that I thought I might need if they started trying to tell porkies or to avoid the subject – all that sort of stuff that you need if you're going to hold a politician to account and try to fact-check while you're live on air. If you're very well prepared, if you obviously know your stuff, it's very much harder for a politician to spin you, and they realise that. That sometimes leads them to give you more genuine responses and to engage more.

Let me give you an example of interviewing [then Prime Minister] John Howard in the run-up to the 2007 election on *Sunday*. Interest rates were in the news and I'd suggested Howard had broken a promise he'd made in the previous election campaign – that a re-elected coalition government would keep rates at thirty-year lows. There had been five interest rate rises since that promise had been made. Howard was resting on a claim that, well, there might have been a Liberal Party ad, but he had never actually said it. In the interview, he said that the promise had not come out of his mouth. I was able to produce from the notes on my clipboard a direct quote from him in the 2004 election campaign: 'The promise did come out of your mouth, Prime Minister.' That's the advantage of intense research.

How much did you trawl through old press conferences or interviews politicians had previously given?

I wanted to know what they'd said before and where I might take that, how I might develop it and learn more, or learn something different, about why they did things. So yeah, I used to look at what they'd said. But I'd also just look at the hard facts as well. I had Julia Gillard on *Sunday* in 2009 when she was Deputy Prime Minister. A couple of asylum-seeker boats had just been detected in trouble and were on their way to Australia. The then opposition was getting into the government over it. I held up a document to Gillard, and I said, 'I've got here a shadow minister's press release headed, "Another boat on the way, another policy failure." Do you agree that every boat with asylum seekers that arrives represents a policy failure by the government?' Thinking it was from the current opposition, she ripped into them and made excuses for what was happening. And then I said, 'Well, it was actually issued by you when you were shadow minister a few years ago.' [That line of questioning] is a bit tricky, and some people tut-tut and disapprove, but it exposed hypocrisy. Politicians use trickery themselves. They have big media staffs and media training on how not to answer questions. I think to do a bit of trickery and bluff is necessary for journalists.

Did you speak to sources or contacts as part of your preparation?

I used to talk to the people I was interviewing or people around them. I didn't want to just invite politicians on so I could do them over. If they had something to announce or some view they wanted to express, I thought it was my job to give them that opportunity and I think that's legitimate. But that didn't mean I couldn't then rebut them. I would also talk to the opposing side about things that might be worth raising, also sometimes interest groups. The more research you do, the better.

Building rapport and establishing warmth with a celebrity interviewee is important. It's not necessarily something you have to do with a politician, although rapport with anybody helps make it a watchable piece of television, doesn't it?

It does. Sometimes with a politician, you also want to frighten them. I didn't always want rapport. It can help to unnerve a politician a bit. For example, with Joe Hockey – I think it was his last budget as treasurer in 2014 – I did a budget-night interview with him. I'd learned that before he went into the budget speech, he'd been in his office with his wife and son, and to amuse the son he'd been dancing and singing to 'The Best Day of My Life'. And that was my first question to Joe: why were you dancing to 'The Best Day of My Life' before your budget speech? And he had to admit it wasn't going to be the best day of their life for people affected by health cuts and social services changes. That was a different way of getting at the problems with the budget; it was much better than sticking to the talking points. The more unorthodox way you find to ask a question, the more likely you are to get an interesting answer.

Did you subedit your interview questions the same way you subbed your television news scripts? Did the same rules about active language, brevity, and so on apply?

Certainly for brevity. Short, simple questions are the best. The more complicated a question, and the longer it is, the more ways there are for a politician to distort it or get around it or ignore parts of it.

What did you look for in an opening question?

It depended on the interview. With the Joe Hockey interview I mentioned, I did want to set him back on his heels and shock him into saying something a bit different from what he was saying in all the other budget interviews. Sometimes I did try and put politicians at their ease, so I would start off talking about what they wanted to talk about before I got to the things that I'd actually requested the interview for, where I could probe and hold their feet to the fire, if you like. The more they relaxed, the more talkative they were, and that helped.

What do you think are the biggest mistakes political interviewers make?

One of the biggest ones is forgetting who the audience is. I've probably been guilty of it as much as anybody. Sometimes you have other journalists in mind rather than the viewers, when you should be asking questions on behalf of your audience, rather than trying to impress your peers. It's a bit of showing off that should be avoided. I love an aggressive interview as much as anybody, but it shouldn't be the default position, and I think there's probably too much of that.

Did you ever find it a challenge to set your own opinions aside in an interview?

I try not to push my opinions, but on something like racism, for example – my view of that came out when I was interviewing people on stuff like asylum seekers – everybody knows you've got an opinion, but my opinions weren't party political opinions. I think I was a bit hard to put into a left- or right-wing box because my opinions on things vary. You shouldn't put your opinions on display more than you have to. The interview is not about you. The interview is not about the interviewer, it's about the interviewee.

If you've got the audience in mind, generally you're asking questions of people in power on behalf of people who don't hold power. Therefore, whether it's Labor or Liberal, your position should be to attempt to hold them accountable for the decisions that they're making.

That's right. At times, you have to be devil's advocate, even if you don't agree with the point of view of the critics of a politician. You owe it to the audience to put the criticism to the politician, to put them on the spot and force them to explain and justify what they do, or what they think, or what they believe. I've often questioned politicians from a direction that I didn't necessarily hold myself, but which a lot of people did. I thought it was my job to represent them.

When you do that, it does also give the politician the opportunity to persuade those people in the audience to a different view; it's actually a good opportunity.

Yeah, it is. But these days, because things have become so weird now with social media, the journalist is condemned for asking questions that represent a view that some of the audience don't agree with. It gets ridiculously nasty. It's getting much harder to do a good political interview, because journalists are, rightly, wary of the response they will get. It's one of many things that are going wrong with democracy in our country.

Television is an extremely exacting medium in terms of the time given to various items. You can be told that you have nine minutes or six and a half minutes and you're expected to land as close to that as you possibly can. How did you manage time?

A lot of people get used to pre-recording, so they lay down as much as they want and cut out what they don't want and keep the good bits. I never had that advantage because I was live. It wasn't hard for me to adjust to the idea that you've got twelve minutes and you've got to get as much as you can, and as you want, in that time. I didn't find I often ran out of time. I would usually steal a minute or two and ignore the producer's voice in my ear. But mostly, because I'd done all that preparation and I had a clock in the studio, I was able to give proper weight to the issues I covered without running out of time. I very rarely finished thinking, 'Oh god, I didn't get to X or Y.' You develop the skill, you develop the habits that you need to do that.

One of the things that I do is mark up my interview. I'll have a note on the side that indicates I should be at this particular point by halfway through; I have brackets around questions that I think can be first drops, and asterisks next to things that I consider must-asks. Did you use any devices like that?

I used to have coloured pens. I would mark the essential things on the clipboard. It was so crowded with typing and scribble that I needed that anyway, so I could quickly find the bit I wanted.

By far the most common question young journalists ask me about live political interviewing is 'How do I know when to interrupt?' How would you answer?

You've got to let politicians give their view but when they keep giving the same view, or when it gets boring, you are entitled to interrupt. I think you need to be polite. There are ways of doing it that don't disturb the viewer. They're seeing what you're seeing, they know: 'She said this before, this is getting boring.' There's a British interviewer called Jeremy Paxman who's famous for asking the same question twelve times in one interview, and that did vividly demonstrate that the interview subject wasn't answering the question. But Jeremy Paxman could have got out of that after the third time and still made the point to the audience. I think you can overdo those things. That, I think, is another example of an interviewer showing off. You don't need to do that.

Along with the question about how to interrupt, the other thing I'm most commonly asked is 'When it's been an interview in which the politician has not performed well, what is the atmosphere like in the studio afterwards?'

There was one interview I did with John Howard and it was in two parts. We stopped for a commercial break in the middle. He was going well enough, but the questions were tough and he was obviously getting angrier and angrier. I threw to the commercial break and he and I sat there for the two minutes or whatever it was, three minutes, not talking to each other. Jim Waley, the anchor of the program, was sitting there squirming and he couldn't stand the silence, so he said, 'Mr Howard, the weather's been good lately.'

It does get tense. There have been times, actually, when I have felt sorry for an interview subject. I remember one shadow minister, when Kim Beazley was opposition leader, had been allowed to appear on the program but with orders he was not allowed to discuss one particular issue. And of course I homed in on that issue and it was just agony watching; he was sort of curling up in the foetal position. I cut that interview short by about four minutes because I felt sorry for him.

How about standing up to ask a single question at a press conference or at the National Press Club? What makes a good question in that context?

Again, I'd go back to short and simple is the best, but then the question of mine most remembered at the Press Club ran for three or four minutes, when I confronted Julia Gillard with a detailed account of her late-night meeting with Kevin Rudd where, in the end, she told him she was going to challenge him for the leadership. So, look – what's a good question is what's newsworthy, what exposes hypocrisy or dishonesty. Usually, a short question is still the best way.

That example of Julia Gillard at the Press Club and you giving a long spiel: those kinds of questions can be very interesting because what is said is probably just as interesting as the politician's face while the question is being asked.

Yeah, I think that's right. I must admit, I wasn't watching Julia carefully when I was asking her that question. I had notes and

I was making sure I got the facts right, to make it impossible for her to wriggle away.

Often when there's a leak, there's an assumption that it's come from a minister or a rival or somebody powerful. How often is that not the case?

Oh, look, all sorts of people leak and sometimes for funny reasons. The best source I ever had was a down-the-line bureaucrat that nobody had ever heard of. Sometimes his job would include shredding documents, so he got to see them – or sometimes he forgot to shred them. I got some quite good stories from him. His motivation was just the excitement. He liked the buzz of leaking and the risk. There was no political motivation at all. He only leaked stuff that should have been leaked, where there was injustice or people being mistreated, that kind of thing. Politicians, of course, and a lot of other people, leak for political reasons, either to promote themselves or allies or policies, or to stab enemies.

Can a political journalist be friends with a politician?

Yeah, within reason, and it probably won't last long. I've had politicians who were friends but then I've done stories or interviews with them and the friendship has ended. The problem is you can't really hold back because the politician's a friend, if you're doing your job properly. Bill Hayden is still a friend, and I wrote some very tough stuff about Bill. I remember when he was opposition leader, I nicknamed him 'Bellyache Bill', much to Dallas Hayden's annoyance. She still talks about it! Some friendships survive, but it's very hard.

One of the thrilling things about being a political journalist is that you do get to associate with these people up close. People like Paul Keating are unique, and it is fascinating to get to observe them and to speak to them.

It's a privilege. I've regarded journalism as a privilege. I think it's essential to our democratic system and I think we've got to remember that. I haven't always done wonderful things in journalism. I have plenty of critics and a lot of them are probably right. But I do feel that the profession matters.

Tracy Grimshaw

Tracy Grimshaw was the anchor of the Nine Network's A Current Affair *from 2006 to 2022 and before that she was the co-presenter of the* Today *show for almost a decade. She has conducted tens of thousands of interviews in her forty-year career, and anchored coverage of many milestone news events, including the 1997 Thredbo landslide and the death of Princess Diana. She has a Walkley Award for interviewing, and in 2018 was nominated for the Gold Logie for Australia's most popular television personality.*

Tracy, I want to talk through the different kinds of interviews that you face, starting with celebrities.

I find celebrity interviews harder than most of the others, to be perfectly honest with you. When you're not an entertainment reporter, these folks aren't coming into your orbit regularly, so you don't build rapport with them. Usually you walk in, sit down and you've got half an hour. You go from cold to a hundred miles an hour, because you really want every minute of that half-hour to work. You have to build trust with someone who's got all sorts of walls up, and usually you've been told by the publicist that there are no-go zones, and you think, 'Oh god, I've got to navigate no-go zones, I really want to go there.'

Often, they'll want to talk only about their album or their movie. You'll be happy to do that, that's why you're doing the interview, but you'll want to talk about some of the other stuff going on in their lives, too. And you want them to trust that if they break down those walls with you, that it'll be treated with respect. I just try to be as relaxed as possible, so that they get a sense that I'm not an avaricious interviewer. It's more a vibe – giving them a sense that you're not looking to dish the dirt.

Let's go to the other end of the spectrum: the person who has no media experience but suddenly finds themselves in the news through no fault of their own, usually because of a tragedy. In that scenario, do you speak to the person before you're interviewing them on camera?

Yes. I really want to talk to them before I interview them. Normally, I will make sure I've got plenty of time before we sit down to record. Just half an hour to relax them, to find out why they're doing the interview – because very often you don't get a chance to ask them. And very often they actually don't have to do the interview. In 98 per cent of cases, no money's changed hands. They're not doing it for the bucks. They want what they have learned to help somebody else. And in those situations, you owe it to them to know exactly what their objective is by talking, so that you honour that.

If the person says to you, 'I'm doing an interview so that nobody else goes through this,' does that influence the kinds of questions you ask?

Absolutely. Also, if people haven't done interviews before, it's the most scary thing. The minute the cameraman tells you he or she's rolling, the room goes silent. You've been sitting there bustling along, crews have been talking, everything feels like normal human interaction, and suddenly it's this unnatural silence. That instantly puts people on edge. So I like to tell them how that's going to play out, to not worry about everybody else in the room, just think about us. I want them to be as relaxed and as informed as possible about how this is going to feel and how it's going to go, so that nothing surprises or frightens them.

I also want them to know that if they mess up a sentence, we're not live and we can do it again. I don't want to make them look stupid. I want them to know that they're in safe hands and that they can trust the process.

I might tell them, 'I need to take you through this, this part will be uncomfortable, I might ask you the same question twice – it'll only be because I'll think you had more to say, not because I wasn't listening the first time. Just trust me. And if I haven't given you a chance to say everything you wanted to say, let me know, because I'll give you that chance.' I just want it to be really collaborative.

How do you hope they feel about the process at the end of the interview?

I always hope they feel it was cathartic. Usually in those situations, we're talking about incredibly traumatic things and I don't want them to be further traumatised at the end of it. What they've been through, it's been traumatic enough. I'll never end the interview if they're sobbing. If they cry during the interview, I'll always try to give them a break, I'm not going to push ahead. I don't have a right to go in there and make it worse. Very often, people will tell me after an interview like that they feel like the load's a little lighter.

Your mindset as the interviewer going into the interview is important as well. I never refer to 'my story' – journos will very often talk about 'my story'. It's never your story, it's theirs. I always go into it thinking, 'This is their story, I'm a conduit of information.' What I ask really isn't critical, it's only critical in terms of how it elicits the information that needs to be elicited.

When traumatic events are being recounted, there's often a moment that's the climax. Take Brant Webb and Todd Russell, who were the survivors of the Beaconsfield mine disaster: there'll be certain moments in their story that are particularly difficult for them. How do you tackle those moments?

Everyone's a bit different. Those boys took strength from each other – the two of them were sitting there next to each other during the interview just as they were in that hole in the ground for two weeks. They kind of tag-teamed; when one was struggling in the interview, the other stepped in. And they did that underground as well. So, in a two-header, when there's been a shared experience, they'll very often support each other. It's more challenging when it's just one person, cos you have to be their support act. You have to really intuit how to navigate them through. And you just learn by doing it a lot. And also, bringing some empathy in.

It can be hard to contain your own human emotion. How do you process that during and after the interview?

Look, I often feel quite wrung-out after big interviews. Increasingly so. And it doesn't really matter whether it's someone recounting a trauma or an adversarial interview – you leave it all on the floor. Usually, it's just the two of you in that space for half an hour and you don't stop concentrating. You're listening to every single word and thinking about where to go next. It's a very intense process.

There are also adversarial interviews in which somebody's held to account, usually for how they're using or have used their power. I can think of a couple you've done that are very well known. I wanted to start by talking about the one with Don Burke, a former Channel 9 star, who'd been exposed as an alleged serial sexual harasser in the workplace. Talk me through your preparation and decision-making process for that interview.

I didn't have much time to prepare. We'd heard at the weekend that these women were going to talk, and a big story was going to break on Monday. When Don's wife Maria met me at the door, she said, 'He's going to tell you that he was unfaithful to me. Don't worry about it, I'm fine.' I thought, 'What? Does he think he's going to change the narrative with the big revelation "Don Burke: 'Yes, I was unfaithful to my wife'", and all that other stuff is going to be swept under the carpet?'

If you look at it, he drops [the unfaithfulness narrative] very quickly. I thought, 'No, you don't get to do that, this is just deflection.' I could never understand why he did the interview.

You don't strike me as a confrontational person. Do you have to psych yourself up to go into an interview that you know is going to be confrontational?

Yeah, you do. I mean, I don't go through life looking for arguments. That's true. But I'm not a shrinking violet. What I never want to do is get so passionate that I raise my voice, because then you lose it. So I'm always moderate in an interview. If you keep moderate, you keep your heart rate down, and things stay on a fairly even keel. That's my trick – never to get so worked up that I'm a player. Because I'm never a player, I'm always an observer.

For me, there's something in the prep that enables me to psych myself up to go in there. Because I know that even if it is confrontational, I'm armed with facts and I have thought through what they might say.

You're absolutely right. You've got to do your homework; you have to know ten times more than you will use in the interview. I'm boringly exhaustive about preparation for interviews. I'll always want to know ten times more than I need to use, cos you never know what direction it's going to take.

Another adversarial interview you've done was with former rugby player Matthew Johns, who'd been the subject of a *Four Corners* investigation into a group-sex incident in New Zealand. When people are accused of doing – or have done – something wrong, they're often at their lowest point because of the shame and humiliation that comes with the exposure. How do you judge the balance between going hard on behalf of an alleged victim or the public and concern for the wellbeing of the person being interviewed?

It's hard. It's a fine line, and it's one of the challenges of the job. Matthew Johns had, for some time, been a Nine person, and was a great television talent. So I had a bit of history with him and I liked him. Fast-forward a few years, and the *Four Corners* story came out with that young woman in New Zealand. And you could see that, seven or eight years later, she was still broken. I editorialised the following night and said he should talk – and the next day, bugger me, he talked.

If you go into an interview thinking someone should talk, that's because you know that there are questions to answer. So you're going to put the questions out there. The interview took place in our Sydney boardroom, and it was packed with people. He had supporters, we had three camera crews, we had lots of people from the network. I met with Matt and [his wife] Trish briefly before we went in, and I said to Trish, 'My main concern is why are you here, because I'm going to ask Matt some really tough questions. I'm concerned about you.' And she said, 'No, I want to be here.' So if he thought it was going to be friendly or easy, by the time we walked into the room to do it he knew it wasn't going to be.

Often it's a competitive thing to land people for big interviews. Do you personally lobby?

It depends on the circumstances. I didn't personally lobby Matt – although I did editorialise, and that was my idea – or Don Burke. Those negotiations took place separate to me. But with the Beaconsfield mine disaster, I was desperate to meet those boys. I'm claustrophobic and every night I went to bed thinking, 'They're still under there. They're a kilometre underground. They've got rock right on their noses. How the hell are they still lucid and able to talk?' I thought, 'I desperately want to know how they did this.' So when that interview was being considered, I did try very hard to insert myself into the process.

We've discussed a number of different kinds of interviews. Are there skills that are common to all of them?

You really have to listen, it's the critical thing. You see lots of interviewers who are constantly concentrating on their next question, and you think, 'Ah, you have to learn to stop doing that.' I know that some people have their questions on autocue now, but I always have my questions handwritten, by me, on a piece of paper in front of me. No one else writes my questions. I don't want to be thinking about the next question, I want to be thinking about the answer.

That's exactly how I do it. I view that piece of paper as a security blanket, it's what lets me get out on the highwire. But I have to be prepared to just chuck it out depending what the person says.

Correct. Absolutely. I'll have people who are nervous about their interview say, 'What are you going to ask me?' And I'll say, 'Look, I've got this page of questions, but truthfully, it's just key points that I want to hit. It's just a framework. Because you'll give me an answer that'll take me in a whole other direction.'

You've interviewed tens of thousands of people over the course of your career. What makes an interview memorable to you years later?

I think it depends on the interview. There's one I'll always remember because of the sheer honesty of it – the unvarnished honesty that you don't very often get. It was with Shelly Walsh. I've interviewed her once since – she made me cry in the first interview, and I made her cry in the second. Afterwards, she said, 'Now we're even.'

Shelly was a policewoman who had separated from her husband, with whom she had two kids. She'd gone to do a night shift, left her children with her parents, and her father killed her mother and then killed her children. She came back the next day and her father greeted her at the door. She's walking through the house asking, 'Where are the kids? Where the kids?' and her father's just saying, 'Do you want a cup of tea? Do you want a cup of tea?'

First of all, she found her mother. Then she had to use her wit . . . her father's still saying, 'Do you want a cup of tea?' And she's thinking at a hundred miles an hour, 'Where are the kids? Where are the kids?' I get chills up my spine as I talk about it. She goes into the bedroom, she finds the kids and then her father attacks her with an axe. She has to fight him off. He takes off and then gets arrested hiding out in a hotel. I'll never forget that day. I'll never forget Shelly telling the story. God, it was traumatic. She was so honest, so unvarnished and so brave to tell her story. That is the interview that will always stay with me. Always.

When you interviewed her later, what was it for?

Many years later, I went back to check on her. She'd gone and seen her father in prison to ask him why he did it. I said to her, 'Why? He doesn't know why! He's a narcissist and a psychopath. Why would you do that?' And she said, 'I just needed to know why.' Of course, he didn't tell her why, he just shrugged. It was just another form of torture – he not only didn't know why, he didn't care to tell her, he didn't care about her feelings, he just trampled on her.

Oh god.

I know, Leigh. She's a remarkable woman to come through all of that. You never replace your mother or your kids. How do you ever put that behind you?

It's good that you went back to interview her. The shows we present often capture people on the worst days of their lives. It can just be a parade of awful things happening to people. And the reality is, human beings are unbelievable in terms of what they can adapt to and what they can live with. As you say, the pain never goes away. But often, when you revisit people a year later, five years later, twenty years later, it's astonishing how they've been able to carry on.

Yeah, I think so too. The ordinary people who were just bumping along, living their lives, who find themselves in extraordinary situations? They're always the interviews that are far more reve-latory to me than celebrities or politicians. It's how ordinary people navigate the extraordinary that keeps me doing the job.

Richard Fidler

Richard Fidler is a host on the most popular interview program on Australian radio, ABC's Conversations. *He has had an incredibly diverse career, hosting television shows such as* Race Around the World *and* Vulture, *presenting ABC local radio in Brisbane, and writing acclaimed books, including* Ghost Empire *and* The Golden Maze. *He first rose to prominence in Australia in the 1980s as part of the globally successful musical comedy trio The Doug Anthony Allstars.*

Richard, you're considered one of the best interviewers in the country, so I fear your judgement: 'Mmm . . . this isn't how I would have opened.'

Let's be heavily critical of each other's interviewing techniques, just nitpick each other all the way through. I think that'll be a really rewarding experience, not just for us, but for the readers as well, Leigh.

Conversations is constantly at the top of the most listened-to podcasts in Australia. It attracts millions of downloads each month. Is there an ethos that drives the guests you invite?

Yes, and it goes right back to the founding of the show. This was an ethos that the community would be maybe dimly aware of, or not aware of at all: 'unfamous' people who nonetheless have seen and done extraordinary things. There's something about radio in particular – as opposed to TV, which puts so much of a premium on how you look – that's very egalitarian, very democratic. Someone who you've never heard of can sound easily more impressive than a very powerful, wealthy, incredibly hot-looking, successful person. We found, right from the start, that listeners would always respond more strongly to unfamous guests than they would to famous people, because they felt they could measure their own lives against them.

The challenge of unfamous guests is finding them.

It's not easy. Often it's word of mouth, often it's someone that one of our producers has heard of or I've met. We have a 'suggest a guest' thing on our website, but we won't choose very many at all from that list. We get a lot of suggestions for people who have been saints in their communities. They're obviously wonderful people, but they might not necessarily make a good guest on the program. We really do need narrative, we need incidents in a life to make it work.

Once you've got a seed, by what process do you decide whether a potential guest will actually proceed to a program?

This is critical, and where the producers become really important. Our producers are outstanding – they make contact, then do a very long pre-interview with the guest and help them order the events of their lives into a single narrative, which is nearly always chronological.

There's a lot of pastoral care involved in that process. Our show's a beast to feed; there's a lot of responsibility involved in dealing with people who are unfamous – who've never been in the media before, who might be intimidated by walking into a building like the ABC. We have to offer them a lot of care, reassurance and respect, invite them to reflect on their lives, then trust that reflection. It's a very, very careful process, and it has to be done with great sensitivity, insight and imagination.

How do you decide what you're going to ask?

If it's a guest for whom a producer has written the brief, I'll go over the brief. I like to let it sit for a day before I write an introduction. Then I'll come back to it and just focus on what's interesting to me. I'm confident that I can infect listeners with my curiosity about things that may seem banal at first. There's that old line of Henry Miller's about staring at a blade of grass for long enough and seeing a whole cosmos inside it – I try to take that approach. If you can reacquaint yourself with your inner eight-year-old, who looks at the sky and wonders why it's blue, then suddenly the world is revealed to you again as wondrous. There's a certain amount of joy and relief in that.

How much of your conversation is free-flowing versus following a designed structure?

I've always got the structure, the narrative thread, of it in my head. Otherwise it'd be a mess. But having that in my head allows me to stop and go, 'What did you just say? That's amazing.' I did an interview yesterday with this extraordinary woman from the Northern Territory, a paediatric cardiologist. She's going into Aboriginal communities, finding all these kids who've got heart disease from untreated strep infections, and she supported herself through her postgraduate medical degree by playing high-stakes poker in Crown Casino. She told me this amazing story about how she had to pretend to be someone else. She showed up at the casino wearing a Homer Simpson shirt, and one of her competitors said, 'So, what do you do?' and she said, 'I don't want to talk about it.' He said, 'Why?' and she said, 'Cos I've just been released from prison, and I don't really want to talk about it.'

Everyone was awestruck by that. With this mathematical gift for calculating probability, she stayed at the poker table till 8 a.m., made quite a bit of money, walked away, went straight onto a shift at the hospital, and a man came to her with his daughter for a consultation. Of course, it was one of the men she'd been sitting across the poker table from that night – here he was thinking he was handing his daughter to a criminal, and she said, 'I think I'm going to hand you over to another doctor.'

She remembered that story part way through the conversation. When that happens, you just relax and enjoy it. Let yourself enjoy that tangent like a listener, keeping always in the back of your mind where it is you're gonna have to come back in. You can hear when an interviewer can't quite do that, when they *have* to get back on track. You can hear them getting nervous and frightened, and they won't let the guest tell that story about pretending to be a hardened criminal at the poker table. You can hear them: 'Oooh, can we just get back to . . .' It always sounds awkward and boring. You go, 'No, no, no, no, let her talk! This is great.'

When I listen to *Conversations*, something that strikes me often is that you are very knowledgeable and yet your questions never make me feel as if you're attempting to convey how smart you are. You never in any way make it about you. Is that something that you're conscious of?

I think you have to wear your erudition lightly. There's a problem you sometimes find in public radio, where everyone is terrified of being accused of dumbing something down. So there are awkward displays of erudition in the body of a question that was never a question. It would be like 'Leigh Sales, you presented *7.30* for twelve years, you were a journalist and foreign correspondent, you wrote on national security and trauma, and you're greatly troubled by the unfolding situation in Ukraine.' Now, all that does is reveal that I've done my research. It's not a question, and the only answer to that comment is 'Well yes, Richard, I have.' You hear that all the time, and when an interviewer does that, they're not acting on behalf of the listener. They're acting to shore up their shaky credibility.

Do you have any particular techniques to build rapport?

Yes. Part of that is the art of hospitality. It's like when you have guests to your house, you welcome them in, and in some ways, you mirror them. If they're shy, you don't smother them with your personality. You're gentle, you bring them in, you're polite and you show a bit of humour.

On the other hand, if you're talking to Miriam Margolyes, you've gotta not pitter-patter around her. You gotta kick the footy to her pretty firmly, because she'll mark it and kick it straight back to you and hit you in the head with it if you're not careful. So I always seek, as a broadcaster and as a writer, to be hospitable to the guest and to the listener.

You have a comedy background. Is being able to reach for wit useful?

Yeah, I think so. But not in a performative sense. Comedians often don't go well on my show, unless they're prepared to drop that little demon they have in the back of their head that says, 'Forty seconds have gone past and we haven't had laughter, better do something about that.' It's very hard to get comedians to drop their performance persona and talk like a normal person. The kind of humour I try and bring arises naturally and spontaneously. I never write gags.

If you do have somebody in performance mode, how do you try to break it?

Oh, it's hard. When it's happened to me, I've instantly realised, 'Ohhhh, I should never have asked this person on the show.' You try and step on their rhythm, or slow right down to break the rhythm of the 'gag, gag, gag' thing they're trying to knock out. Slow it right down, ask them questions, ask them to be reflective.

I remember listening to you interviewing Brenda Blethyn and I had to pull the car over because I was laughing so uncontrollably. She was telling an anecdote about being at the Golden

Globes. She was nominated, really nervous, and was wearing a long gown. Then she went to the bathroom and accidentally weed on her dress. When her name got called, she could see the steam rising from the urine on her gown under the stage lights.

If you look at her getting the award, Nicolas Cage is presenting and he's got this priceless 'Can I smell piss?' look on his face as he's handing it to her. When we finished that interview, we walked out of the studio together and were still in hysterics, just crying with laughter.

Often on your program, you'll have somebody telling a story that is incredibly moving or deeply personal. It gets to a point in the story where you feel like you're in a kind of sacred place, but obviously, once they've finished saying something very poignant, you as the interviewer can't allow the silence to go on forever. How do you push the conversation forward delicately?

I rely on instinct. There are some times when people have said something that's just so profoundly and beautifully sad, in relating something that's happened to them, you feel something like grief or deep sorrow and compassion sort of rise up through your stomach and your chest. You have to just let it pass through you – let it come up, sigh, wait a beat and then start again. Rather than try and step on it.

Most of the time, listeners are feeling it too, and they need that moment to breathe it out, reflect on it and move on to the next thing. There's always a moment where you know when it's right to start talking again. It's not that hard to know when that moment is for me. I don't know why, I just don't get frightened by the silence. And on TV it can be even more beautiful, because you can look at the person's face and study it and just let it sit there for a bit.

Every episode of *Conversations*, you're using a skill set that is critical to journalism, but you're not a journalist yourself. And you don't come from a journalism background. What advantages do you think coming at this job from a non-journalist's perspective gives you?

In my twenties, I was a comedian. I was in a comedy group for years and years, and I think that gives me a nice sense of absurdity. I hope it does, anyway. Also, a large part of my early life was spent reading in the back of a touring van. I've read widely, I've read a lot of history, and so I'm just curious. I've always tried to foster that sense of curiosity that I think journalism, all too often, tries to turn inside out. There's a demand for a certain kind of worldliness in one's tone as a journalist, I think. And journalists try and draw authority from that sense – like, 'I've seen it all and done it all, I know everything to begin with.' And I know I don't. And I know my listeners know I don't. Also, I'm not a foreign correspondent, Leigh. I'm not in Ukraine. I'm not in Syria. I've never been in those dangerous zones. I don't have the authority that comes from being in the middle of a place where the worst things in the world are happening. So I think I'd feel like an imposter if I tried to sound like an authoritative journalist.

Journalism, like all professions, has a culture. Certain things that are valued; for example, objectivity and impartiality. From

your vantage point, is there anything in journalistic culture that you think stifles the ability to do a good interview?

Yes. I used to see a lot of this, where journalists would talk about optics. That need to sound like you're part of that savvy conversation. Journalists would talk about how a politician was going over 'out there'. What the hell is that? You're supposed to be out there. They're inside, you're out there. The need to sound savvy, like, 'Oh, I was at a drinks party when I heard the vice-president say this.' Yuck! That's revolting.

I'm lucky I come from a local radio tradition too, which has a strong values system, an idea that you are not 'out there', you are in here, you are in the middle of this community. You're broadcasting from the main street of this community, whether it's a big city or a small regional centre. Your loyalty is to your listeners. Whereas the press gallery has always sounded like it's coming from the press gallery. And the architecture of Parliament House in Canberra – surrounded as it is by two moats, State Circle and Capital Circle – doesn't help that. There is that feeling of 'Oh, the country is out there, and we are in here.' I think there's a danger for journalists in trying to sound like they're reporting from 'in here' rather than 'out there', if you know what I mean.

Is there anything else you feel would be useful for people to know about the art of interviewing?

Yes – and this doesn't happen to me very often – but it's what to do when you're talking to someone and you go, 'Oh my god, I'm interviewing a giant dickhead.' I think this is something you and I both have experience with, Leigh. And that's when I become much more of a journo. My questions become much less friendly – much sharper, shorter and more interrogative. My bullshit detector has to ratchet right up, and I press them much, much harder. And then I go, 'Oh, this is quite fun actually, I'm enjoying this.'

I have a fantasy that one day I'm going to go, 'You know what? You don't really seem to enjoy being here, and I'm certainly not enjoying speaking to you. So let's just bring this to an end, shall we?' and then I'll just stand up and walk out. To be honest, by far the more common thing is anticipating that somebody might be difficult and they turn out to be lovely. The one who springs to mind is Harrison Ford, who in all of the research was portrayed as really grouchy. So I spent a lot of time thinking how I was going to build rapport with him. I thought the best thing I could do was offer him a minute to himself while the crew mucked around with the lights. He sat down, we shook hands, and I said, 'Look, the crew's gonna take two minutes to fiddle around on the lighting, you've probably been talking to people all day, so I'm very happy for you to just sit here in complete silence, it might be the only two minutes you get to yourself all day.' And he said, 'Oh no, not at all. I'd love to have a chat.' And then I mentally went to pieces: 'Oh god, I haven't pre-gamed the small talk for Harrison Ford!'

Yeah, that has happened to me a few times as well. But I think a large part of that was you being in the same room as him. Whether you were conscious of it or not, you might have been mirroring his body language to some degree. And this was your show as well. He's your guest. Maybe you were projecting a certain kind of authority and hospitality in that moment that made him feel calm and relaxed.

The worst kind of guests you can have in those circumstances are those I call the 'and uhhhs'. They go, 'So I went down the street and uhhh . . . went to the milk bar and uhhh . . . bought a loaf of bread and uhhh . . .' and you're waiting for them to get to the end of this story. And you know how it always ends? They go 'And uhhh . . . yeah.'

Live Broadcasting

Public speaking is one of the most well-known human fears, so a job that involves talking unscripted for an indeterminate period of time to an audience of hundreds of thousands would be many people's nightmare. This is the art of the live cross.

Senior general news reporters, rounds reporters, foreign correspondents and anchors are often required to fill time on air for hours as major news events unfold. Sometimes it will involve crossing live from disaster zones or the scenes of breaking news, where the information conveyed to the community can be a genuine matter of life and death. One of the scariest things about live reporting for a journalist is the need to be as accurate when speaking unscripted as they would be in a carefully written story. There is little margin for error. Inaccurate court reporting can have particularly devastating consequences.

Adding to the difficulty of live broadcasting are the external unknowns: an environment can turn dangerous, the unexpected might happen or technology might fail at a critical moment. In every one of those circumstances, the reporter must keep going as best they can.

No matter how much rehearsal a reporter might do, nothing can replicate the pressure of live performance. The only way to truly learn how to report live is by stepping onto the highwire and actually doing it. It is undoubtedly a challenging task but there are tools and strategies that can make the task easier.

David Speers

David Speers is the host of ABC TV's Insiders, *where he interviews leading political figures and explores issues with an expert panel. David also writes political analysis for ABC news online, appears across TV and radio platforms, and has regularly hosted* Q&A. *Before joining the ABC in 2020, David spent nineteen years as the Political Editor of Sky News Australia. He has multiple Walkley, Logie and Kennedy awards, and has also been named Press Gallery Journalist of the Year.*

How many times have you gone on live TV without knowing how long it will be for and without knowing what is going to happen?

Dozens and dozens of times. For me, it's usually a big political development or scoop that involves that sort of live coverage. But there have also been other stories, terrorism attacks – 9/11, London, Indonesia, smaller incidents in Australia – events that require that big, rolling coverage. My comfort zone is politics but the common thread is you don't know how long it's going to run or when it's going to end.

What goes through your mind when a producer says, 'David, this is happening, we need you to go on immediately'?

Often it's happened to me when I'm already on air, so you literally have no time to think about it or prepare; you're told in your ear this has happened and away you go. Sometimes you're told, 'We need you to get on right now,' and that gives you a small amount of warning. What goes through your head is 'What do I already know?' Then you do the process of starting to think ahead to where the story might go next and what you might need to know and who you might need to get in touch with to sustain the ongoing coverage.

Do you suffer nerves?

I've been fortunate in that I haven't suffered from nerves as much as some others, but I still feel nerves from time to time.

I find once I'm actually broadcasting, there's so much to think about that there's not a lot of space for nerves to come in. The anticipation is far more excruciating than doing it.

I would agree with that entirely. The nerves for me are when I think too much about whether I'm going to get everything right, whether I'm going to be fair, whether I'm going to make sure I neither over-hype nor undersell, all of these things. The nerves are about whether you're going to perform how you want to perform. But if you start thinking too much about how it's going to look, that's where it can really get you.

My approach is to always try to remind myself that I've done the preparation, to be confident in the work that I've done to get to this point, knowing that I've done it before. Then absolutely, once I start the live coverage, a lot of that disappears. There is the buzz, the adrenalin of a big live story, but there's also the focus once you're on air of really concentrating on what's happening.

What does it mean in live broadcasting when somebody tells you to pad?

It's about talking and talking until something happens, or more importantly until a relevant guest arrives who you can go to in order to find out more about what's happening. Padding requires information, first and foremost, plus insight, interesting comments. Some do it better than others. My favourite person when it comes to padding has always been Stan Grant. I think he is outstanding, whether he's been on CNN or the ABC. You can tell it's padding because they're scrambling for a guest, but he can sustain really insightful, interesting discussion while on air talking alone, and he doesn't miss a beat. He is incredibly eloquent and very good at it.

You need a few things. The first is the basic information that has caused this rolling coverage to start. The second is that bank of background information. For me, when it comes to politics, it's about the context. Something big has happened, what's the context for that? Why has a leader resigned, or someone challenged? Usually you have a pretty good sense of why things have got to this point; you can unpack that and discuss it. You can draw on history and your knowledge, having covered this patch for a long time: how is what we're seeing different or similar to what has already happened? What are we seeing now that is unusual? You also have the knowledge of who are going to be key players as things unfold from here, and you try to get information from them to stay ahead of where the story is going.

Do you have any special tricks that you use? For example, I sometimes jot down four or five points on a piece of paper so that at any time I can say something like, 'Just a reminder of Bob Hawke's key achievements: he floated the dollar, he created Medicare,' so that at any time, if there's a lull, I have something to reach for. I may never use those points, but it's like a security blanket I can reach for if I need to.

Dot points are key. Each one of those dot points will be a launch pad for different ideas, arguments, discussion. Coming back to the basic facts that have brought on the rolling coverage is really important. It might be a statement from a politician, it might be a statement from police; you've got to remember that viewers are constantly joining the coverage, they haven't watched from the beginning and you need to bring them into the loop to let them know what's going on and bring them up to speed. That can be a safety net as well: just reset the conversation.

So you're not too worried then about repetition over the course of a broadcast?

It's a balance. You do have to repeat the basic facts every now and then, but hopefully people are sustaining their viewing and so you don't want to be *too* repetitive. The other thing to do when it comes to a big political event, if you do have the warning before the coverage starts, is text as many contacts and sources as you can, people who might be relevant, and let them know you will be looking for any tidbit of information, because even a small bit of information can give you another piece of the puzzle.

Even a contact texting, 'This is a bit like 2006, when XYZ happened,' can be extremely helpful because it might trigger another five or ten minutes of discussion.

Exactly. A second brain, or two or three extra brains, on a big rolling story can be enormously helpful. Sometimes, if you don't have a colleague to do it, you bring in what we call a presenter's friend, who might be an expert in this area – terrorism, earthquakes, whatever it is. Having someone you can keep talking to for a long period of time will trigger fresh thoughts of your own and keep the conversation going.

There's pressure to be first in journalism. Say for example you've got a leadership spill and you get a text message that says it's Morrison and the numbers are 52 to 49. Will you go live with that information on the basis of one text message? Normally you would try to get verification first.

Look, I have done that but it really depends who it is. If it's somebody I absolutely trust and know, and they're in that room and I know there's no chance they are using me – because what's the point of giving me a false number – yes, I have. But we all know that if you're wrong with something like that it's a real scar on your reputation, so you don't ever want to be wrong. Fortunately, I've never been in that situation.

Even when you do trust the person, it can be quite scary to make the declaration straight down the barrel of the camera, because you know that ultimately it rests on you.

Absolutely. I still remember one of my early jobs in radio, reading the news when Princess Diana died. People might remember that there was the car crash, then speculation went on for a number of hours – was she alive or dead – and then finally the networks in London, the BBC and Sky, and so on, all claimed they had the official confirmation. I raced in thirty seconds before the bulletin and read it out. Even seeing that confirmation, I still remember the nerves I had making such a big call. It is a big moment to say something dramatic if you're simply taking it from a number of sources rather than directly. You have to trust your information.

Have you had any live experiences that went so wrong you are still chilled to the bone thinking about them?

I've had plenty of experiences that have chilled me to the bone, not so much live. I had a flight cancelled when I was trying to get to the White House for my one and only interview with the president, and that threw me into fits of panic! I've done an interview with a prime minister in another country where I didn't record the sound, so we had to do it again. Those things are horrifying for a journalist.

During big leadership dramas, the biggest concern, the biggest panic, is being given dud information, being played, being used. Has that ever happened? Sure, I've been told things that didn't turn out to be true, but nothing that I still look back on and think, 'Wow, that was a whopper.' I was able to show just enough caution at the time around that information.

If somebody is attempting to use you, does that negate any obligation on your part to preserve their anonymity as a source?

No, I still protect the source. Sources will tell you something and then say the opposite in front of the cameras, but it doesn't mean

I'm going to blow their cover and reveal their name. It's just one of those ethical things as a journalist where you have to suck it up and then you remember it. But I won't reveal them as a source.

It just perhaps informs your thinking about them *as* a source in the future.

One hundred per cent. It just means you'll take it with a big grain of salt the next time they tell you something.

What would be your advice to a young reporter doing live broadcasting for the first time?

The best way to learn is to do it. Now, that's easier said than done. But any experience you can get is great. For me, it was while I was still at university doing community radio. For those who are already working in the industry but haven't done as much live, I guess it's about watching those you do admire, techniques they use. I also keep coming back to information, arming yourself with as much information as you can. Read, read, read. It all helps when you're in the hot seat.

Stan Grant

Stan Grant is a journalist and author who, most recently, has been the host of ABC TV's Q&A. *After starting his career in the Australian media, he moved to CNN for a long-term stint as Senior International Correspondent. Stan has written six books:* The Tears of Strangers, Talking to My Country, Australia Day, On Identity, With the Falling of the Dusk: A Chronicle of the World in Crisis *and* The Queen Is Dead. *A Wiradjuri man, he wrote the film documentary* The Australian Dream *about the racism directed at AFL footballer Adam Goodes. It won both the 2019 AACTA (Australian Academy of Cinema and Television Arts) and Walkley awards for best documentary.*

Stan, for much of your career, you were a foreign correspondent for CNN. That meant that with zero notice, at any time, you could be told you're flying to any country, where you may not know anyone, where you don't speak the language, where a disaster might have rendered basic communication and amenities hard to come by. Then, when you land, you might be

expected to immediately start doing live crosses to CNN. How do you do that?

You've gotta have a good team around you: people that I really trusted, who had my back. The cameramen, the fixers on the ground. CNN had a really good network of those people at the places I would often be jetted into at a moment's notice. So if I went to Afghanistan or Iraq or Pakistan or Somalia, there were people there we knew could be trusted.

The other thing is that there is no substitute for being unbelievably prepared. I know it's hard to be prepared for the unexpected but I made a point of knowing as much about as many places as I could. To be able to have institutional knowledge, historical knowledge, to know the politics of these places so that when I hit the ground, I could do something.

You're right – many times I would land and they would want me on air before I cleared the airport. All you've got is the knowledge you've brought. You also get very, very used to finding people to talk to immediately, and airports are good for that because you're seeing everyone come and go. So as soon as I landed, I was talking to the baggage handler, I was talking to the people who worked at the airport, people milling around, any of the taxi drivers. That would get me through the first crosses and then off you go.

In between assignments, how much work were you doing to maintain those local contacts so they would be there when you needed them?

All the time. I was constantly in contact with the people in places where I spent a lot of time. Apart from anything else, we were close, they were friends. These were people that you worked with twenty hours a day, that you ate with, slept with. They were people who shared hours and hours of journeys in cars across the country, our interpreters, our drivers. People you'd been to horrendous scenes with, that you had witnessed death with, come under fire with. The relationships are really, really close and I was constantly in contact. I still am. They're a very special breed, fixers as we call them, and without them we couldn't do our work.

It sounds like this kind of reporting cannot be treated like cramming for an exam.

No. It's not enough to just follow the headlines. You can't just know what's happening day by day, you have to know the history. If you're going into Pakistan, you have to know: what is it about Pakistan that makes Pakistan the way it is? What was it about partition in India that created Pakistan? Why is the civilian government in Pakistan historically so weak? What is built into the idea of Pakistan that defines its identity? What's the role of Islam? What's the role of the military? Who are all the various terrorist groups and how do they all fit together? What's the power structure? Why is it that a country like Pakistan, a Muslim country, could elect a female as prime minister before that ever happened in Australia? The same for North Korea, the same for Afghanistan, for Iraq, for any of the places I was going to a lot. What was it that made those places unique? You need deep, deep, deep knowledge. That means reading. There is no substitute for reading. Especially at a place like CNN, Leigh, because you never knew what you were going to do. Once you were on air, you never knew when you were going to come off.

Once, we were in Beijing and we were waiting for Xi Jinping. He'd just been sworn in as President and we were waiting for him to come to do his first speech and introduce the politburo, the seven most senior figures in the communist party. The timing was that I'd come on at ten minutes to the hour, he would come on at the top of the hour, he'd do his thing, then it would come back to me and we'd wrap up the program. We thought it would last, at most, about an hour. *Two hours* after he was meant to have appeared, he finally appeared. I had to tap dance for two hours. At CNN, they wouldn't just go away from it, because it [the speech] could happen at any time. There was just me. You have to know about Xi's past, his father, the Chinese communist party, what led up to the revolution, who were the significant figures, what happened post-Mao, what role Deng played, what happened during the reform era, who are the major players now, who was likely to be in the politburo, what their backgrounds were, how this fitted into the rest of the world. You must have that knowledge all at your fingertips – nobody can come in and give you a piece of paper. Nobody can come in and prep you, you're there and you're exposed.

Even as we're talking now, you didn't know what I was going to ask you and yet you were able to reach for example after example off the top of your head regarding Pakistan and China. But we're just chatting, and so there's not the pressure of being on live TV. If we were live, would you have the confidence to do what you did just now without having notes, or would you need something in front of you?

A hundred per cent without. I started this way from very early in my career. I think it's got something to do with the way I grew up and my education. I was really lucky to have had very little structured, formal education. People are often astonished when I tell them this, but I really did not go to school in any significant or meaningful way until I was fourteen, and even then it was pretty ordinary schools. I was moving around so much. We were a poor Aboriginal family, itinerant. I'd turn up to school for a few weeks, we'd then move on because Dad had found a job somewhere else, or I wouldn't go to school at all because we weren't going to be in a place long enough. I went to at least thirteen or fourteen different schools by the time I was in high school, so there was no continuity. Nobody was taking me through the grades, moving me in a structured way through the various stages. I got to rely a lot on my own wit and instincts and I read ravenously. I was this nonstop reader because that was all I had. Mum would bring books home that she had picked up in the cardboard boxes at St Vincent de Paul's or The Smith Family, where we got our clothes. She'd just put her hand in and pick up ten books and I'd read them all. I absorbed information.

By the time I got into high school, we'd settled down a little bit – I still went to six different high schools – and I found that I had this ability to retain and recover information. Whatever I read, it went in. When I went into journalism, I would make a point of going to a press conference and not taking notes. I could come back and remember everything. I could go to wherever things were on the tape. I'd have my scripts written in my head before I got back to the office. Everything came together: a great memory, an ability to recall information, and a confidence that I had that ability. So when I got on air, I just never doubted it.

I remember once when I was on air, and I'd been on for half an hour or so, I had this incredible feeling of calm and I remember smiling to myself, sitting there thinking, 'Right, I'm like a football player in the zone. I don't need to rehearse this play or sit down and map it out, I know exactly what I need to do.' I felt so calm. In other aspects of my life that isn't always the case.

Learning and retaining information is one thing, but you are also particularly amazing at speaking fluidly. You look entirely relaxed yet you also sound authoritative. Was there anything else in your background that helped you learn how to speak like that, so eloquently?

In church. I was raised in the Aboriginal churches on the missions and my uncles were the pastors. These were guys inspired by the likes of Martin Luther King Jr. Their social justice movement mirrored the black rights movement in America, in the churches of the South. These were people with very limited formal education who could stand there and give these incredible sermons that could last for an hour without missing a single beat, quoting scripture, crafting a narrative, speaking to you emotionally and powerfully and politically. There was always a political message. I just absorbed that, being around those figures who were commanding speakers with incredible presence, with charisma, with the incredible ability to reach out and touch you. This was my real education: being around those people and seeing the way that words mattered, and the way they landed those words, the command and the confidence and the passion they brought to it. That's where it came from.

Sometimes when a reporter is in the field and the newsroom crosses to them, they might be told they have five minutes, or they might be told forty-five seconds, or they might be told it's

indefinite. How do you develop a sense of timing and know when you're hitting your duration?

I visualise a lot of things. When I'm recovering information, I can see it in my head like a book, like I'm turning the pages of a book. It's the same thing with time. I visualise it, I see the second hand of the clock. I can feel what five, ten, thirty seconds, a minute feels like. It has become really innate. I can land right on it. That mental clock is ticking down while I'm speaking.

Do you ever think about who you're talking to?

I hear people advise to think about a specific person. I never did that. I was much more interested in the story, wrapped up in that, finding what I thought was particularly compelling and important, imparting that knowledge, connecting the dots. I was much more absorbed in that in the moment, rather than who I was talking to. People respond to your knowledge, how authoritative you are, how calm, how confident, how engaging you are. I wanted people to be wrapped up in the story I was telling.

What you're doing in a live cross is a form of storytelling, unscripted storytelling.

Things never come out right for me if they're scripted. Even writing books, I will often compose the entire book in my mind before I've written a single thing on the page. Sometimes when I'm starting a book, I'll go for a drive and I'll put my phone on record and I'll speak what I want to say in the book. As I'm speaking, the ideas start to form, the words find themselves.

It's like improv jazz. You know your instrument. You know how to impart that feeling and connect with people musically, and then you just let it all go. I've always liked the idea of working without a net. I didn't need something there to catch me if I fell. I knew I could catch myself. I had enough knowledge, I had enough ability, I never doubted that. I've always worked much better in a less scripted form. The moment it's captured on a page for me it loses some magic. And I lose something.

I've never felt I was one of those TV performers or presenters who could deliver a script, or somebody else's words. Whenever I filled in doing *7.30* or something, I felt like I wasn't coming through the screen. As you know, Leigh, it's hard to go through the camera, it's hard to get from this side of the television to the other side of the television. People are sitting at home, you're competing with so much background noise and distraction. I find it difficult when something is written for me, when it's somebody else's words, to bring enough of myself to punch through the screen. If I threw everything away and just freestyled, then it felt like me. It's not a sense of arrogance, it's the only way I know how to do it. Words in a script in front of me is like sheet music in front of a self-taught guitarist: it just doesn't make any sense. I can't deliver that, I've never been able to.

When you were starting out, did you have to fight to use this approach?

I was lucky. I've been fortunate in my career, I've walked into places where people saw something in me and really backed me. It must be hard to work in a place where you can't be yourself. And I have done that. I found when I worked in commercial television, it was so not me. Every bit of it rubbed against me. I wasn't it and it wasn't me. I could never be the sort of person they wanted me to be. Some people do it spectacularly well.

People like Karl Stefanovic, in many ways I kind of look at and envy. I think, 'Wow, he's got so many gears, he's entertaining, he's affable, he's bright, and he's the epitome of that commercial TV act.' I never had that.

But the places that have worked for me have been where all that other stuff came together. CNN worked for me like nothing else. The moment I walked in there, I felt like, 'I've got this, this is who I am.' The people I worked with there, people like [foreign correspondent] Christiane Amanpour, who in every way is not your polished television performer. She'll turn up and her hair will be blowing and she'll have no make-up, and she just brings so much gravitas and passion and knowledge. When I walked in there, I thought, 'This is for me. I can breathe here.' When I was at Channel 7, it was so manicured. The words were never mine and I felt incredibly constrained. It was a lesson in learning who are you and what works for you. There are things that work for you and things that don't. I've learned over the years who I am.

It's a real lesson, isn't it; if you can hold true to your authentic self and find the path that works for you in journalism, it's the way to do it. I know myself, I couldn't do the kind of reporting you do because I'm too anxious, I couldn't function in war zones. I have friends in journalism who feel like frauds because they've never done investigative journalism. But there are many different paths, many of them behind the camera, that certain personality types lend themselves to.

You can't be all things to all people and you can't overthink it. If you know who you are, you do your best, and you surround yourself with people who can bring that out in you, that's enough.

Melissa Doyle AM

Melissa Doyle has more than thirty years' experience in journalism and is best known to Australians as the founding co-anchor of Channel 7's Sunrise, *a job she held for sixteen years, taking the show to number one in the competitive breakfast timeslot. She has hosted the live broadcasts of innumerable major national and international stories, including four Olympic Games, the Queen's diamond jubilee, Victoria's Black Saturday bushfires, multiple state and federal elections, the inauguration of Barack Obama, and the election of Pope Benedict. She has also presented Seven's flagship current affairs program,* Sunday Night, *as well as* This Is Your Life. *Melissa is the weekend breakfast host for radio station Smooth FM, and juggles an extensive list of other media and charity commitments.*

I want to start by talking about when you went live for a lengthy time with a story that moved at a painstakingly slow pace. That occasion was the Beaconsfield mine disaster. What did you require to do that?

You have to have a team you trust, whether it's a director or a producer in the studio. We used to have this saying that they will never leave you flapping in the wind. You have to know that if it all falls apart and you have no idea where to go or what to say next, there's somebody there to give you a prompt or suggestion. I would always say to the producer, 'As long as you let me know where to get to, I will get us there.' It's like knowing where the next cross street is.

There's more to talk about than you probably realise. There's always something happening around us. I saw my role in those situations as being the representative of the viewer. They're at home in their kitchen, lounge room, watching. They not only want to know what's happening, but also what it's like. So whether it be Beaconsfield, or a bushfire, what is the atmosphere? What are the sounds? What are the smells? Who are the people? What is the tension? What's going on around us? You can always fall back on some of those descriptors as a bit of padding when you don't have any new or breaking content.

With Beaconsfield, we were there for ten days and every day when I came off air, I would go around and gather information. I'd wander around the town, see what shops were there, who runs the bakery; there was a lovely lady down there I remember who was making a lot of soup and coming and feeding the media. Find out who are those people, how long has she lived in town. What are the local schoolkids doing, what is the community doing? You then have this stockpile of anecdotes you can rely on. The next day on air, you're like, 'Yesterday I was chatting to Martha, who was making soup and feeding the locals.' If you don't need any of it, that's okay. But I always feel like the more information I have to draw on, the more relaxed and comfortable I am.

The preparation is a security net under the highwire.

I remember doing a papal election and there were the top ten candidates and I'd done all my research and tried to cram them all in. And then the smoke goes up and they announce Pope Benedict, and he wasn't one of the favourites. I was like, 'Oh, shit! I haven't fully briefed myself on him. We weren't expecting him.' And then of course, because we're standing in St Peter's Square, with five million other journalists from around the world who are clearly putting a strain on the Roman internet, I couldn't get any signal to access Google on my phone. I had an amazing producer in my ear giving me all the facts and I just spat it out. There are always situations where no matter how much work you've done, and how prepped you think you are, it falls over.

I'm imagining you going, 'We have a new pope and it's Pope Benedict, but let me tell you about Archbishop So-and-so, he's the guy who came in third.'

Let me tell you about the ones who didn't get elected!

What's the difference between going live on a breaking news event versus a staged event like a royal wedding?

There's a lot more prep for a staged event. For example, for a royal wedding you have a great array of experts that you can call on, you probably have a bunch of packages already done, the history of royal weddings over the years, the history of Harry and Megan's romance, et cetera et cetera, so you know you have those things ready to go at any time. It makes it a lot easier to take a breath.

What makes padding *not* sound like padding?

I think it's those important touch points, just the reminder of why we are there. Not going off on some long ramble. Just that constant update of where we're at, this is what you need to know.

You also must know when to cut something off and not pad. I remember during the Lindt siege [in 2014, a group of Australians were taken hostage in a Sydney cafe and two were killed], we had this guy who was an expert in Al-Qaeda terrorist tactics and he started talking about beheadings. It was day one, and I remember thinking, 'This is not appropriate.' Knowing when to pull out of something is important, or conversely, when to let something breathe. In the Black Saturday bushfires, this man came up to me by the name of Sam and he couldn't find his wife and children, and he just came up live on air and said, 'I need to find Tina, here's my phone number,' and he was kind of pleading with viewers, has anyone seen Tina? Moments like that, that kind of leave you reeling, you have to let them happen and unfold. You're not going to cut somebody off in that situation.

Sometimes we feel like we need to keep talking and keep padding, and actually we don't. We can take a pause, we can let the natural sounds be heard – sporting events especially, or big events, like the Queen's jubilee, when there are sounds, when there is cheering. I don't want to hear a reporter talking over it. Sometimes I want them to shut up so I can hear the true sounds.

If you have a producer you trust, them saying 'Shush for a minute' can really help. You might be caught up with what you're doing. Another person objectively telling you to be quiet is good. But when you're in the field, you can actually see what is happening, so you may bring better judgement to it; you may be able to see somebody or something coming towards you.

When you said that someone might tell you to 'shush for a minute' or 'be quiet', that's the kind of language you wouldn't use in a normal workplace because it would seem rude. Is that literally the way you communicate in the live environment?

Yes. It's fast-paced. You can't have somebody saying, 'Mel, darling, would you mind just taking a moment.' It has to be simply 'Shut up!' And I think that's fine.

If you've been standing in the field for hours talking, sometimes adrenalin keeps you going and other times fatigue takes hold. Do you have any tips for when you start flagging?

When I'm in the moment, I'm in this weird zone. I'm never going to be an athlete but I imagine it's the closest feeling to when you're in a race or something. It's all you think about. For some strange reason, you can keep going. I've always found the harder ones are when you get to five minutes to the top of the hour and the executive producer jumps in your ear and goes, 'We're going for another hour.' They were the moments, I'll be honest, where it was like, 'Oh god.' You can pace yourself better if you know how long it's going to be.

For me, it's stuff like election night when you're waiting for somebody to show up to do a concession speech. You try to seem fine on air, but in your own brain you're going, 'Please, come *on*.'

And the mics are all set up and it's good to go, and it looks like it's imminent and you think, 'Oh beauty, they're about to come out,' and then it's waiting, waiting, waiting. That ten minutes can feel way longer than the previous hour!

I remember covering Kate and Will when they were having Prince George. She was late and I was there every day talking about the same thing. That got hard. There was only so much new information I could have after the first four or five days. You've used all your good stuff and she's still not in labour. I remember *The Telegraph*, one of the papers there, had this thing on the back of the paper, these finger-puppet cut-outs of William, Kate and the baby, and I remember I cut those out on air. I was thinking, 'Oh my god, this is the end, I have peaked, I have nowhere else to go.' There was nothing else to talk about!

One of the questions people most commonly ask me about this stuff is to do with the physicality of it: when do you eat, when do you go to the bathroom?

Bathroom is usually never. I'm probably over-sharing here, but sometimes when I came off air after long stints, I would feel so revolting the next day because I was so dehydrated. You just don't eat or drink. Or you just have things like jelly snakes for a bit of sugar. Or maybe you're in a bushfire zone and somebody brings you a meat pie covered in sauce, which normally I would crawl over hot coals for, but if you're standing there in TV attire, the last thing you can do is risk eating a pie with sauce.

I remember being outside when Schapelle Corby was released from Kerobokan Prison and it was so hot and humid. I was trying to look half decent and maintain a bit of hair and make-up. Trying to keep yourself looking alright is very hard, and as you know, the second you start looking a bit dishevelled, people start commenting. Covering Lindt, I wore black because I thought, 'This has to be really sombre,' and somebody wrote on the socials, 'Great dress, where is it from?' I remember thinking, 'That's your takeaway at this point in time?'

Everyone who works in live broadcasting knows that things go wrong. How do you handle missteps?

I believe in handling them as they are, acknowledging them. It looks silly if you just ignore them. If you're standing in a bushfire zone and somebody doesn't have audio, that's okay. You just say, 'Sorry, audio wasn't working there, we're doing our best here; Leigh is standing in a paddock five kilometres from me with no phone signal.' You just apologise and come back to it. I don't mind a bit of ropey television myself when it's live because it reminds people that it's real.

It's also very important to set the tone when you're on air. I think again back to Lindt, and the importance of my language. We were all in major panic, we thought the city was about to blow up, that there could be bombs everywhere. It's very important in those situations for journalists to be mindful of the words they're saying and how they're delivering them.

What helps you choose the right tone?

I think the sense of my responsibility in the moment. Experience gets you to a point where you recognise your responsibility. With Lindt, Man Monis [the terrorist] might have been watching, the families of the hostages might have been watching. I didn't want to alarm them any more than they were already.

The Victorian bushfires, it was terrifying, we didn't know the full extent. You don't want to alarm people about something that we don't yet know, but you also don't want to downplay it.

When you started at *Sunrise*, it came out of nowhere. *Today* on Channel 9 was very dominant. *Sunrise* was scrutinised, but there perhaps weren't the stakes that are there once you become the number one show in a time slot. Did it help that you were able to learn about live broadcasting under the radar?

Definitely. When we started, it was the old ratings where they had numbers. We used to get an asterisk. Nobody watched except our parents, and that was the best thing because we were able to find our way in a really natural, organic fashion. I can only imagine how many mistakes I made and how often I stuffed up, but hardly anyone was watching so nobody knew. By the time more viewers found us, we had hopefully got a little bit slicker. I always thought it was one of the best advantages that we had, that we could start under the radar and just let it evolve. We were never plonked in a situation and told, 'Do this, say this, make sure you have chemistry.' We were just told, 'Okay guys, there's a desk, off you go.'

The scrutiny now is ridiculous. People are so quick to judge. Especially when people are doing live commentary, and somebody highlights one line that they've said. I think, '*You* sit somewhere and talk nonstop about something live for an hour and never get a word wrong, or say something that you didn't quite mean, or that came out the wrong way.' That's human nature. We are a bit too quick to be harsh on live commentators.

What do you think about reporters trying to memorise what they're going to say live, to avoid making a mistake?

Don't. Because then if you miss one word in the middle of it, you're stuffed. It all unravels. I will always make notes and circle a few key words and they are my prompter words. And there's nothing wrong with looking down at your notes. It's natural.

In a normal conversation, you don't hold unbroken eye contact for the whole time.

That's right. And you're going for the feeling of a normal conversation. If you look at your notes, nobody is going to go, 'Oh, she doesn't know what she's talking about.' They're going to go, 'Oh good, she's checking detail.'

One of the hardest things about live broadcasting is that the only way to truly learn it is to do it, because even if you practise, there is no way to replicate the stress and pressure of performing live. What would be your general advice to a journalist facing that?

It's funny, because I love live. I love the adrenalin rush of it. If I'm pre-recording things, it's never as good. The adrenalin helps me perform.

I think, 'Go easy on yourself, and remember that most people watching you are a lot more forgiving than you might imagine. If it doesn't go 100 per cent smoothly, it's okay. It's okay if you stumble, it's okay if you lose your train of thought.' We all do that. Just go with it in a way that's natural. 'Hey, while I think about what I was going to tell you about Leigh's career, let me tell you about what's going on over here.' If it's not as slick and perfect as you want it to be, that's okay.

Also, live broadcasting is not for everybody. And that's fine, there are other jobs in journalism.

I say to people, 'Don't get so caught up that you think a job in front of the camera is the only one. It's the visible one but it's not by any stretch the most important.' I've worked with some of the most incredible, brilliant producers, and there is a particular skillset in being a production person who pulls it all together. There's a different skillset again in being a great researcher. On *This Is Your Life*, oh my god, the research is like a book. It is an amazing talent and I don't think I could do that. They give it to me on a silver platter and say, 'Now you go deliver it.' And I'm good at that, but that would be their worst nightmare! So yeah, find what makes you comfortable and what you're good at.

Telling a Story
with Pictures

Any journalist will tell you that landing a skilled camera operator, photographer or video editor to collaborate with on your story is as highly prized as the assignment itself. A talented one can transform a good story into something first-rate and rescue a poor or mediocre offering. Many journalists today shoot and edit their own material, and learning visual storytelling from experts is crucial. It involves far more than pointing and shooting. Only an amateur expects to sort things out in post-production with filters and digital editing.

In the field, a camera operator or photographer needs visual intelligence, street smarts, and a winning way with people to talk themselves in and out of places. They have to show the greatest courage of anyone in the crew, often putting themselves in the centre of the action, including danger, to get the best material. They also need the judgement to understand where to draw the line so they don't put themselves or others in harm's way. For video, the operator may also need to gather audio, another crucial part of the storytelling process.

The editor is the person tasked with cutting together sound and pictures to a script. Their creativity, ability to stay cool under pressure, and sense of rhythm and energy are critical.

Renee Nowytarger

Renee Nowytarger has more than twenty years' experience photographing history-making news events and profiling some of the world's most influential people. Her work has been hung in Australia's National Portrait Gallery and has appeared on the front pages of major mastheads, including The Australian, The Sydney Morning Herald *and* The Australian Financial Review. *She is that rare talent who is equally at home in the field or studio, with candid or posed images, in the media or corporate worlds. She is a two-time winner of the Nikon-Walkley Australian Press Photographer of the Year and has also been awarded Portrait Photographer of the Year.*

Camera work is critical to many of the stories that journalists write and tell. As a photographer, how much do you think in storytelling terms?

All the time. When I'm on an assignment, I want to encapsulate the environment: where somebody lives, who they are, what's happening in their life, the effects of what's happening in their life. I want to portray the true reality of what's there. You can shoot things in different ways to represent them differently. For me, being able to tell the real story through my pictures is very important.

I hated being in a hotel room filing. If you're in a room, you're never out amongst it. So, as much as I could, I would file from the car and go back out and walk the streets or start talking to people.

When you're working with journalists, it's really important to visualise what people will read. A lot of readers have never travelled overseas or have no idea what it's like after a tsunami or an earthquake or civil unrest or a coup, and how much it affects people's lives. When you can visualise that, you can show the emotion of the people affected.

When you're out in the field, there is an infinite number of possibilities to frame with your camera. How do you decide what actually makes it into a shot?

For me, it's about people. So it's real life, it's not set up. There's never really one thing. During the day it progresses. We start very early in the morning, and we finish very late at night. We just work all day. And as the day progresses, we meet new people, see new people, see new things. And the story changes, it evolves, it's never set in stone. It's always organic. Towards the end of the day, you look back and think, 'Well, what is it that we need to portray out of today that really tells the story?'

Do you think of every single shot as potentially a complete story?

I don't. I think of each shot as it is. I don't want to tell something that I can't. I just want to portray the reality. Not all the time can you tell an entire story. This is a basic example – you might have a woman crying over here, and a wedding going on over there. Is she crying because somebody is dead? Or is she crying because she's happy about her child's wedding? You know what I mean? Sometimes you can't always tell the entire story in one image.

I just don't think you need to force it, especially in this day and age where we have features online and we don't just run one photo, we run a series. You can tell a story through different images.

I still think the one photo that does run needs to be strong. It needs to tell the story. But 100 per cent of the story? It's difficult to do.

When somebody says, 'Oh, she really captured something in that frame,' what do they mean?

It means that it's emotive, it's environmental, it's descriptive. For me, it's personal. It brings the viewer into the image, it makes them feel like they're there, it makes them feel like they understand what the other person is going through, or what the other family is going through, or what's happened to the environment. It makes you feel. That's the most important thing. When I file photos, I ask myself, 'Is this visual? Does it tell a story? And will it bring the true emotion out in people when they look at it?'

Is the goal for the viewer of the photograph to experience the same emotion that exists there in the real-life scene?

Yeah, I believe so. I think it's to bring people that aren't there into the scene.

If a newly elected prime minister is making his victory speech on election night, on stage with his family and a crowd of faithful watching, how much do you focus on the central action versus the periphery?

In that situation, if you were one photographer, you would try and do both because you have to. That's the hard part – trying to be everywhere at once is impossible. You would probably try to cover some of the speech and then get out and see what's happening in the crowd. Like from one extreme or the other; it could be riots or it could be joy. You want to represent everything that's happening in that news story. If there's more than one of you, you could allocate people to different areas.

How much fear do you have in the field that you'll choose to focus on one thing and miss something else?

All the time. I don't even know if it's fear. When I'm photographing, I'm just focused. It's like I tune in and I switch off everything else. I'm thinking about what's going on, and then I'm thinking, 'Is there another angle that I should be coming in from?' It's really hard. You literally can't be at two places at once. I could also be four metres to the right of another photographer and completely miss something because they've turned to the left. You know? And that's the picture of the year that's just happened. And you're like, 'I got the back of it.'

It's also experience. Knowing where the right place is and getting to it, that's a mark of experience. I was always working with big blokes, but because I was little I'd always shuffle through the middle, through the cracks, and get into where I needed to be.

One of the few advantages of being a woman in a male-dominated field!

Definitely.

I think I suffer a bit from magical thinking around this kind of fear. Say if I'm covering court and waiting outside for somebody to emerge, I fear that if I go to the toilet, they'll definitely come out.

You'll miss it! You just don't go to the toilet, do you? I've had that experience, it was awful. They sent me to the *New York Post* for four months as an exchange. I thought it was going to be amazing. But I'd gone from travelling all over to being put on street corners in the middle of the snow, photographing houses where celebrities lived. I had to stand there twelve hours a day, just in case they came out. And the one time that I went to the toilet, we came back and the only person that ever came out came out of this frickin' house. And the other photographer got it.

The lesson for media rookies: you need good news instincts and a bladder of steel.

Yeah, basically!

How much of your job relies on people skills?

Every part of it. It's huge. Communication, and making people feel comfortable with having you around. A lot of our job is portraiture, so we need to make people that have never been in front of a camera like ours feel comfortable. You need to make them feel they can trust you so they're relaxed. You need to be able to portray them for who they are, not in this state of fear or discomfort. I honestly think it's ninety per cent of our trade.

When you photograph someone who's never been photographed before, what are the things you do to try to put them at ease?

For me, it's all about conversation. I'm quite a chatty person anyway, it's probably quite annoying for people. For portraiture, I'm quite happy to sit down and have a cup of tea beforehand, to just chat to them about their family. I'm intrigued about their life. Depending on the situation, I like asking questions. When I went to the Northern Territory, I'd get involved as well. Like if they were playing cards, I'd just hang out and play cards with them. Or I'd go to the shops with them and buy a snack, just little things. It wasn't intentional to break in but having a connection with people helps.

Does that affect the photograph?

Oh, absolutely. Because people trust you, they feel comfortable in front of you.

What about when you're shooting the opposite kind of person – a celebrity used to having their photograph taken all the time?

It's very process driven. A lot of the time it's very quick. The environment's pre-chosen, usually a hotel room or stage setting, and you've literally got five minutes, or ten minutes max. Most are just so professional that they know what to do. I try and push the boundaries, that's what I love about doing those jobs.

Like with Jerry Hall, I got her to lie on a bed. Ben Eltham, I was trying to get him to jump in a bath or something. Things like that. Ninety-nine per cent of the time they say no, but that one per cent that say yes, it's pretty cool.

Tell me a bit about your thought process when your assignment is a portrait.

I love environmental portraits. It's about looking at the person and looking at the environment. A lot of people blow the backgrounds out; I'm quite the opposite. I love depth of field, I love showing where they are, I love showing where they live, I love the angles around them. I tend to prefer natural light over studio light. I would choose to use natural light all the time. I like people to be in their own environment so they feel [the photo is] representing them. It's all about the expression in their face and telling their story. Everybody's life and who they are, you can see in their face, in their eyes – the way they look at you, or in the way they look off.

It's quite funny – because photographers are so used to looking at people closely all the time, you pick up little things. You might pick up when somebody is actually a little bit upset with somebody else. They're not really showing it but you can tell by their mannerisms. I think it's because we've spent so long looking so closely at people.

In 2006, you took a photo of Mamdouh Habib – one of two Australians who'd been imprisoned at the US military prison at Guantanamo Bay – smoking a cigarette in the Sydney CBD. It was a finalist in the National Portrait Prize. Can you tell me about that photo?

He's an interesting character, isn't he? We were in the city, I only had a few minutes. It was a really quick, simple portrait of him. There was nothing really around. I said to him, 'Look, I found a laneway,' and he said, 'I just want to have a cigarette.' And I said, 'Okay, can I just photograph you as you are having the cigarette? And then we'll do some other portraits after?' And he went, 'Yeah, fine.' That was how I got that photo.

I asked one of your former editors, Clive Mathieson, formerly of *The Australian*, what kind of assignment he put you on, and he immediately said, 'She's legendary, I would literally use her for anything,' and then he specified any job involving families that required empathy and compassion. He said I should ask you about your coverage of the 2004 Boxing Day tsunami in Indonesia.

Yep. So, I went in with the journalists. One of the stories I think he's referring to is when I was at the hospital – I met this family who had lost their young daughter. I ended up chatting to the dad. I just started chatting to him in the hospital because he was upset. I asked him if he was okay and he went into the story. They then gave me permission to document her funeral. It was incredible. I was invited into their home to photograph the embalming, the wrapping of the body, everything. She was probably twelve. I am very empathetic. I am very compassionate. And I think that's really important, right? Because people are going through enormous trauma. Enormous.

The trust required to let a stranger come in and shoot that is unbelievable.

Still to this day I think it's amazing that they did let me into their home, they did make me feel welcome. They actually wanted me to be there. That's what was incredible about it.

Why do you think they wanted it documented?

Just to document that she lived and it mattered. Even though so many people had died, it mattered.

When people give you access to the most intimate parts of their lives, does the responsibility weigh heavily on you?

It definitely does. I always come out of doing a story like that – and this is very honest – feeling very lucky. I'm not in that situation, I'm not going through anything that they're going through, I go home. I'm given the amazing ability to show the world what they are going through. It makes me feel privileged.

How do you look after your personal safety in the field when so often you're focused on what you're seeing through the lens of the camera?

Sometimes safety's a bitch. You take into account that there's no point getting injured or dying in the field, because you don't get your work out anyway. Your mind changes as you get older too; you're a bit more gung-ho when you're younger. You also rely on a team. There's not one person when we go: we've got myself, the journalist, we have a fixer generally. You all work together to look after each other.

All the media look after each other too, whether you're competition or not. Nobody wants to see anybody get injured. It's about teamwork, it's about analysing the situation, it's about looking at what a safe situation is, what is not safe, and whether it's worth moving forward. It might not be, and if it's not, wait a day or reassess it.

How did you become a photographer?

I always loved photography. When I was a little kid, I used to borrow my dad's Canon camera and just take arty photos. I did photography at school and took photos for the school newspaper too. I did work experience at *The Manly Daily* when I was about fifteen. When I left school, I did a photography course. And then every two or three weeks, I'd send Cumberland newspapers, [publishers of] *The Manly Daily*, a newspaper that I'd literally drawn up myself. I'd go out and take photographs, put all my photos in [my newspaper] and send it off to try to get a cadetship. Looking back, it's a bit dicky, right? Finally, I got the interview, I got a cadetship at *The Manly Daily*. I reckon I learnt more in my first two weeks at the paper than I learnt in my course at TAFE.

Was that from watching what other people were doing? Or did more senior people look at your work and say, 'No, Renee, you need to do it like this.' Or 'You should do that'?

Both. There was definitely a lot of mentorship. One thing I think is really sad nowadays is we just don't have that. It's definitely going to affect all businesses. People are working from home, there's nobody to mentor those coming through. We used to work in the darkrooms together. You'd all process your film and go, 'Oh, which one do you like?' You'd look through the negatives together, you'd do a print and you'd show the other person, and they'd say, 'You need to put a bit more contrast into that.' And you learnt through asking questions, watching what other people did.

Working in news photography, how many other women were around?

It definitely grew, but there weren't many [when I started]. I grew up with two older brothers – I'm quite a tomboy – so I didn't have an issue being around guys. I grew up on a six-acre property not far from the city. We had horses and pigs and mountain bikes. So for me, slotting into those male-orientated environments felt quite normal. I was never treated differently, I was always given opportunity.

If I picked up your iPhone, would it have some bad photos on it?

Yeah. I post really bad photos online. One of my girlfriends, Janelle, sends me text messages all the time: 'Your photos are crap, Renee. They're not even basic standard. It doesn't make sense.' It clicked for me: I'm either really in the zone, totally focused, or I'm not at all. Then, I don't want to be behind the camera. I'm enjoying the environment I'm in.

Levent 'Louie' Eroglu ACS

Louie Eroglu is an award-winning cinematographer and one of the most experienced news and current affairs camera operators in the world. He has many honours, including Walkley awards and Australian Cinematographers Society awards. Louie is a two-time White House Video Photographer of the Year, an award presented to him by President Barack Obama. He has been based in the ABC's North America, Russia and Middle East bureaus – he made ten trips to Iraq to cover that war. He is much sought after by journalists for assignments because of his peerless ability and experience. He is currently with the ABC's Four Corners.

Even though you film news and current affairs, do you draw many visual ideas from TV and film dramas?

A lot. I go to galleries too, to see photographic exhibitions or paintings and stuff. I get inspiration from magazines. I loved film clips as a kid. What I do watch lately – SBS movies. Some of those European, South American cinematographers: delightful.

French cinematography, Italian cinematography, Spanish, Turkish, Iranian – the kind of movies that aren't based on big epic scenes, car crashes, but are more to do with the power of silence and how to tell a story when it's just a face in a room, with the viewer filling in the blanks. I tap into that every now and then with real people that we film.

When you watch something, are you going, 'Oh, that framing, I could try that?' Or lighting? What are you absorbing?

Framing, lighting, mood. The first movie that inspired me to become part of cinematography was *Apocalypse Now*. That opening scene where Martin Sheen is having a shocker and he's just imploding. It starts with The Doors [playing] and helicopters going past – a big scene, no CGI. It's done beautifully and there's a bit where the helicopter blades dissolve into the fan on the ceiling. It just transitions. I went, 'This is so cool, this is brilliant.' I thought, 'Okay, rather than doing a hard cut, you could make things a bit more seamless, a bit more clever, to shift from the past to the present. I just understood it straightaway.

Let's discuss a three-part series you shot for *Four Corners* on allegations of Russian interference in the 2016 US presidential election. Talk us through the way you decided that series would look.

The first thing I've gotta realise when I'm approached for a story or an assignment is it's not my story. I didn't come up with the idea to do Trump/Russia; the journalist approached me. What I do is implement my visuals for it. The first thing with the assignment, whether it's one or two parts, is that you've got to vary it a bit. And so, two angles: wide and tight.

For filming the interviews?

Yeah, for the interviews. Two angles every time, wide and tight, just to break it up a bit. And also, it's a way of seeing the environment, you know, especially if you've got a nice big, deep room. You see a bit more, then boom, into a close-up. With *Four Corners*, some episodes are more interview based, some are more picture based, and some are lots of archives and stuff. This one was mainly interview based. So we start with that.

I did another thing I like, it's quite stylish, it's to go both smooth and rough. So doing things where you do a shot locked off on the tripod – for example, of New York, shot from Hoboken, from the other side [of the river], looking back. It's really lovely. You can do time lapses and whatnot; that's smooth. And then boom, you go off-the-shoulder, into the streets of Manhattan; it's rough. And so it's a full-on mash, smooth and rough.

And what does a mash achieve?

It can give you a sense of edge. That something's about to happen. Or it can enhance the fact of New York. When you're watching New York from a distance, across the water, it's quite serene. But as soon as you come out of the Lincoln Tunnel, it's like aarrgghh! That scream can be replicated audio-wise and visually, by quick edits. And you keep the camera moving. Then you add music; it all builds tension.

If you're shooting a war, it's very visual and you are overwhelmed by choice. This story was not like that. It was about computer hacking. How do you come up with ideas to illustrate something so visually dull?

Well, you might have some archive, FBI press conferences and stuff. Once you've got what's available from archive in your head, you can find ways of making the transition from the present to the archives.

The other thing we can do is stylise things. We don't go too literal with the re-enactments, cos we weren't there. We shoot in a way that, hopefully, people can fill in the blanks. And we did that a bit with the Lindt Cafe story. We had access to the Lindt Cafe and I didn't want any artificial re-creations. We got in there at night. I had that window pane into the street, the emptiness, and I'd seen the archive of the night stuff during the siege; I knew that the streets outside were empty. I just placed myself into what the hostages may or may not have been seeing and smelling and hearing. I tried to get their point of view. Chairs, shadows and stuff, without being too artificial; I didn't light anything. I left it the way that they would've seen it.

The way you shot it gave the viewer a claustrophobic sense of being in that building and looking out but knowing you can't get out, you're trapped.

That's right. Trapped inside. And [I had the camera] getting down low, under the tables, through the legs of the tables. A vignette of the kitchen. And the other thing I noticed too was the silence, Leigh. In the silence of Martin Place, all you hear is the *boop, boop, boop* of the traffic lights. And the *d-d-d-d-d-d* when it goes on walk. That's just endless, maddening. You've got an ibis, the odd homeless person, the odd cup just rolling around or something. In the silence, there were visual ways to replicate the barrenness, the feeling of it.

The audio, so important.

Sometimes we camera operators who focus on the cinematography don't realise how important sound is. I could have got just a street shot, and I did get that street shot, but that street shot with that sound, the madness of the repetitive *boop, boop*: that changes everything.

I try to capture every dimension I can, and sound is a critical one. It's how you do it without a big Hollywood recreation of what happened. Cos let's face it, nothing is gonna ever replicate that real-life event.

Technology for camera operators and editors has changed drastically since you started. Are the core skills still the same?

I think people aren't tapping enough into the basics. There is a lot of technology, a lot of gadgets to enhance the so-called production values. But I think sometimes you've still got to get back down to the heart of it, and this is why I like those European movies.

What do you think are the key basics?

Framing, not over-lighting, shooting as natural as possible. I always tell people, 'Get your basics first and, if you've got time, then get your art and your vignettes.'

How did you come to be a camera operator?

Well, I wanted to be an astronomer as a kid, and that didn't work out. Then I wanted to be an air force pilot, but I haven't got the eyes for that. I was at uni doing a bachelor of business, not a good fit. Anyway, a job as a researcher came up in the western suburbs for a show called *Beatbox* – just like to say, I'm a Westie – and that was my foot in the door. And from there, some camera-specific training opportunities came. I did outside broadcasts, I did football, I did rugby league. And I was so grateful. I couldn't believe it. But I'll tell you one thing, though, even though I'm trained, I'm still training. I'm not trying to sound like a wanker, I'm still training. You can never rest on your laurels in this job. It's happened to me where I've gone, 'Oh, I've got this,' and you come back and watch it on TV and you go, 'Oh my god, no, I've stuffed it.'

A story I did just recently in Hawks Nest, I'd get up every morning at five to get the sunrise at 5.30. Is one sunrise enough? Sure. But it's *Four Corners*, you've got forty minutes on one town. I decided to go every morning and I'd meet people, and they're like, 'Oh mate, what've you got there?' And I like talking to people. 'Where you from?' '*Four Corners*.' 'Oh, what are you doing?' 'I'm getting the sunrise, a few shots of your pretty town.' 'Mate, you should go to such-and-such. There's that hill there and you get a really amazing view at this time of day.'

Not only do you get to meet the locals, you get to find more stuff to shoot, cos they know, they've got info, they've got the home ground advantage.

You and I have mostly worked together on news and live events. Something that's always struck me is your ability, in a massive media scrum, to get right to the front and centre and hold the best angle.

Well, I don't know if I'm tapping into my days of dreaming to be a winger for the Parramatta Eels, but yeah – I was hard to catch!

Do you have to be pushy?

There are some scrums where you're getting squashed, and you're like, 'I can't breathe, I can't talk.' You try to not block other people. You don't want to be the person in the group of fifty that pisses everyone off. You've gotta be polite but you've gotta stand your ground too. You've just got to get in there nice and early, hold a spot.

When you first started, were you shy putting your camera into someone's face?

Yes. Yes. Yes. Yes. I was so freaked out. You've got one chance to get [corrupt policeman] Roger Rogerson coming out of court, and everyone's there, and they walk fast backwards and you've gotta make sure that you know who you're meant to get a shot of. So, yeah, there can be pressure and the expectation. I just thought, 'I'm gonna sit here and watch the others, I'm gonna watch what the others do.' And then I'd watch the news that night. And I'd go, 'Ah! I was there too but I didn't see that shot!'

So you'd watch your competitors? You'd watch Seven and Nine and Ten and see what they had?

Yeah. I still do to this day. I start with Ten News, then I go to Nine and Seven, then I watch a bit of SBS and I watch ABC then 7.30. Still.

With technology now, you don't have to be anywhere near somebody to get a close-up of their face. What's the difference in the result between using a long lens from a distance versus being 50 centimetres from their actual face?

That is outstanding, that question. If you shoot someone on a long lens, like a telescope, you can still get the face. But the perspective, the *something* between the foreground and the background – [from that] you know it's been shot from far away. It's quite a clever way if you wanna give the impression of something being further away, or you want to do something with the background. Being up close is literally you're in someone's personal space. You know, that sort of 'Whoa! Can you move back a bit mate?'

What I try and do with the media scrum when you're right in there, and for example [corrupt politician] Eddie Obeid is coming out, the viewer's convinced because of that angle that they're right in there with him. And they go, 'Okay, wow,' and sort of feel Eddie and the media scrum and what it's like to be there during that five-second walk.

How much detail do you like a journalist or producer to give you about a story?

Detail is important. I didn't realise it until maybe a few years into it. I was probably too busy worrying about the mechanics of the camera. But if you listen to a story that's being given to you to capture, you can understand things and work smart. You can say, 'I know that at some point, I've got this scene that can help with your line there.'

I remember once, in Washington, you came up to me at the end of a press conference with John Howard and George Bush and said, 'I've got a pull focus starting on the Australian flag and ending on the American flag. But if you want to start by talking about America, I've done it in the reverse direction too.'

That is the most incredibly useful thing for a cameraman to give me because it means I've got options for structuring the sentence.

Ha, the reason I did that was it took someone to come up to me and say, 'Mate, you know how you went from right to left? Actually, I really could have used the other way.' Taking it to black at the end of the shot, that's another tool I can use. I pan off into black and then you can dissolve into something else. That's one thing. But if I do it the other way, it's also a reveal. So I get two birds with one stone.

How do the best journalists help you do your job?

They understood my role in creating their narrative. Just understanding one another. I guess particularly in hairy situations, where you know you could probably run, but you choose to shoot it anyway.

That can be very hard, because people assess risk differently. I know you really enjoyed working with ABC journalist Mark Willacy in the Middle East because you were in sync about when things were too dangerous but also about when to push through. If you were working with me in that context, we would not fit because I'm way more risk-averse than you.

Yeah, that's right. That's a good point, cos even though you and I are like-minded, if at any point one of you doesn't feel comfortable, it's all over.

How do you manage your fear on the road?

The adrenalin does kick in. And I won't say I enjoy it, but I get a buzz . . . is it a buzz? Your heart is pumping and you think, 'Okay, I've gotta be on my game here.' I was a well-oiled machine. I still am, I think.

What is the scariest situation you've been in on a story?

Jeez, there's been a few. There were the markets in Iraq with Mark Willacy when we were chased by a young fella with a pistol, shooting. He was pointing it at Mark, actually, and firing.

Another time in Afghanistan, [ABC journalist] Tim Palmer and I, we realised we could've been driving through a minefield.

I've had three near-death experiences, where you think it's all over, and the one I most remember was with [ABC journalist] Trevor Bormann and Mark Willacy. We were in a car and we were stopped by US marines. I was dressed in black. We were in a Toyota Crown. Trevor and Mark were in the back with our translator, Balsam, and I was in the passenger seat next to our driver, Bassan. I was filming out the front window and I remember Trevor saying, 'Louie, Louie, put the camera down, put the camera down.' And I turned around and I saw these two marines with weapons straight on me. At that time, the American soldiers were being attacked by insurgents and there were kidnappings, beheadings and whatnot, so things were very, very sensitive.

A broadcast camera can look like a large weapon from a distance. And there probably would've been a bit of racial stereotyping because you're Turkish?

Exactly. It was all of it together: the Toyota, me dressed in black, brown man, the camera out the window.

The thing I remember from that incident is that you were all hauled out of the car and put on the ground, but you kept the camera rolling. You put it on the ground next to you, and the viewer can see Mark Willacy's desert boot and him lying spreadeagled in front of it. There's only that cut-off image with this very tense audio. Not being able to see the full scene was almost more chilling than witnessing the whole thing. Your calmness and foresight to keep rolling in those circumstances speaks enormously to your skill.

Thank God the marines had the professionalism to just hold back, cos that could've been . . . If someone was trigger-happy . . .

When we're old, are we going to annoy everyone in the nursing home with tales of these adventures we've had?

Haha! Yeah, Salesy! They can tell us about their office politics.

Fred Shaw

Fred Shaw is a video editor at the ABC's flagship nightly currently affairs program, 7.30. His career began in the 2000s in London, fetching coffee and sushi for advertising executives in Soho. He worked his way to editing award-winning global television commercials. He joined the ABC's Sydney newsroom on 7 February 2009, as Victoria's Black Saturday bushfires raged, a challenging introduction to the intense world of nightly news. He edits a diverse range of stories for 7.30, from investigations to features, and has a collection of awards that testify to his skill.

If somebody asks, 'Fred, what do you do?' how do you explain it?

I tend to say that the journalists who I work with go off and work hard on stories and they bring me back a big bunch of material. And then it's up to me to help make sense of it and help present it in its best possible form, so that it engages the viewer. When someone's sitting down and watching the story, you don't want them to look away. You want them to be tuned in to what they're hearing, to what the video is saying, to the stories people are telling. Any distraction from that I see as a weakness, not necessarily of a story, but on my part as an editor. My job is to make that viewing as seamless and engaging as possible.

Is your involvement always at the end of the process?

Typically, yes. I'll turn up, and I don't know what's going to be on my plate that day. Which is good and bad. It's nice in that it keeps you on your toes, and every day's a little bit different. But sometimes you do wish that you'd been involved a little bit earlier in the process.

What can you bring if you get involved early?

Well, I'm often not involved in any kind of editorial or legal discussion. So my opinion is very much an outsider's opinion, which means it can be a fresh, different perspective on something that people have been chewing over for a while. I'm also across what our executive producer expects of the show. I know they will ask me, 'Oh, did we not cover that?' or, 'Why isn't there this shot?' So it gives me a chance to help make sure the journo or the producer is across what needs to be done. It gives me ownership as well, and it makes me think ahead.

One of the things that stresses me the most when I contemplate your job is that you can only work with what's dished up to you on that plate. It's not an option for you to go, 'Actually, what I'd like are some better shots of this.'

Yeah. Though we do have a team of archivists from the library on hand too, and I'll often go to them at the last minute: 'I need morning sun through gum leaves, help!'

Tell me something that can be distracting to a viewer, using audio as an example.

You want it smooth. So if it's a series of shots from the same scene, could just be a street scene, if you take the individual audio from every shot and change it every time, it jars. I would just lay down one long street-scene chunk of audio, that would maybe be synced to the first shot, and let it play under. One continuous bit of natural sound underneath allows the voiceover to flow on top of that undisturbed. It minimises any harshness from edit to edit.

In the field, when an audio operator asks everyone to be quiet so they can record 'atmos', what do they mean by that?

Atmosphere track. It's maybe thirty seconds of field recording of the natural sounds occurring where you're shooting, whether that be a quiet room after an interview, with a bit of aircon buzzing away, or maybe a place where you have planes flying overhead. The editor can use that as a tool to smooth over edits and help massage grabs into place. Ultimately, it helps the viewer have an easy viewing experience.

What would you say are the basic ingredients storytellers need to gather when they're in the field, so that a story can be well edited?

I'd say a shooting script is important. I was talking to Tom Joyner, an ABC video-journalist who shoots his own stuff. He's brilliant at what he does. He always does a shooting script because it allows him to go into a situation and get X, Y and Z shots. There's a bare minimum of what's needed – maybe a wide shot to give a sense of location, a sense of the event we're witnessing.

There are other little things I recommend. For example, if a piece to camera (PTC) is being used, it needs to be there for a reason. Also, film around that location as well. When that PTC pops up in the story, if you've got a few shots and a bit of natural sound to introduce that scene into the story, it adds value. I often find pieces to camera can be the most abrasive element of a story – all of a sudden the faceless voice appears, and you don't know why.

Natural sound is really important too. Not atmos, but natural dialogue. If you have time to sit back and record someone talking naturally and comfortably, it's often a lot better than having an interview grab where someone's saying things more consciously and unnaturally. I really enjoy editing stories where there's a natural element and you get to see people living their usual lives. You get a lot more engagement with the person, the subject matter, if you see them being natural.

Louie Eroglu told me that he tries to capture a sense of the location he's in so that somebody watching feels what it was like to have been there too. Your approach to editing seems the same.

Yeah, for sure. Things that I can put throughout a sequence add a bit of depth to a character: an ashtray that's got a few butts in there; a pair of dusty work boots by the front door, suggesting that this person is a hard worker who's up at the crack of dawn.

There are things around a scene that don't involve the subject but are really powerful to use and which people can relate to. You may not relate to the person talking but you can relate to a pile of dishes in the sink that haven't been washed. That can tell as much of a story sometimes as the people.

What is meant by a sequence?

In a traditional news sense, a sequence is the images you film after an interview that can cover a voiceover. The word 'sequence' to me suggests something slightly contrived, but it doesn't have to be. If you are an inexperienced storyteller, and you've done a shooting script, you would have thought ahead to, 'Okay, what can I capture this person doing that best helps illustrate their story? Or their purpose in being here.' On our show, we try to avoid the making of a cup of tea, which is too formulaic.

You can ask the subject what kinds of things they like doing. Do they go to a yoga class? Do they mow their lawn every weekend?

Then maybe they're more comfortable on camera than being told to walk fifty yards down the street and past a camera as naturally as possible while in a three-piece suit. Those things stick out to me as an editor if I'm watching at home. I'm probably not going to listen to what the voiceover is saying at that point, I'm going to think, 'That guy doesn't look real.' It's taken me out of the viewer experience and before you know it, I've lost the train of the story. That's exactly the opposite of what I'm trying to do.

The sequence that ruins it for me is people walking on a beach, even though, sure, lots of people do love walking on the

beach. But it's become a bit of a cliché, where someone has had a traumatic experience and we film them walking alone on a beach, looking pensively at the horizon.

I know. Yeah, yeah, yeah. And then you want the scene when they're trying to get sand out the back of their car, cursing, like the natural beach scene!

Are there rules of editing that can't be broken?

When viewers tune in to our show, they expect a certain type of story. So we can't really reinvent the wheel, we're not avant-garde artists. And it's like I'm saying, we're serving the public, we're serving the story. We don't want to do anything that would distract from that. I try to avoid repeating shots, although that's probably better than five seconds of just void space. The one rule that can't be broken is that [the video] needs to be editorially correct, and I put my faith in the journalists and the producers that by the time it arrives on my desk, everything is watertight.

There's probably no job that carries more pressure as a program approaches its deadline than the editor's. How do you deal with that when you're watching the clock tick down minute by minute? You often have multiple people hovering over your shoulder and there's a tangible feeling of tension.

Everybody in my line of work will go through a very, very bad day at some point. You only have to dip your toe in once or twice for some people to go, 'Nup, not for me, thanks. I can earn the same amount of money having a very easy life just a few edit booths down.'

How do I deal with that? Through experience. You can often see these things on the horizon. Our deadline is 7.30, that's not going to change. If a couple of hours before, you still haven't seen your material, it's a case of 'What can I be doing now to make two hours down the track smoother?' It's having the experience and the foresight to know.

Who makes the call about something not making it to air?

We will often take it as close [to deadline] as we can. That often involves what we call live rolling, which is when it's too late to send the story or the interview [to the studio]. It might even just be a grab from a press conference that's happened at 7.40. That story is played out live from my edit suite. That happens quite often.

I feel confident enough to be able to say to my bosses that something isn't going to make it without that necessarily being a reflection on me doing a bad job. When it gets to that point, we've all done the job long enough to know [it's a case of]: 'Tell me now and we'll run with plan B.' It's about being communicative because it's down to seconds at that point.

It is, and it's also down to extremely fast, clear decision making.

Whether or not it's the right decision is another question, but a decision has to be made.

Any decision is better than no decision.

I think so.

I know these things are not matters of life and death, but even having this conversation is making me feel physically ill . . . Just from that feeling of having been at the crunch of it, many a time.

I don't know about you, but on those days when, yeah, it is a live roll, or when your adrenalin's pumping, I'll stare at the ceiling in bed until past midnight, chewing over what's happened. Kind of reliving it a little bit, still on that adrenalin buzz.

What personality traits do you think make somebody suited to work as an editor?

You need to be patient, collaborative, decisive, and clear with your choices. You need a good sense of humour, especially after those days when you've had a nightmare. If you can come in the next day and make contact with whoever was around at the time and reflect on it and have a laugh about it, that will set you up better for the next time a bad event comes along.

It's important to realise that sometimes tempers get frayed. In the heat of the moment, I can sometimes be a bit short with people, just because stuff needs to get done. The next day, I'll try and find that person and say, 'Sorry about yesterday,' and often by then they're happy with the story, so they're like, 'Oh, don't worry about it.' I think it's important that no matter what you've gone through the day before in the news cycle, you try and reset with individuals.

In an ideal environment, what do you consider to be best practice from a journalist or a producer with whom you're working?

It helps if they're enthusiastic about the story. If someone comes to me and says, 'Listen, brilliant footage, there are some great moments here,' that feeds back into me and I'm like, 'Oh, we've got a good story here.' If a story's been foisted on someone and it's not something they particularly want to do, I'll still do as good a job as I can, but it helps if the team approaches the beginning of the editing process in a positive fashion. Also, ideally they would have done their shooting scripts so they know what they're about to hand over to you.

Trust us, give us space and time to do our bit. No editor enjoys a backseat driver. Let me focus for a while; if there's an issue I'll come find you. If there's something you're not happy with, we'll talk it over, look at options, collaborate.

Another thing I've found quite important is being on the receiving end of gratitude, and in turn, trying to pay it forward – having people reach out when they've seen a story and just give you a one-line-email pat on the back. When it's someone you respect that just out of the blue gets in touch and says, 'Oh, I watched the show last night. Great job,' you go, 'Wow. Brilliant. Thank you.' I assume the journos get that a little bit more than the crews and resources do. It doesn't take very long to do. For me, it's important. It's probably kept me in the job longer than I would otherwise have been.

I remember once how captioning got your name wrong when I was giving you a credit on a story you'd edited. I said, 'That story was edited by Fred Shaw,' and captioning wrote, 'That story was edited by a French whore.'

I did two years' worth of laughing in the space of one evening. It's very rare that editors get a mention, so for that to happen . . .

Finally, your massive contribution is acknowledged and that's how it ends.

Yeah, that's how it ends!

Commentary
and Analysis

Some of the most famous and widely read journalists in the world are writers of commentary and analysis: think Maureen Dowd or Thomas Friedman at *The New York Times* or Marina Hyde at *The Guardian*. The best opinion writers apply the same tools as straight news journalists: chasing contacts, uncovering new information and connecting dots. By contrast, the weakest peddlers of media commentary are those who simply broadcast their own opinions without any real expertise or effort to explain complexity to the reader.

The difference between a straight news story and a piece of commentary or analysis is not only in the content, but also in the form: the writing in the latter is less formal, sometimes even humorous, and the piece will provide significant context.

One of the challenges for journalists who work in this space is that they will often be assigned a weekly or regular slot, meaning they are constantly on the hunt for ideas to sustain considerable copy or air time. A well-regarded columnist is always granted prominent real estate in a publication, so there's pressure to ensure that every piece they file justifies that status and attracts traffic. This is not something required of a regular news journalist, who may sometimes have a page one scoop but won't be expected to be one of the publication's most-read or watched bylines every time they file.

Niki Savva

Niki Savva writes one of Australia's most influential political columns for Nine newspapers. She has spent almost her entire career covering or working in federal politics. Her cadetship was at The Dandenong Journal *and she joined the Canberra press gallery in the 1970s, writing firstly for* The Australian *and later for* The Herald Sun *and* The Age. *She worked for the Howard government for most of its term in office, firstly as press secretary to Treasurer Peter Costello and later as an advisor to the prime minister. She is the author of four books,* So Greek: Confessions of a Conservative Leftie, The Road to Ruin: How Tony Abbott and Peta Credlin Destroyed Their Own Government, Plots and Prayers: Malcolm Turnbull's Demise and Scott Morrison's Ascension *and* Bulldozed: Scott Morrison's Fall and Anthony Albanese's Rise.

What do you consider the job of a political columnist?

I always try to tell people something they don't already know: an anecdote, a bit of colour, a few new facts, even just a different perspective. There is so much news around all day every day, there's no point rehashing what people already know. I only get one go at it a week and I always try to make it different. I try to speak to as many people as possible, from different places – serving and former politicians, staffers and officials. I like to have my opinions tested. And it is still surprising to me how many people are willing to share.

How do you find something new?

It's not easy, given how many people are out there chasing the same thing. You try and squeeze as much information out of people as you can. I ask them as many questions as I can possibly think of and I'm not frightened to ask them uncomfortable questions either.

I'm a voracious consumer of politics and news so I watch everything from breakfast TV and radio right through to *7.30*. The 24-hour news channel is on all day. Something will happen, or someone will say something and I will think, 'Well that is absolute BS, I'm gonna chase after that and see what really happened.' Or it will trigger an idea that I will also pursue.

How often do you use primary source material, such as a complete press conference, question time, senate hearings, and so on?

All the time. I work from home so I'm not in parliament house, which means I don't have the access others do. That's both a curse and a blessing because I'm separated from a lot of the everyday that they have to pay attention to . . . or can get influenced by. I listen to and watch as much as I possibly can. I know: I'm pathetic! I have a pathetic life, Leigh!

Oh, I'm the same, it's addictive and it's routine – like brushing your teeth, right?

It is something you have to do. You have to keep up. I don't have kids, it's just me and my husband, so I can devote myself to it. I only write once a week but I try to keep up with everything, because, as I say, something can happen that will trigger an idea. Every piece of information that you watch or listen to could be valuable, or you could miss something that's important. Then you have to spend time catching up, or you have to reconstruct.

Do you keep notes on a daily basis or do you hold it in your head? For example, we are speaking right now during an election campaign. I have two files on my computer that I open every day, one for Morrison and one for Albanese. I cut and paste things into them, or jot down a particular thought. I might never use them, but when the big interviews come along, I have a bank of possible ideas. Do you do anything similar?

I open a file for my next column. I start thinking about my next one almost as soon as I'm finished the last one. So if somebody says something I think might be pertinent, I will cut and paste. I do make notes if I hear something of interest.

How soon before deadline do you start writing your column?

My column appears on the Thursday. I will begin talking to people in a serious way on Sunday. Then Monday is usually spent also talking to people and just putting lines or quotes into the computer, which may or may not last. The most important thing, as in a news story, is the lead. Once I have that, I relax a bit and have a better idea of where to go, and who I need to speak to in order to get there. By late Tuesday I really need to have most of it written. The tweaking and the rewriting and the refining is constant.

I send an early draft at 6 a.m. or 7 a.m. on Wednesday morning. Then I spend the rest of the day refining, adding or deleting, trying to get it to one thousand words, because that's all I've got. Then I email the final thing at 4 p.m. on Wednesday.

Do you like, or take, feedback from an editor?

Do I like it? Not always! [*laughs*] But often they will pick up something. A good subeditor can save your life and prevent you from making a mistake. If they were to come back and say, 'I think it would be better if you said this,' and it's a factual thing, then I will obviously accept that and be grateful for it. If they were to say to me, 'We think you've gone too far there,' then I may or may not take that kindly. There have been times when superiors have made suggestions not to my liking. My response is, 'Run it as it is or don't run it at all.' My words, my name, my reputation. If it has my name on it, I want to be able to say I stand by every word I wrote, not what my editor thought I should write.

Do you have a particular audience in mind?

Anyone who is vaguely interested in politics. That's it. When I send copy off, I never think of people reading it. I just think, 'Oh, nobody's gonna read this, they're not gonna be interested, they're not gonna be bothered. I kind of – this is gonna sound weird – I write it to please myself because I know what I like to read, as somebody who is interested in politics. I know the columns that I love and the writers I really admire.

Who are they?

Maureen Dowd [*The New York Times*], she's number one. Marina Hyde from *The Guardian*. Here, Sean Kelly [Nine newspapers] is very good. I used to love reading Laurie Oakes. He's no longer writing and I miss his contributions a lot. Greg Sheridan [*The Australian*] I read because even if I don't always agree with him, I respect his points of view and what he has to say.

One of the things you raise there which is very important is reading people with whom you might disagree. That can be a rich source of ideas, and spark your thinking in a certain direction.

That's right. I will read – I won't name people here – somebody on a competitor's newspaper and I will think, 'That is a rubbish view,' or I think it's biased or self-serving. I will then write something that counters that view, or tries to give a more accurate account of what happened, without actually saying I'm writing in response to it.

We mentioned before that your columns are far from straight opinion. They include a lot of reporting and information that people have told you. How useful then are the skills you accumulated in your years as a news reporter?

Invaluable. Leigh, I never wanted to do anything else apart from be a journalist. I loved it from the very first day I was lucky enough to get a cadetship. I was blessed to work with brilliant people who taught me all the basic skills and also put me in my place. They educated me in all sorts of ways, about how to cultivate contacts, how to write, and how to be an old-style reporter who went out there and spoke to people and got information and then put it together in a coherent and hopefully interesting way. I wrote a bit about that in my book *So Greek*.

You know, another thing: I've never forgotten where I grew up, which was on a housing commission estate. I was the daughter of working-class parents. My father and mother worked in a factory. They were illiterate. I have never forgotten where I came from and just how hard it can be for people.

Early in your career, when you weren't far out of that upbringing, you were in the Canberra press gallery. It was heavily male and Anglo-Saxon and you were nicknamed 'Ethniki'. How much do you think things have changed?

When I got there, I could count on one hand the number of women in the press gallery. It has changed in that respect. But I look around now and there are still too few women running the joint. In news bureaux, mainstream newspapers, commercial free-to-air TV – all male bureau chiefs. There's still a bit of catching up that needs to happen. And there needs to be more diversity in another sense, not just gender. When I was there, I would look around the room and I'd be the darkest person there, and I have olive skin. There does need to be a lot more diversity in the press gallery.

Class diversity too, because you wonder how many people there today would be the children of illiterate factory workers.

Yes, and I never went to university. I started as a cadet when I was seventeen. Maybe there's too academic an approach to reporting and that needs to change.

For many years you were a political staffer, working for Peter Costello. How do you think that inside experience helped your journalism when you returned to it?

I never wanted to be a press secretary but it was something that happened for a whole heap of reasons. Looking back, it was invaluable. I learned firstly about the nature of politicians: what they're like, how they think, what motivates them, how they go about making decisions. I also learned about crisis management and how they go about handling really difficult situations. The most important thing I learned was just how powerful journalists are and how journalists can influence the thinking and behaviour and performance of politicians. I've never forgotten that. You have so much more power as a journalist than you think you have.

Through what you're writing or just by asking questions?

All of it. You can up-end an entire press conference with one question. Then spear it off in a different direction with the final product. What journalists tend to forget is the impact their words can have on people who make decisions.

In *So Greek*, you characterise politicians as 'blabbers and users'. What did you mean by that?

You know, when I wrote that, I thought my career was over, right? After the 2007 election, I could not get a job for love nor money. Not anywhere, not doing anything. Not even waiting on tables. Certainly not as a journalist. So I wrote it because I thought I had nothing to lose. In a lot of ways, that's how I still approach things today: like I have nothing to lose.

What I meant, when I wrote 'blabbers', is that there are people who are just dying to tell you things, if only you ask them. They will spill their guts if only you give them a call and ask them in the right way what happened and why it happened. There are also the 'users', who have different motives in revealing information – quite often, it's to shaft a colleague, or to shaft someone on the other side, so they use you as their vehicle to achieve their objectives.

You might know you're being used, you might know they have an agenda, but they still may provide useful information. How do you gauge whether to use it?

That's a judgement you have to make at the time. Really, you can't dwell too much on the 'why', often it's just the 'what.' The information they're giving you is valid in its own way, regardless of what the motive is – so long as it's accurate and well informed. You have to learn who you can trust, and often that is hard. I have known journalists who refused to accept off-the-record information. I am the complete opposite. You never forget what you've been told, and often down the track it will fit into a mosaic. Also very valuable for knowing who doesn't trust who.

How do you keep contacts when you write something they don't like?

I am their worst nightmare because I have nothing to lose. I don't care if I get sacked. I'm certainly not in it for the money. I care about my name and my reputation and also about trying to tell people what is actually going on and why. If that means some people no longer talk to me, well, so be it. I don't care whether they like me, whether they hate me – it's irrelevant. What I try to do is just keep talking to as many people as I can. Obviously I have lost a lot of contacts along the way. And friends too. There are people who won't speak to me. Well, bad luck for them. I try to keep making new contacts and finding new people to talk to. All the time. It is constant, whether you are writing news or columns.

As I said, after *So Greek* came out, I thought nobody would ever speak to me again because of the way I wrote it and what I wrote. But in a funny kind of way it helped my credibility, and there were people who respected that. I think people still do because I try to be honest. I don't have to appease people, I don't have to protect anyone. I think in this job, if you do it properly, you basically end up with no friends. Hopefully, you do end up with people who respect you.

I often remind myself that one of the great things about covering politics is that if I do blow through contacts, I only have to wait until the next election cycle because then there's a change of personnel.

That is dead right. The other thing is: you and I are still standing. And a lot of the people who didn't like us, or in my case tried to have me sacked, are now feeding the pigeons. We're still here, Leigh.

Having been a staffer, what's your advice to political journalists about dealing with staffers and how to have a productive relationship?

To recognise your power and to use it, and to be fearless. Never be afraid to ask a tough question or an uncomfortable one. Never be intimidated by people you are covering. You do have to be obsessive and dedicated and have a thick skin. Recognise that staff have a difficult job. They might tell you something – not everything, so you have to go beyond them to the prime source.

As well as being fearless, what do you think are the keys to being a good political reporter?

The key is to find out the stuff they don't want you to know. The best story is always the one they don't want you to get. Too often these days, I think people just wait for the press release or they wait for that background briefing. The Morrison government has excelled at getting people on the drip. You keep reading all these stories that have 'exclusive' attached to them that are really just press releases.

Is it possible to be too cynical covering politics, to believe they all have a hidden agenda, that they're all power-hungry, that they would all sell their grandmother to get ahead, and so on?

Yes I think so, but I think it's also possible to be too trusting. Can I give you an example where I was too trusting?

Sure.

Okay, insiders years ago would tell me they never liked or trusted Scott Morrison. But I did. I used to think, 'Oh don't be silly, he's good at what he does.' I thought, 'You give Scott Morrison a mission and he will accomplish it.' It wasn't until the coup against Turnbull in 2018 that I realised they were right about what they said about him and the way he operated and what drives him. Sometimes I look at myself and I think, 'God, haven't you learned anything after all these years?'

Waleed Aly

Dr Waleed Aly is a writer, academic, broadcaster and lawyer. He co-hosts Network Ten's The Project *and won the 2014 Walkley Award for commentary and analysis. He lectures in politics at Monash University and his PhD was on global terrorism. Waleed also writes a column for Nine newspapers and co-hosts a program on ABC's Radio National called* The Minefield. *He is the author of* People Like Us: How Arrogance Is Dividing Islam and the West, *and two pieces for* Quarterly Essay, *'What's Right?: The Future of Conservatism in Australia' and 'Uncivil Wars: How Contempt Is Eroding Democracy', co-authored with Scott Stephens.*

Waleed, when you're writing a column, do you have anyone particularly in mind as your audience?

It varies. Sometimes the audience is me. By that, I mean I find writing anything – a column or something longer – a good way of learning what I think about things. Sometimes you think you know your argument and you go to write it and you suddenly run into all the holes in it. So sometimes it's a working out of my own thoughts.

Then there are times when I think of the eventual reader. I tend to assume, which is not always wise, that they're reading in good faith and that whatever their view is, they're interested in learning something new or thinking about it in a new way.

I do have a concern about the way that opinion writing or commentary generally is going. It is becoming increasingly solipsistic, where you write for your tribe, and really what you're doing is just trying to give the sharpest, most emotionally laden expression to that tribe's views. You're not really writing for anyone who might think differently, and you aren't interested in including them in the conversation except as an object to lacerate. I would rather read and write stuff that is a bit more cross-cutting than that.

You address this in your *Quarterly* essay, 'Uncivil Wars: How Contempt is Corroding Democracy'. What do you mean, that contempt is corroding democracy?

It begins with the feeling that everyone seems to have that there's just something new and wrong about the way we conduct public debate. Often it's distilled as anger but it's not simply anger. Anger is a temporary emotion: you feel it and it goes away, you become happy and then that goes away. This is different. It's a stance we take towards one another, a standard way of doing debate, and it is contempt. We hold ourselves out to be morally superior to those with whom we disagree, which implies we feel we stand in a position to judge people's character. We read into their character [according to] certain positions they may take on something, even though sometimes our understanding of their positions is a caricature. The evidence is that this dynamic is playing out on more and more issues.

It's bizarre, isn't it? Even scientific questions polarise on a political axis.

Yes. It's a good example, because science doesn't resolve social and political questions. It informs them. Science might say X is the consequence of Y, but it doesn't answer questions like 'Is X acceptable? Is the cost of avoiding X too high? And what would the best policy be to avoid X, anyway?' These are political questions, where answers aren't always obvious and reasonable minds will differ. But if we pretend they're purely about science versus ignorance, they descend into culture wars.

You write a column for Nine newspapers. How do you come up with what you're going to write about?

Mostly in a panic! That's the thing about a column, you have to write it at a particular time, and I'm always annoyed when I have a great idea but it's too old by the time my column comes around.

I write Wednesday night going into Thursday, and because of my broadcast schedule I tend to start writing at 10 p.m. Wednesday and I'll finish maybe 3, 4 a.m. It's the only time I can do it. I start to think about the column on Monday. I pay attention to anything I can see in the news cycle that triggers a bigger idea. If I come across a story where I can go, 'Oh, that is a gateway into something much deeper,' that's when I know I have my idea.

An example is a thing I wrote in the middle of 2021, around the time the Morrison government was in some kind of stoush with Google or Facebook, maybe both. At the same time, something happened in the trade relationship with China. These things seem unconnected but what struck me as interesting is the different kind of power that each of these actors has. You have one of the biggest nation-states in the world with one of the biggest militaries, and you have a company. Yet it's far from clear once you crunch through the details who actually has the most power. That's interesting because it says something about the changing nature of power and how we can't think of it any more just in terms of states.

That's a one-sentence idea, though: 'There are different kinds of power.' How do you take that to a thousand words?

Sometimes it comes to me clear as a bell and I know the steps: I know where I have to finish, and to get there I have to go through this hoop, that hoop. Other times you force it out by just writing *something*. I tend to write from beginning to end, rather than start in the middle. It works best when I force myself to just get something out. The worst case is when you think you have an argument and then you see that you don't. Then it's a bit of a crisis, because what do I do now?

I'm very fortunate because I have a friend in the UK who is a professor of politics, and I will usually send him something to read. It's great, because he's really good but also he's awake at the time I'm doing it. A good reader is an important part of it.

Tell me what you want from that kind of reader.

Somebody who can engage with the ideas on the page. The worst kind of response is 'Why didn't you write *this* column?'

Somebody who can spot problems in it: 'You can't say this in paragraph three if you want to get to what you say in paragraph seven, because they're contradictory or different ideas.'

Sometimes what I find beneficial is him saying, 'I like the way you've made X point,' and the way he distils it is interesting. Now he's paraphrasing my argument back to me: do I recognise it or not? If I do, has he distilled it in a way that's clearer or identifies part of the argument that I need to bring out more? You're after a reader who's attentive: not one who reacts, but one who attends.

Do you like the pressure of the deadline?

I don't enjoy it but I think it brings out the best. It brings a certain intensity in focus. If I'm just left to my own devices, I might wander and meander and it will take me a lot longer to get to a place that's not that much better.

Do you map out a structure?

I often will have it in my head that I will go from A to B to C. Then there are times where I discover [the structure] as I'm writing. Either way, no matter how many words I have on the page, or when I think I've finished, I then think structure. I think, 'In order to make this point, have I explained everything that needs to be explained to get to here?' When I feel a piece has succeeded – which I must confess is rare – the argument unfolds in such a way that the conclusion feels inevitable from what has flowed. I'm not urging you to accept something that requires a leap: all the ducks are in a row. The structure was set out in such a way that you have to go, 'Yes I accept A, yes I accept B, C follows from that, it has to be D.'

That's almost a legal argument.

Well, I am legally trained!

How does a newspaper column differ from an editorial for *The Project*?

It differs slightly less than you might immediately think. You're still trying to marshal evidence to build an argument. Structure is still unbelievably important – perhaps more so for television. But they're different media so they have inherent differences. Television is a more emotive medium. It's a shorter form. You couldn't do an 800–1000 word editorial very often – it would be too long in television. You also can't have long slabs of uninterrupted text on television. It has to be broken up constantly by grabs or vision or something. You're limited in what you can quote by what's available as a visual clip. It's also much more of a team effort. You've got editors, producers: TV is a very cumbersome medium and to do anything requires a lot of hands. For that reason, there's always an element of compromise involved that probably isn't true of a column.

But I always try, if I'm doing an editorial on *The Project*, to avoid just bashing you over the head with my conclusion. I'm trying to walk through how I've got there and I'm trying to earn the conclusion. I can't perhaps incorporate the same level of nuance I could in a column, but in a column I can't have the same level of nuance as I would in an essay or a book.

Do you give any thought to whether what you write or present is going to deliver a lot of clicks?

I try desperately not to think about that at all. I fully understand the irony of me saying this, but I think virality is the very worst goal. The thing that worries me about the machine of virality is that it seems to me to reward all the wrong things. When I do something and it goes viral, that to me is a cause to stop and reflect on it, not a cause to celebrate.

Why?

Because so much of what goes viral is terrible. We send things viral for bad reasons: because they allow us to designate and attack an enemy, rather than because they offer something enlightening or subtle. They almost always have to be negatively inflected in order to go viral. It's not the kind of content that I think is the highest calling of commentary.

But I'm assuming newspaper editors love it if they get a column that goes viral, so how does this fit with the media business model?

That's an excellent question, and a question I choose not to think about, because it's not my problem. I'm not making any decisions about media business models. I'm noticing, though, that more and more conversations I'm having with editors and journalists, they're saying, 'We're took the wrong approach, clicks are the wrong way to understand success.'

What effectively happened is that media companies outsourced distribution to the internet. When you do that, the way to measure success *is* distribution: it's numbers of readers, viewers. Now I'm starting to hear more talk about subscribers, therefore we need to deliver what they value – quality, not just viral information and passions. I've definitely noticed among media practitioners, especially ones who've been at it a while, a sense of retreat from that 'easy' model. Going viral is no longer as exciting as it once was.

It's also often a sign that people are reducing your argument to a caricature of itself, so they can squeeze it into whatever trench war they're involved in. I wrote a column recently about the Albanese government doing an inquiry into Scott Morrison's secret ministries [the portfolios he took over during the pandemic without informing Cabinet]. I wrote that Albanese really should explain precisely what we would get out of this that wasn't already plain, because this cannot be political revenge, and if that's what it is, then there are reasons to be suspicious of an inquiry.

That column exploded, and from what I gather, there was a lot of consternation about it. Of course that was going to explode, because all you had to do was say, 'Here's a story about Scott Morrison and how good or bad he is.' Which it wasn't. It wasn't a defence of him at all, but it becomes read that way because that's what people are looking for.

When we started doing editorials on *The Project*, around 2015, it was a different environment. Virality often was celebratory. That didn't necessarily make it good; I still maintain that position. But now virality tends to overwhelmingly mean being at the bottom of a pile-on.

The point is, it's not that hard to achieve. Select your topic, choose the right words, take a stance that will enrage or inflame people, it's not that hard. It's not an achievement.

Annabel Crabb

Annabel Crabb is an author, podcaster and journalist with the ABC, specialising in politics. She has written and presented seven seasons of Kitchen Cabinet, *revealing the personal side of top politicians, as well as other popular programs, including* Back in Time for Dinner, Ms Represented *and* The House. *She co-hosts the culture podcast 'Chat 10 Looks 3' and has written for* The Age, The Sydney Morning Herald *and* The Advertiser. *She is the author of books including* Losing It: The Inside Story of the Labor Party in Opposition, The Wife Drought *and the* Quarterly Essay *piece, 'Stop at Nothing: The Life and Adventures of Malcolm Turnbull', which won the 2009 Walkley Award for feature writing. She has also co-authored two cookbooks,* Special Delivery *and* Special Guest.

Annabel, what do you consider the job of a columnist to be?

There has been a diversification of roles that columnists perform during the twenty years I've been a journalist. There are a lot more columns now, a lot more opinion – and a lot more vacuous opinion too. I've never been so in love with my own opinion that I think it alone can fuel twelve hundred words of copy.

The job a column should do is reveal something, or provide an angle or insight, that the reader might not have encountered before. Traditionally, a piece of analysis sits next to a news story in newspapers. I've never abandoned the idea that analysis or commentary should be about contextualising news events, and trying to furnish the reader with tools to help understand what's going on and why it is important.

That can be hard to do, because certain policy areas are very difficult to explain – and it's impossible to write a column about something if you don't understand it clearly yourself.

Right. And that's one of the pitfalls political analysis can fall into when it's around a subject that is diabolically complicated. You'll see columnists employing an accepted set of words to dispense with the policy detail that they're discussing, and then move straight onto the politics. One of the primary jobs you have as an analysis or commentary writer is to pre-digest difficult things, and then to at least have a stab at explaining how they work, rather than just skipping straight to the politics and assuming the reader will understand every detail of climate policy or super-annuation, or whatever knotty area it is.

Talk us through how you consume news over a week, and how you percolate an idea if you're doing a column.

I wake up and I read the papers. Then I usually listen to *Early AM* on Radio National. I'm not necessarily writing about everything

I'm listening to. I'm latching onto interesting interviews or moments that I think are pivotal. That's where you get ideas for columns or analysis – you hear someone being interviewed and they seem to be saying something a bit different from what they normally say, or maybe they're flagging a change, or you hear them being exposed on a point where they don't know what they're talking about. That is the stuff that lodges in the brain and you think, 'Is that a signifier of a broader shift? If so, can I write something about it?'

You mostly write on Australian politics, but how broadly do you read beyond that?

I read a lot – nonfiction and fiction. Heaps of that has nothing to do with politics, but I find there's something about being a broad reader that really oils the synapses in your brain, if that is even a physiologically appropriate thing to say. Often, if you're writing analysis and commentary, the most important part of the process is the noticing. It's noticing something that needs to be pointed out or explained. And the noticing powers in your brain are kept in good nick by reading other stuff.

What happens when you're writing a weekly column, it's deadline day and you don't have a good idea?

It's a terrible, sick feeling. The truth is, when you have a good idea, you can write a column in half an hour. If you don't, it takes days – most of which are spent swearing and crying and ripping things up. And look, it's impossible to be happy with everything you write when you write a weekly column. I don't think you would ever find a weekly columnist who hasn't, at some point, hit *send* with a sense of nausea, thinking, 'Well, this is absolute rubbish and crap. I can't bear it.'

Do you keep a couple of back-up ideas?

Yeah. When I was writing a weekly Saturday column for what was then Fairfax, I had a couple of terrible, in-case-of-emergency-write-about-this ideas. My friend Miranda used to tease me about it because I was always threatening to write a column about the humiliation of getting nits as an adult. One weekend I actually filed it, and she texted me saying, 'Oh man, times must be tough.' And I was like, 'Don't judge, man.'

Once you have an idea and a sense of what you want to write about, what is your actual writing process?

I start at the beginning and type until the word limit is reached. That sounds like a joke – but honestly, I've written an 800-word column so many times, I don't even have to do a word count. I know exactly the shape of that word limit.

It's funny, isn't it? People think there's some great secret to writing. But it literally is as you've described: sit down, start to write and force yourself to keep going.

That's it. I normally have breaks along the way for excessive research and disappearing down rabbit holes, then realise after an hour that not all that stuff can be crammed into eight hundred words. That is an important part of the process, all joking aside. If you have an idea, and you know the point you want to make, one of the great distractions is researching and turning up all sorts of delicious oddities. Then you stand back and realise you've got five thousand words of interesting things, so how do you choose between them?

With journalism, you have to start off as an intelligent igno-ramus. You go into work and you're sent off to do a story about somebody in an industry about which you know nothing. Your only asset is your curiosity and your capacity to learn quickly. You spend the day racing around learning everything there is to know about this area. At the end of that process, if you're any good as a journalist, you'll have got up to speed reasonably quickly. You could probably go to a dinner party and hold forth about the horse-racing industry – or whatever it is that you're writing about. The trick then is to write something that is intelli-gible to people who are one stage behind you. I think one of the errors that people writing analysis make is to assume that every-body else has been on the journey with them and knows the ins and outs of the story as well as they do.

It's a frequent characteristic of sports reporting. You know, 'The Reds defeated the Blues in a whitewash.' What sport are we even talking about?

Right. And that is one of the dangers of a round – you get so deeply into it that you're really only writing for other aficiona-dos. That's an understandable mistake but it's a bad one, because it means you're alienating a huge proportion of the population.

Whenever I write about politics – I don't mean to sound holier than thou here, I'm convinced that I've committed this error countless times – I try to make my purpose: 'Will this piece of writing help anyone get a better understanding of what's going on? Will it throw out an invitation to people who, if asked, would say, "I'm not interested in politics."' And that's why, ever since I was allowed to start writing commentary, I've tried to use humour as much as possible; that way, I genuinely think you get people tuning in who might not show up just for the raw politics.

You are well known for your use of humour: is that something you had to work to develop? Or has it simply been a case of getting your authentic voice on paper?

This idea of authentic voice is very tricky. Among younger or newer journalists, there's always an enthusiasm to establish a voice. The truth is, I don't think I had a very distinctive voice until a decent way into my work as a journalist. You really have to assemble the bare bones of structure before you can start playing around with it. It's like Jimi Hendrix – you've got to learn to play the guitar before you start playing it around the back of your head and smashing it up.

Sometimes I really work not to put jokes in, because it can look flippant if you put in too many. I've definitely been guilty of that in the past.

What are the other risks with trying to inject humour?

That you joke about something that's not a laughing matter. Or that bitter humour can make you look a bit sadistic and undermine the insight you're hoping to deliver.

You now have a distinctive, identifiable voice. How do you think you developed it?

Just by reading widely. Actually, the way that I got interested in political reporting was a powerful influence on the way I write.

Many years ago, I took a year out from my law degree and went and worked in a fruit and veg shop in Scotland. I used to read *The Times* on my lunch break. Matthew Parris was writing a political sketch at the time and I found myself being drawn into British politics purely because of the quality of his writing. He made the characters and individuals so clear to me. His writing was comedic but it gave you an insight into what was going on beneath the surface, in an irreverent and entertaining way. It meant I suddenly started reading more broadly and was interested in British politics. I always thought, 'Wouldn't it be amazing to be able to write like this?' or be able to perform that service. And when I started in journalism, I never forgot that lesson – that I had been a bystander not at all interested in politics, really, and I had been drawn into it by this magical and well-structured, intelligent, entertaining and informed writer.

Do your columns necessarily reflect your own opinions?

Oh, no. I have areas of interest that I write about; gender and workplace policy is one of them. That personal interest is influential in some of the writing that I choose to do beyond straight politics. In that case, I guess it's loosely powered by my opinions, but I try never to be incredibly didactic about it.

I'm a firm believer that you don't get change, you don't get insight, you don't get progress, if you're just tub-thumping your narrow opinion. One of the great geniuses of the democratic system – as well as one of its most perplexing and challenging aspects – is that everybody gets a vote, right? You can't just browbeat everybody into agreeing with you. I'm always suspicious of writers who work like that – here's my opinion, and here's me smashing everybody else, ripping the shit out of people who don't agree with me and trying to humiliate people with whom I disagree, and that's how I'm going to convince you of my point of view. I'm *never* convinced by writers or advocates who use those means.

In truth, most consumers of journalism, I think, are more like me. They're full of doubts about what they think on certain things. They're looking for information, they're looking for context, they're looking for insight. They're not necessarily looking for somebody to shout at them until they surrender.

I know that there's a huge business model that revolves around shoutiness. In our current environment, there is a flight to tribalism, where people who feel uncertain about lots of changing things in the world, anxious about their own place in the world, find comfort teaming up with one extreme or another. But I think there is a vast central group of people who probably would settle somewhere in the middle. And for those people, a calmer, rational piece of analysis might be more useful for them to gather background and context and make their own decisions.

Anchoring

An anchor of a podcast, television or radio show defines how the program is viewed by the public. On a news or current affairs show, the job is a mixture of journalism and performance.

Unlike a reporter, who covers one story in depth and then moves onto the next project, an anchor usually has to be across many different subjects at the same time. They must be able to think on their feet and react in split seconds. The ability to listen carefully and to constantly remain in the moment is crucial.

One of the most important skills for an anchor is managing performance anxiety, in the same way as an actor or musician. At all times they must appear calm and relaxed, even if things are going wrong in the broadcast, or if they are required to suddenly deliver traumatic or alarming news.

If a presenter is unable to connect to an audience, if they cannot hold their nerve, or if their persona does not adequately reflect a show's brand, the venture will either fail or the anchor will be replaced. That is part of the reason why anchors of prominent programs are usually highly paid. The position is subject to intense scrutiny and can be short-lived. Failure can result in the loss of many people's jobs and permanent reputational damage to those involved. The flipside is that a skilled anchor can turn their programs – and themselves – into beloved and trusted public institutions.

Kumi Taguchi

Kumi Taguchi anchors the highly respected Insight *program on SBS. She initially studied classical violin at university and her first job in the media was at ABC TV's 7.30* Report, *where she picked up dry-cleaning and ran other errands and answered the phones. She used that opportunity to build a diverse media career spanning more than twenty years, from anchoring on Star Television and Asia TV in Hong Kong to hosting* Compass *on the ABC. She has been the face of major events coverage at the national broadcaster, including the Australian of the Year Awards and the Invictus Games. The 2019 ABC program* Kumi's Japan *explored her Japanese heritage.*

Kumi, explain the premise of *Insight*.

In a studio, you have a group of people who have a lived experience that's similar – or a connection to a topic – but who might have totally different interpretations of that topic and totally different reasons why they want to be there. The dynamic between those people, that's part of the magic of the show. A lot of the time, the people who are in that studio have never spoken about that topic before, so it's a vulnerable space.

How do you come up with the topics?

We have a hierarchy of producers – supervising producers, then producers and then associate producers – who come to a commissioning meeting and pitch two or three ideas. One producer will work on a show for six weeks, so every six to seven weeks they're pitching a bunch of new ideas. We all discuss and go, 'Yes, what do we think?'

There was a great article the other day in *The New York Times* about children whose parents are in prison. I said, 'Have we ever done anything on this before? Is there an Australian angle?' But we'd done something five years earlier.

The producers need a sense of 'This is why it's an *Insight* program' – and not a documentary, not a *Q&A*. There's a very specific feel of *Insight*. With those pitches, they also have to pitch who they might try and get on the show if it's commissioned. We have a very robust conversation – what could some of the angles be? Is it interesting? Are we in our little bubble and it's just us who think it's interesting?

As we're having this discussion, Australia is experiencing major floods. A very easy and obvious angle for *Insight* would be people who've survived disasters. How much are your program ideas tied to the news cycle?

Not on any level. There are so many other outlets doing that important work. I always think of that Christopher Hitchens quote, 'Beware the dogs that aren't barking.'

Something that stuns me with *Insight* is the ability to fill a room with people who will talk about something you'd think nobody would want to publicly air. An episode that springs to mind was about families where one child is favoured over another.

That episode comes up so often. People will say, 'I love that episode.' We think the taboo topics are sex and drugs and affairs, but actually, I think the taboo topics that are most interesting are the ones we all know to be true but don't say. I think the favourite child one really taps into that.

We have about 250,000 people on Facebook and we put up shout-outs such as, 'Were you a favourite child in your family?' Or: 'Did you ever think you were not the favourite child in your family? Are you parents and secretly have a favourite but don't want to talk about it?'

Our producer may speak to experts in that field and come up with another angle. So at a check-in meeting, maybe halfway through the pre-production process, the producer might say, 'Look, we thought this was an interesting angle, but actually, no one's talking about that.' We prove ourselves wrong a lot of the time – we flip and change the direction of an episode because we don't know everything, right? [The talent] might say, 'Well actually, that's not a big issue. *This* is the issue that's at the heart of the topic.'

We have a lot of younger associate producers who are just amazing, they're starting to find really great talent on Reddit threads. We found some talent for a show that's coming up called 'Forgetting Fatherhood', about men leaving fatherhood behind. And there were these really weird, closed-off, fascinating forums of young guys chatting about it on Reddit. We spent a couple of weeks just chatting on these threads, finding a few people who might be willing to talk. It's a long process of building trust, then getting people comfortable to the point of actually coming into the studio and feeling safe in that space.

You mention the studio being a safe space. Frankly, having to talk to a roomful of strangers about something really intimate, in front of eight television cameras, is about as unsafe an environment as you can imagine, right? As the anchor, how do you make people feel secure?

I often think about that, and it's all to do with the team. By the time people get into the studio, they feel safe within the team of *Insight*. They feel looked after, heard, and that they're going to be treated with respect. We're also very open about the opposing views in the room; we'll say, '*Insight*'s a place where robust, honest conversations can take place, with differing points of view.' We never want people to feel like they've been blindsided. We brief people really carefully.

Do you meet or speak to any of the people in the audience before you walk in?

I deliberately don't. I set boundaries around that. It's not to avoid people, but I don't want anyone to start sharing their story with me. Otherwise, by the time I get to the studio and into that part of their story, they feel like they've told it to me before. I want that to be fresh.

I learnt that the hard way. I learnt it from big events like Australian of the Year; I've been on planes where you're sitting next to half the people you're meant to be engaging with in eight hours' time. I have to be quite open and honest with people now and say, 'Look, I'm going to have to put my headphones on and tune out.

I need to preserve my batteries because my job's at 6 p.m., and I'm really looking forward to chatting with you then.' I say it up front now, and I speak more about my energy and my need to just be in a bit of a zone, and people are quite fine with that.

It's a balance, isn't it? Between it being fresh and wanting people to be at ease.

It really is. Two hours before I go into the studio, all our guests will have arrived. Producers have met everyone and settled them in. Then I check in with the producer and say, 'How's everyone going?' You just don't know what's happening in people's worlds when they're on the way to the studio. I will note down a few people I need to quickly check in with before the recording starts, particularly the person who has to go first in the show. I'll generally go up to them and say, 'Hey, how you feeling? You're going first, you're going to be fine, but thank you so much.' I find those conversations are fine because they're pragmatic, they're making that person feel seen and valued.

Anchoring a complex program like *Insight* requires a real clarity of your mental space, and making small talk is a draining thing to do.

I agree one hundred per cent. The small talk thing is the most difficult. I'm quite rigid with how I structure the time up until I go into the studio with my team. There's very little time to eat, I've got a five-minute window here, a ten-minute window there, [between] camera checks, promos, make-up checks and things.

I put headphones on and send a message to the team: 'It's headphone time, I've tuned out for half an hour. Send me a text if it's urgent.' And they're literally all around me. It sounds a bit odd, but I really feel like I need that time to listen to music. I've got a pre-show playlist that makes me think about the bigger perspective. I take my mind back to why we wanted to do this show in the first place. Why it's important. It's so easy to get caught up in the minutiae of the story and the scripting, and when you're churning out episode after episode, it's too easy to go, 'I've done that episode, what's the next episode?' They're not episodes, they're fifteen people with huge lives who are investing a lot of their time and emotional energy with us.

I do quite a bit of mental gymnastics to reset. I visualise every person in that room, and I'm just grateful for their humanity. I think that's vital for me.

It's such a rushed environment, you can feel like you've got to finish the recording. And I really don't want to have that attitude at all. I feel that studio needs to have a calm, respectful energy. And it helps me too, to question people I internally find challenging or disagree with. When I look at their face, I think, 'Okay, you're a whole human being with your right to how you view the world, your feelings are your feelings and they're valid.' And, hopefully, it helps me come across as curious about every single person's experience, even if they're on opposite sides of the spectrum with what they believe.

When you go into the studio and start the program, how carefully have you structured the direction it's going to take? For example, the order in which you ask the questions, or the order in which you go to people.

Incredibly forensically structured. When I first started the job I thought, 'Come on, where's the room for just riffing? A bit of spontaneity!' I learned very quickly there's a reason for the high level of structure. We have three segments: segment one's usually 'What is this thing we're talking about?'; segment two's often 'Where are these nubbly bits?'; and segment three's 'Okay, so this is what we've learned but where do we go from here?'

I'd say 95 per cent of it is the structure that we've put in place: really thought-through nuance about how we transition from one guest to another. And then 5 per cent is conversations unfolding in a way that you don't expect. Someone will reveal something that they said in pre-interviews they weren't going to reveal. There'll probably be about six or seven moments in a recording of two hours where I'll have that gut feeling of 'I just need to go one little step further into this.' But I've learned to really trust the structure. It's kind of magical how it works.

Do you think there are any tricks to reading naturally from an autocue?

I've thought about this since I started doing voiceovers for all my reporting in Hong Kong. I would listen to my voiceovers and I'd just go, 'What? Where is my normal voice?' I'm suddenly this other version of myself, which is this preconceived notion of what a news reporter is.

To retrain myself, I'd pretend I was having a conversation with my grandmother on the phone. I'd go, 'Hi Granny, I'm doing a really cool story today about some protest marches in Hong Kong and I just want to tell you about it.' Then I'd literally walk into the booth, pretend I'm talking to her and start reading my script. It's like I had to cut that barrier, that weird thing that happened between being normal and being abnormal in front of the microphone. We don't have any autocue at *Insight*, so that's easy. But I worked really hard to be normal when I was doing three hours of daily news a day.

It's incredible, isn't it, how difficult it is to sound natural. The key to it is being relaxed, but that is so easy to say and so difficult to do when you're talking to a piece of machinery.

I enjoy looking down the camera lens now because I imagine a person sitting there, and that we're looking at each other.

How difficult do you find it to control your emotions if you're hearing from somebody who's telling a sad story, or you're anchoring a tragic story? Do you have any techniques you use to try to stay on top of that?

I've found it difficult at times. Because the news is so factual and you've got to be a bit stoic, it's almost easier. I've found *Insight* much harder. The first show I recorded, the parents of Sara [Zelenak], who was killed in the London Bridge attacks, were in the studio. I remembered anchoring that story years before, hour after hour after hour. I knew the parents were going to be in the studio, I knew their backstory, I knew what they were going to talk about; they're scripted in, it's all very pragmatic. I remember walking into the studio and just seeing the father's face – that I'd seen dozens and dozens and dozens of times – literally a metre in front of me. And I just remember turning to my EP and going, 'I don't know if I can do this.' Because it's one thing to hear someone's story through sound bites, but it's another to have them really there, particularly for a couple of hours in quite a challenging space.

A few times I didn't know how to handle it. In a sense, it wasn't until I was in that space that I knew where my vulnerabilities were. I thought, 'I still need to be empathetic,' but I also felt very strongly that I needed to hold firm so other people could be vulnerable. Because that's my job.

Have you ever seen that crappy movie *Maid in Manhattan* with Ralph Fiennes?

No.

He had to give a eulogy for his mother's funeral, and he was worried about breaking down. He got some advice: 'Get a paper-clip or something sharp and twist it open, so that there's a sharp bit pointing out.' And you literally hold that in your hand. When there's a moment where you feel yourself welling up or getting quite emotional, you just shove the spike into the palm of your hand.

It's been the most brilliant tool. And so strangely enough, I often keep this fingernail longish on my little finger because I know I can just press that fingernail into one of my other fingers or into the palm of my opposite hand. It's become a little bit of a habit now, my body just tends to do it when it needs to. Physically, it's the best thing I've ever learned to do.

There's a bit of a cliché of the female reporter as this hard-nosed, feisty, aggressive kind of operator. You're not like that at all. Did you ever feel pressure coming up through journalism to be something that you were not?

Yeah, I did feel pressure. I was told I'd never make it because I wasn't tough enough, didn't look the right way, got started too late. And I never had that aggressive bone. I did have a belief in my intuition about people and the world. I'd just have a feeling about something and ask something. And I started to trust the way my brain worked in this hyperspace. As a result, I think my career's been quite self-selecting. I would love to have been an amazing investigative journalist or something, but I just know that it's probably something I'll admire from afar. It's not due to lacking confidence but just knowing where my strengths and weaknesses lay.

It did bother me a lot because I thought, 'How am I going to make it?' I felt like I didn't have the right ingredients on so many levels. Even now, I'll go to events like the Walkleys and I still have that feeling of being so kind of . . . underdone. A lot of people are just quite tough – so certain, so determined.

Journalism does reward that personality type. If you're aggressive and a bit of a salesman-type person, you're going to land good interviews and all the rest of it. But the reality is that journalism needs all personality types and all kinds of backgrounds. Otherwise you're going to end up with this very narrow cohort of people with a very narrow worldview, and miss a whole lot of what life's about.

Exactly. And you know, we're lucky that the industry is so diversified in terms of how many ways you can tell a story. I'm quite fascinated with the opioid crisis in the US at the moment; I'm reading this fat, amazing book. But looking at something like opioids or drug addiction, you could read a book like *Beautiful Boy*; watch Steve Carell in *Beautiful Boy*; read this thick tome that I have, written by this incredible *New York Times* journalist, about the Sackler family and the opioid crisis; watch *Euphoria*, a [TV] drama about addiction; read an amazing article; listen to a podcast. What I love is that people can reach that story in a way that makes sense to them. Not everyone's going to read that fat book, not everyone's going to love *Euphoria*, not everyone's going to watch *Beautiful Boy*. But each of those pieces of content appeals to a different audience and in a different way.

I feel like that with our industry. We've got so many wonderful avenues now for different personality types to be and exist.

You studied classical violin from age five. What lessons do you think music has given you for your life and career?

So many. I think it's been the biggest gift to my career. The discipline of doing something over and over and over again, knowing that you get better. That things take time – playing an instrument and mastering it takes a lot of time. I was a very shy kid, and I'm quite an introvert. But having to perform was one of the best things the violin gave me. Also: not stopping. When you perform, it's like, 'No matter what happens, don't stop.' Whether you stuff up or you forget a note or your bow flicks off. I remember feeling my cheeks going red, the pianist still going, you're catching up, and that 'never stopping' thing. Something wires that in your brain – that once you're in performance mode, you keep going.

The other thing that's been invaluable with music is orchestra playing. I love the fact that you're just one instrument in a whole bunch. It takes every single little instrument working together to make something incredible, which is what a lot of journalism is – it's that team. I love that aspect of the jobs that we do, like the multitasking that your brain has to do in an orchestra. You're playing your instrument, you're reading music, your brain has learned over many years to look at a note and not even have to tell your fingers what to do when they see that note; it's bypassed about five different pathways in your brain. Your fingers just do it, which is the most extraordinary thing. At the same time as you're playing you're listening to whether you're in tune – there are about fifty things going on just in that action. You're looking over to the cellist who's about to give you a cue, or you're looking over to your fellow violinist and seeing that you're in tune with each other. You're looking over to the conductor, you're listening to how loud or soft you are compared to everyone else around you. It is the most extraordinary multidisciplinary multitasking action that your ears, eyes, brain, [body] can do. When I think of intense moments like live crosses, live TV, massive hosting events, where everything's going pear-shaped – there's no autocue and everything's physically being blown out by lightning strikes – there's something about that hearing of people in your ear, reading the autocue, listening to someone talking to you and nodding at the same time. It's like performing music, where it all comes into play.

Karl Stefanovic

Karl Stefanovic has been the co-host of the Nine Network's Today *breakfast show for almost twenty years. In 2011, he won the Gold Logie for Australia's most popular television personality. He has also hosted shows such as* The Verdict *and* This Time Next Year, *and reported for* 60 Minutes. *He studied journalism at the Queensland University of Technology and began his career in regional television, before moving up the ranks at Nine, including a period as US Correspondent.*

For many people, the thought of going on live TV five mornings a week, for more than three hours at a time, and talking off the top of their head to hundreds of thousands of viewers would be their idea of torture. What do you think it is that equips you to step onto that highwire every day?

Oh, experience. Even doing university stuff on radio and TV at QUT, I would get nervous. Years later, doing on-the-road stuff for WIN TV and then back to Channel 9 to read the news, I was terribly nervous. Sweating, sphincter-tightening nerves; your voice is shaking and you feel that you're just not going to be able to get through it. Something horrific is going to happen. The autocue is going to go down, you're going to be embarrassed . . . and then all that stuff does happen. So your worst nightmares become reality.

After that, it's just about getting those on-air miles up. Now I actually look forward to it. I love it because it makes me sharper. I like the adrenalin before a big national broadcast.

So it's like you've come to think of it differently and channel that anxiety a bit better.

Yeah. I've come to accept that I'm going to go through it, and in a strange way, it makes me more focused. I'm able to think clearly. I'm thinking two or three seconds ahead. I've had that thought process going while I'm speaking and I can actually sort of be outside of myself. It takes a long time, though. Like I said, it's just repetition – hour after hour of grinding away.

I think one of the hard things for people starting out is there's really no way to learn how to anchor except by doing it. You just can't replicate the feeling of driving a live broadcast.

It can be overwhelming. And you can really hamper yourself in those nervous moments. You can go over things too much in your head. You've got to do your research, you've got to know what you're going to say, you have to have faith that you're going to be able to remember it, and you have to stay calm. If you're relaxed, you have clarity of thought and then it comes out of you a lot easier.

When you're anchoring in the field, you often need to improvise. What kind of notes do you have in front of you?

It depends what you're doing. I remember one of the first jobs I did anchoring from the field was when [former US President] Ronald Reagan died. There was the big procession in Washington DC and I was just down to do the news crosses for the *Today* show. But I just had a feeling it was gonna be a spectacle and that once [the network] saw the picture, they would want more. So I spent hours taking clippings from newspapers and writing notes about what we were going to see, going, 'Okay, when I see this particular guard, these things on their sleeve mean this and that.' And so, when it came time to do it, I knew that I was off and running. I could relax into it because I'd done the preparation. The only way to do those big set pieces and the big broadcasts – from a royal wedding to a US election – is to be prepared.

For me, Reagan was the big one. A few years later, in Brisbane in 2011, during floods, I did eight hours on my own without any ad breaks. And that was with no notes, just keeping notes on the run – where we're going, who the talent is, who the talent is next.

Sometimes when I'm anchoring, I feel as though my brain is split in two: there's the part that is managing what's actually on air, and the part that's listening to what's happening behind the scenes, anticipating where I'm going next and how much time I've got. I'm trying with that first part of my brain to not show on my face what's going on in the second part.

Yeah, I think that's true. I'll be thinking about being present with the interview or opinion, and making sure that's clean, and I've got my mind on the clock. I know I've got to hit the break four and a half minutes to the half-hour or at the top of the hour. I'm going into openers next, I know that the floor manager is giving me a count, the producer's saying, 'We've got it, move on,' or, 'We've got to ask this before we go, plus there's a back announce.' But again, that's just experience.

Somebody who reads the autocue well looks like they're just talking to you. But if you see somebody who doesn't do it well, you can really tell they're reading. What do you think is the key to a natural delivery reading from an autocue?

This is going to sound like I'm so up myself, but when I first became a correspondent with Nine, I started talking to a mirror. I found that if I could watch myself in the mirror and not be distracted in my delivery about what I was saying, and my face was relaxed, I could replicate that on camera. I don't do it now, but I reckon that's a great technique.

When you're starting out, you have to work at looking natural. That's a very peculiar thing to say but you're better off being observant about your movements. I had to work really hard with hand gestures and my looks off camera to make sure that it didn't look funny, because it's how I talk. When you go on camera, things can be amplified. Your facial expressions can be amplified, your vocal tone can be amplified. Little things like that can put an audience off. Getting the right tone is the most important thing that we do. And that goes to facial expressions, hand gestures – all that stuff is about putting the audience at ease. And to put the audience at ease, you have to be at ease. I don't think there's anything wrong with having a look at yourself when you first start out and seeing what works and what doesn't.

All of us television reporters have to overcome the horror of seeing what we actually look like and hearing what we actually sound like.

Yeah, yeah. I remember hearing myself for the first time and going, 'My god, that is just awful.' And I thought I was so good, I thought my shit didn't stink. You should hear some of my first stories on WIN TV. It's like, 'Um, you . . . know . . . so . . . stilted,' it's just horrible. So you just have to get over that.

Sometimes I wonder how much of anchoring is performance and how much is journalism.

Yeah, I think that's an interesting point. I always come back to energy. I think energy is the most important thing – getting the energy right. I think it is a performance in the way that you present individual segments, but also, overall, the whole show needs performance. And in a strange way, you're presenting yourself.

In a breakfast program, where you're interacting with a group of people on set, how important is the chemistry, and can it be faked or manufactured?

No, it can't. You've got to work hard at it. I come in every morning and try to help with everyone's energy, I give a pump-up to the studio crew. I always go straight to the camera operators or the autocue operator. I sometimes wander up to the studio control and give them a big rev-up. Chemistry is not just your co-host, chemistry is the vibe in the studio. It's the vibe amongst the producers. And again, back to energy, I think if you can get everyone motivated and keyed up, it's going to be a lot better show, and you're going to feel better about yourself.

Also, on air you don't know which people you're going to have better chemistry with. For me, I've had chemistry with all the people I've worked with. There are some things you can do during a show, techniques you can use, that make it appear as though there's chemistry. Like turning to your co-host, actually listening to your co-host, listening to an interviewee. If you listen and you're able to react to what they said – rather than thinking about other things and where you're going – that leads to the idea that a certain on-air couple have chemistry.

How do you view the relationship between the executive producer and the anchor? And who is the boss?

Depends on any given day. You have to be respectful of the EP job, no matter how good you think you are. *Today* is a big, big show. And you're not controlling every part, so you've got to let yourself be part of the process a little bit; control what you can control, do a good job of that. If it's editorial, we can talk during the show, and we can decide whether or not we're going to change things. Sometimes in the morning we'll throw out a lot of stuff and just go with whatever's fresh, which I think is really important. And to have an EP who's comfortable with that is a big deal. I think a good EP is a guider, not a dictator. And I think a good anchor is a good listener.

Even though every role in making a television program is essential to getting it to air, in the eyes of the public the anchor is the most prominent figure. What responsibility do you think that carries, and how heavily does that weigh on you?

Very heavily. I think in the last few years with Covid – something that's affected so many people's lives – it's never been more important to be aware and across details. It affected people's lives in a very different way, individually and for families. In my career, it has never been a more important time to have the right information given to people. And that's hard when you have different doctors telling you different things, and such conflicting information on social media. So it's a very sensitive broadcast.

People would write to me and say things like, 'You are the person I've seen the most in the past three months of lockdown.' If I took days off, I'd get tonnes of social media messages asking where I was, and if it was two days it would snowball. It was like my absence was an added stress that people didn't want – me not reliably being in their living room when I was usually there every night. That is a huge responsibility. People feel that you are their trusted friend.

A hundred per cent. And it's a real privilege, I adore this job for those reasons. I've had people who are in hospital, I've had people at home in bed, I've had people who've been so depressed they were contemplating the very worst, and they've written to me saying, 'You are my companion.' What could be a bigger honour, as a craft and vocation, than to have that kind of influence on some person's life? Even though it's TV, it's going to the nation, it's going into people's living rooms, over their breakfast tables with their kids around. I feel a great sense of responsibility to get things right and also a great sense of responsibility to entertain. I feel a great responsibility to make a complete and utter fool of myself. It's a show. If something's been heavy, I break it up and try and have different rhythms, because I'm always thinking about that audience at home.

Indira Naidoo

In 2023, Indira Naidoo began hosting ABC TV's Compass *program as well as anchoring four evenings each week on ABC radio for Sydney, Canberra and New South Wales. Before that, she was presenting the ABC's* Weekend Nightlife *program, which has a million listeners across Australia. Indira rose to national prominence in the 1990s as the popular anchor of ABC Late Edition news, before moving to SBS World News. She has written three books,* The Edible Balcony, The Edible City *and* The Space Between the Stars. *From 2016 to 2020, Indira hosted and co-executive produced three seasons of* Filthy Rich and Homeless *for SBS. She has been an ambassador for Sydney's homeless crisis centre The Wayside Chapel for the past decade, and her journalistic interests in recent years have been on the role global environmental issues play in conflict, poverty and food security. She has spent periods working outside journalism, allowing her to focus on her humanitarian and social justice priorities.*

Indira, you are the rare person experienced in anchoring both television and radio programs. Beyond the obvious need to brush your hair, what do you think are the major differences?

I had no idea how different they would be. One requires you to be absolutely to the core who you really are. And the other one you can get away with a bit. I'll leave it up to you to work out which one's which.

Well, I think people can act like they're credible or caring on television *or* radio, but I think that the audience can see through it.

Yeah, they can. I guess it's more about when everyone is focused only on your voice, and that's the only thing they can access. The voice is so honest. I would have thought when you look at some-one's face, you see it all. But really, you get distracted by their face, so you don't listen the way you probably would when there's only the voice. It requires you to be much more real when it's just a microphone, as opposed to a camera and a mic.

In television there's make-up, lights, outfits – they offer a kind of armour. And you're talking through a piece of machinery, which imposes a distance as well.

When I talk to long-term radio hosts, they say, 'Oh, thank god, we can hide behind a microphone. I couldn't stand in front of a crowd. I couldn't be on stage.' And I go, 'Oh my god, I can do that anytime of the day.' A microphone for me is like the truth chamber. What I'm really falling in love with, now that I'm not so terrified of radio, is that everyone – the audience and you – takes off all the pretence. It's the most intimate conversation that you can possibly have.

I was live on air on Saturday night when Shane Warne's death news came through. Hearing that news while you're actually broadcasting, in the middle of a sentence – plus being a huge cricket fan and knowing the impact his loss would have not only in his family, but the greater nation, the greater world – you just have to follow the ABCD that you know, tick all the boxes. First of all, you have to make sure that it is accurate. Get as many ways of confirming that news as possible, which is difficult at that time of night. You have to fall back into, 'It's not about being first, it's about being right.'

How did you break that news in what you thought to be the appropriate way?

There's not much time to think, and not much time to get yourself together if you're not together. So it has to be off the cuff and exactly how you feel. I haven't heard it back, but I'm sure you would have got the sense that I was shocked by the news. I didn't have to say 'And in shocking news . . .' You would have got that from my voice. But you also need to remember that whoever's listening, they're all alone. So they can't immediately get comfort. It might not be Shane Warne's death, but wherever you leave them, you have to leave them in a safer place, where they can sit for a while until they can talk to someone about it.

One of the most important things is to not pass on your fear. And this is not just for broadcasters, but anyone that wants to play a role of supporting and helping people. It's the easiest thing to pass on, you know? You can't do that. Of course you're feeling it too – they know you're feeling it, you're a human being – but no one tunes in to hear your fear.

On a regular night, when you start your radio program, how much do you know about what is going to be on?

Almost everything. Our show is pretty structured because of its duration – four hours, every night – and the length of the segments, which are large chunks and very in-depth interviews. We start planning three or four weeks in advance, start lining up the talent, the guests, the structure, what sort of points we want to hit.

For instance, someone on our team had a female tradie, an electrician, who came in and did some work and she was just talking about it. I was saying, 'Yeah, I had a female plumber.' We were saying, 'Isn't it terrible that that's an unusual thing that we would comment on?' We started talking about female tradies and thought, 'There's a really interesting chat about why there aren't more. Are there some out there listening? What is the challenge when you're a female tradie?' It was really interesting. We ended up talking to different women – plumbers, electricians and construction builders – from around the world; some of them came from academia and TAFE backgrounds, some were on the job. And then we asked the audience to participate too. We were talking about what their favourite ute is, what sort of tradie has what sort of ute. You can tell a tradie by their ute!

So that can be one hour-long segment, and then we'll have another segment that is about brain plasticity. And we'll have a couple of very high-end Oxford or Johns Hopkins specialists talking about where the human brain and different prosthetic stuff is going – that's another whole hour, which can be an amazing, deep, futuristic thinking discussion. And then we'll just talk for an hour about Aussie slang – 'What are your favourite Aussie slang words?' – and we'll have people contributing from all around. It's so diverse, and all of those [segments] have to be locked in and planned because it's half an hour to an hour of someone's time, somewhere in the world.

When you're doing that segment on female tradies or brain plasticity, do you prefer to go in having done a lot of research, or do you just let your natural curiosity drive the conversation?

Leigh, I've learnt that I over-prepare. It's always been a real failing, actually, because I don't trust that I will be okay to get myself through. *Nightlife* is the sort of show you can't over-prepare for, because you really can't have a PhD in everything that we talk about, even though the people you talk to do.

Sometimes you can ask a really silly question and people love it. We were talking about Instagram influencers, and we had all this research, and I just started off by going to the person we were interviewing, 'Why do I need to know about this?' So many listeners said, 'I was thinking the same thing!' That's something I've had to learn a lot more about, just to trust my natural response.

Do you approach a conversation with a listener who's just called in the same way that you would approach an expert from Oxford University who's been lined up?

Well, that's the thing that I've learnt to do. As journalists, we can be pretty dazzled by people's qualifications and we can forget they are human beings. For instance, we were talking about microcars and some of the more collectible ones, as there was an exhibition at the Powerhouse Museum. We had three experts on microcars, car designers and God knows what sort of engineers from all over the world. It had been prepped, of course, to draw on their expertise, but then I suddenly went, 'Hang on, did you ever have a microcar? What was your favourite? Tell me about it.' And it brought out such a different side of their personalities.

You were identified very early in your career as having extremely good TV anchoring skills. What did you think it was that caught the eye of the bosses?

Honestly, I've never really thought about that stuff. You know, it was just, 'Someone's asked me to do something, so I'll go and do it.' It really was as shallow as that. Obviously, now I look back and I understand the craft a lot more. I never really overthought it. I didn't wake up every day when I was a kid going, 'I want to anchor something.' I think it genuinely was a sense of 'naturalness'.

You cannot host a live television program and never have something go wrong. What did you learn about how to manage those moments?

The viewers love it when things go wrong. They really do. And even though they might complain, they love it, because then there's something to complain about – 'Oh my god, it was so funny when her earring just fell off her ear in the middle of that chat.' As the anchor, we want it all to be slick and the same, so that you can tune in Tuesday today or Tuesday 2050 and I'll look the same, it'll sound the same. But no one [watching] wants that.

In the old cart-stack years, if one cart was put in the wrong place, it was like falling dominoes – every story would fall over. One night at SBS, the second story in the cart stack had been incorrectly labelled. The computer didn't read it, then kept trying to read every one under it as the same story. I had the autocue and the scripts but no package would play after I read anything.

This particular night, the floor manager was quite inexperienced, and he just lifted his hands in the air. That was his support. We had one of those crazy red bat phones next to me, just a stupid prop that sat there, and I thought, 'I'm just gonna pick it up and pretend there's someone in the control room that can hear me.' At least it's something for me to do. So I picked up the phone and went, 'Yes, hello. You're across it? Great. Fabulous.' Just buying time for when I have to actually tell people what the hell is going on. So then I said, 'It's all being sorted out, let's go back to that first story again.' There was still no package – and no sound in my ear – so I went through my script to find something I could just read. Anyway, we finally got it together, but it was about twelve minutes on air, which is just hell. I used to end [the program] by saying, 'This is *SBS News*, I'm Indira Naidoo,' and I ended it [that night] by saying, 'This is *SBS News*, I'm Indira Naidoo, I'll be back tomorrow because I'm an optimist.' It was so funny. I was obviously pretty shattered, but the viewers loved it.

When there's silence in your ear, that's when you know it's really bad out the back. A colleague once told me that often, when something goes wrong, it's a simple thing like someone pushing the wrong button. And if you can buy a little time, that's often enough to fix it. He said, 'It's so much cleaner to just pad a bit and then say, "Let's try it again," than to go to something different.'

That's so true. Radio teaches you that; you have to be a good padder. And now, I can't actually pick when I'm padding. I just start just rambling on and I'm thinking, 'Am I padding? Or do we have the next guest to go to?' Radio is a great format for teaching you those padding skills that don't sound like padding.

The unplanned moments are what I like. We were playing a quiz and asking about a very unusual Serbian cheese that's made from the milk of two farm animals – 'One of the farm animals is a goat, what's the other farm animal?' We had people guessing cows and sheep, and then this young guy rang in and said, 'Chickens?' and it was hilarious. I didn't want to make fun of him, so I said, 'No, I'm sorry. That's incorrect.' But for the rest of the quiz, everyone kept sending in, 'I've just had a glass of chicken milk, it's delicious,' then I'd say something about chicken milk. It just became an off-the-cuff, funny little thing that connected people in more ways than the planned quiz questions would have. That was a good lesson for me too, to go with where it's feeling like it needs to go. You have a lot more freedom to do that in radio than television.

And you get home and think, 'Wow, I didn't know I'd be talking about chicken milk for forty-five minutes today, but there you go.'

I had a glass of chicken milk every day after that.

How about controlling emotion when you're presenting sad or tragic news? You certainly had a number of years with *World News* at SBS with horrific stories night after night.

We had the East Timor crisis, we had Srebrenica. And they were the days when the feed's all the raw, wild footage coming straight in from APTV and WTN. You'd find footage yourself as it came off the feed, so you ended up seeing all the graphic images and then reducing them for the viewers. I don't know if there's much that can prepare you for that.

Did you have anything that you would do to try to insulate yourself emotionally?

Drink, which isn't a good coping mechanism. You know, I was only twenty-seven or twenty-eight. I wouldn't be doing that now, that's for sure. Now I know to not drink, get some exercise, go for a nice long walk in a park.

What's so different about this particular conflict currently in Ukraine is, because we have social media, it's sitting in my pocket all the time, which it wasn't in the late '90s. This is the first war that's actually just sitting in my pocket. It's even harder to get away from because a notification is interrupting even when you're doing something not to do with the war.

During your career, you've had many different jobs in journalism and you've also spent time away from journalism. What have the periods away taught you about how to be a better journalist?

I think you have a certain way of looking at the world as a journalist. You want to know, understand and learn, and then inform and communicate what you learn. But like any industry, you have failings. Generally, as a group, journalists are cynical, sort of dark. You see so much of the bad parts of human nature that you tend to think most humans are like that, which can then infect the way you start looking at stories. You go in a little bit cynical – 'Of course he's gonna say that. Of course she's gonna do that.' You're not open to the possibility that it won't be like that, which I think can infect the quality of your journalism. For me, it was really important to step away and spend time with people who really think they can change stuff.

Journalists forget how much influence and power they have;

they can still see themselves as victims to the system. Spending time with people who really have no access to power and influence and can't get any change happening in their communities is so important.

Stepping away was good, first of all, to remind me what a privilege it is to be a journalist, to be in the media. And how important it is to keep reminding yourself what these people – who you're speaking on behalf of all the time – really want, how they really live their lives.

In the 1990s, you were one of the first serious journalists to start combining news presenting with a broader persona, and you made some regular appearances on a comedy show called *Club Buggery*, hosted by Roy and HG. Was there any blowback at the time?

Within the ABC, it was a very unusual thing to see one of their news presenters or journalists doing something in another forum, particularly light entertainment and comedy. And there's always the concern of 'How is our serious news going to be seen if our presenter is doing a sketch with a bucket on her head?' And because no one had really done that sort of stuff, no one really understood or knew. I didn't think of it very seriously; I never thought, 'What effect is this going to have on this job or career?' It was just about having fun. Some of the news and current affairs bosses said, 'Well, who do you want to be? Do you want to be a serious journalist? Or do you want to hang out with Roy and HG?' Does it have to be an 'or'? It didn't matter to the audience. I've learnt that as long as whatever you're doing, you're doing authentically, it's fine.

Editors and
Executive Producers

Arguably, the most complex and difficult job in journalism belongs to the person who pulls everything together. That person usually has a title like Editor or Executive Producer. Their job is to commission, refine and organise an enormous pile of content, produced by a large group of people with wildly different skill sets and personalities under tight deadline pressure, and then turn it into a newspaper, website, television program, magazine, radio broadcast or podcast series that attracts an audience.

Doing this successfully every day comes with a dubious reward: you get to wake up the next day, where what you did yesterday counts for little, and do it all again.

An editor needs at least cursory familiarity with every major news story in the world at any given time, although breadth alone is insufficient: they also need depth of knowledge about ongoing stories so they can predict where issues are likely to go next and deploy their limited resources accordingly.

As if producing content isn't hard enough, the editor is also responsible for ensuring their programs are error-free, legally sound and ethically blameless. They have to manage a budget and human resources. The worst-case scenarios for an editor are a misstep that costs their network or publisher millions of dollars in court, or finding themselves and their anchor on the front page of a newspaper every day until they are replaced. It is a job that is performed under relentless, extreme pressure day after day. To survive, every editor needs endless creativity, courage, decisiveness and intelligence, along with a staggering work ethic.

Michael Pell

Michael Pell is Senior Vice-President, Entertainment Content, North America for the Seven Network. He is based in Los Angeles. From 2010 to 2022, Michael was the Executive Producer of Seven's breakfast program, Sunrise, *the top-rating breakfast show in Australia for almost two decades. Michael has also served as Executive Producer of* Weekend Sunrise *and* The Morning Show. *He began his career at Sky News and as a reporter for Prime Television, with stints at the Nine and Ten networks.*

TV can pretty much be divided into people in front of the camera and people behind it. Is there any general difference in personality type between the two?

Yes and no. I think on some level, everyone who works in TV is a bit crazy. It takes a special type of person to achieve what you're asking people to achieve in a television environment, under such huge amounts of pressure. Even the most junior person had to fight their way in. They had to put their foot in that door and get

303

in there. So I think you can never underestimate the television employee, whether they work in front of or behind the camera, because it is so hard to get in.

Once you get in, then it's: how do you go about your business? Generally, maybe there is a bit more ego with on-camera because you need that to be able to perform. You have to have that to be able to put yourself out there to the masses and get judged every day. For the person who's reluctant to have that much public scrutiny, behind the camera is the place. Sometimes I see people who were great on camera but decided to be off camera later in their career, simply because they wanted a bit more control. There are some people whose personality types are probably more suited to producing a show, or even being a camera operator or an editor, where you can really craft something.

You mentioned that people who work in TV have to fight their way in. How did you fight your way in?

When I was twelve, I wrote to Sharyn Ghidella, who was with Channel Nine Sydney and who now works in Brisbane as Seven's 6 p.m. newsreader. I said, 'Could I do some work experience?' To my surprise, she faxed me right back saying, 'Yes, we'd love to have you. You're certainly the youngest person that we've ever had in here, but we're happy for you to come. You might want to bring a guardian, though.' So my mum had to come in with me at 3:30am every time I went in to Nine's early news and *Today*. Afterwards, I went and studied journalism and that's when more of those cold letters and phone calls got me in.

Cold calling is a core skill for a journalist – approaching complete strangers and asking for something for nothing in return.

For nothing. That's it. You always get the young people in the team to chase, because they're the ones who are the most persistent. I remember having to overcome shyness, I didn't like talking on the phone as a teenager. I had to leave that at the door and just get over it and do it. When I started working in breakfast TV as a segment producer, it was my job to get that big interview of the day. As a twenty-three-year-old that was a lot of pressure but I had to do it.

The chaser on a television program is a very, very important and valuable asset. Other than being charming and persistent, are there any other particular tricks to it?

It's also about having contacts. It's about knowing where to look. These days, producers are remarkably good at finding people really quickly using the internet, social media, all those things that we take for granted that weren't around when I started. A good chaser can find anyone within about five minutes. And then, once you get the subject on the phone, it's about talking and, most importantly, listening.

You were twenty-eight when the job came up as EP of *Sunrise*, arguably the most important brand on the Seven Network because it sets up the entire day. By the time you took over, it was very successful, it had grown from nothing to a big force on Australian television. It was consistently beating *Today*, so there was a lot to lose if you messed it up. The network boss, David Leckie, even said to you, 'If you're no good you're not gonna be around for very long.'

That pressure does weigh on you. You don't want to fuck it up. You feel like you have a responsibility to the audience, to the network, to the presenters who are fronting that show, who've carried that brand for so many years. For me, that was also a motivating factor, because it was, 'Well, what are you going to do? How are you going to take this show to the next level, while still staying true to its core values? And remembering what the audience wants.' Everything that I've ever done has been about the viewer. How we get there as a production team is our problem.

When an EP talks about the pace of a show, what do they mean?

I'm big on pace. It's several things. In breakfast TV, it's how long segments go for, how much time you devote to a particular package or a live cross, how quickly you get through all the news headlines, how long you spend on particular interviews. I like to think of it as a car ride. If we're on a highway, Leigh, we're going to speed along. But if we're at traffic lights, and there are interesting things going on, we might stop, we might have a look, there might be a bit of a pause. In the same way, TV pacing is all about gear changes.

For example, if we're looking at a 7 a.m. news bulletin, when I started on *Sunrise* it went for about three minutes. By the time I left the show, it was probably about ten minutes, because the world had changed. Information is even more important to the viewer these days. You might then do several other program segments in that hour which are news-of-the-day based, and they might go for two and a half minutes each, which is super-quick for a live interview. Sometimes you're talking to politicians – and they love to eat up time – then we might have an interview with Katy Perry, and I might let that run for twelve minutes. Why? Because we've just had all this fast-paced news, and now we want to relax and see what a celebrity is doing. Pacing is also about all the bells and whistles that add as production elements: graphics, camera moves, music, whooshes, all the little things that make a live TV show a live TV show.

You executive produced a huge broadcast for Channel 7 after the terrible 2020 bushfires in Australia, a massive fundraiser. It was a ten-hour program and you drove it for the entire ten hours.

The Fire Fight Australia concert was a massive event. So many celebrities and music icons joined forces and said, 'Yes, we will be part of this,' because those bushfires had touched and shocked the world. Anything we did with the show had to reflect a few things – the star power, the tragedy of the situation, the hope that maybe through this we can help and as a community we can come together. The opening of the show had to feel all of those things. I think we even used a sample of Queen's 'Bohemian Rhapsody' underneath people talking about losing homes, which sounds weird but it worked. It was also about capturing the scale and the historic nature of that moment in time. Event television is one of my biggest passions because you can actually get excited and bring the audience on a journey.

How important to the pace and tone of that program was the way it was edited?

Really important. Sometimes editors are the unsung heroes of a show. In the Fire Fight Australia concert, the editing was very fast-paced unless we were talking about the tragedy of the situation or telling a personal story. I think there were about thirty tape elements in the show, several an hour to get us between live music acts and interviews. Some of them were incredibly sensitively edited. There's a real slowness there for you to think and digest, as an audience member, exactly what's gone on. And then it's 'But here's what we're doing about it and here's who's coming up next in the show to perform.' And it's whiz, bang, bang, bang, you know? It's really important, which bits are going to be punchy and in your face versus which bits are going to be slow and sensitive and let you feel.

Queen took their time getting to the stage and it was unclear exactly when they would walk out, so you had to fill some time. What do you do as the executive producer in a situation like that?

What you don't do is panic. It's really tricky. You can take a commercial break, but if Queen come out when you're in the break, you've missed the moment. You have to make quick decisions when you're doing live TV. My feeling at the time was the speculation, excitement and anticipation was almost as good as the actual event itself. Basically, you tell the presenters, 'Stretch,' which means 'Just keep talking and we'll let you know what comes next.' One of the key things for a good presenter is the ability to talk underwater. I think we ended up padding for probably seven minutes or so, a long time on prime time, but when there's this thought that the main act is about to come out – the climax of the show – it actually wasn't that bad. It was quite addictive television. It was engaging, you couldn't really look away.

On *Sunrise*, you often had to transition from something funny to something tragic quite rapidly. What is the key to making what's called a 'segue'?

Sometimes you don't always get it right. Sometimes there's no easy way to do it, it can be rough. There are methods you can try: separating or quarantining tougher content from lighter stuff. If there's a really serious story, we would try to quarantine it to its own segment, so it's got a commercial break either side. Sometimes, if you've done a really, really sad story, you don't want to tease anything to the break [promote what's going to be on the program when it returns from an ad break], you just want to do, 'Back with more in a moment,' because it seems the most sensitive thing to do. Sometimes you're laughing hysterically about something and then you need to move to something that's tougher. Something as simple as a time call can be effective – you know, a laugh then, 'Well, it's 7.43 on *Sunrise*.' Or some basic scripting like, 'Well, shifting focus now. . .'

When you were running *Sunrise*, how would you interact with your anchors while the show was on air?

A constant conversation. A lot of it was a discussion about what we thought was the most important news of the day and placement of things in the show. But also I was constantly trying to mirror to the hosts in their ear [via an earpiece linked to the control room] what the audience might be thinking. So if we were doing an interview and I found something funny, I would laugh in their ear. If something was sad, I'd say to them, 'Cannot believe it.' Sometimes just giving a bit of that emotion in their ear could help them know where to steer and navigate something.

What else would you do in the control room other than liaise with the anchors?

Often I would just watch. Maybe talk out loud about how I was viewing a particular interview or segment. I was making editorial decisions on the run – do we need more of this? Do we need less of this? – plus keeping an eye on breaking news, trying to decide what's important for us to cover, what we should lead with every half-hour. And timing out the show [ensuring it ends on schedule].

What constitutes good communication in a live television control room?

It needs to be short, sharp and clear. Tone is really important. That's fundamental in a live television environment: if a presenter or director mishears something that you say, then something might not go to air as you intended. I mentioned tone because I would never want to inject any sort of panic or fear in the presenter's ear. They are the faces of the show. So if I was to get in their ear and scream, 'No, we've got a problem!' it's gonna show on their face and they're gonna freak out on air. When it comes to presenters, you can't sound like you're not sure – you've got to be sure. You can be honest, you can certainly have emotion, but you should have an element of calm and be commanding.

In the control room it's a bit more apparent when things aren't calm. That's okay as long as you're being clear and concise. Live TV is a difficult beast and a control room is almost like a vacuum. Whatever's said in the control room stays in the control room. Sometimes the quietest and most focused control room is the one right in the middle of rolling breaking news, because everyone is listening. Everyone's at their most focused. That's when people really earn their money.

How closely did you monitor ratings? And how much did they affect what you chose to run or not run on the program?

I monitored ratings extremely closely. They're the most immediate feedback and survey of how we're going. Are people liking it? Are they not liking it? If they outwardly rejected us on a particular show, on a particular day, in a particular market, I would listen to that. Sometimes it was nothing to do with what we were running. It was about whether or not people had time for us that morning: whether it was raining and they had to get out of the house quicker; or a public holiday and they got up later; or there was a lockdown and they were working from home. Breakfast TV is heavily influenced by lifestyle factors.

But generally speaking, ratings are a really good indication of how you're going as a show.

TV is legendary for being the domain of blokey, middle-aged alpha males. You are not that. How have you been treated as a young gay man in a very powerful position?

I think in some ways it probably helped because I stood out from the crowd. I think some of the powers went, 'Oh, he's a bit different but he seems to know what he's doing.' But I have always noticed that blokey-ness. Probably less so now than earlier in my career. I've been in TV for more than twenty years and in the beginning it was all male bosses. No one was gay. I think that's changing now. But yeah, it is intimidating when, you know, you're the only gay in the village – or the only gay in the boardroom – and that's happened to me more often than not.

What qualities do you look for in people you hire?

People who are passionate about storytelling. People who like the medium of television. I look for people who are good writers.

People who are not afraid to stand up for themselves, because they're going to have to do that a lot. Also, I'm often looking at who will fit well into the dynamic of the team. What are we missing?

If young Michael Pell walked through the door, would EP Michael Pell hire him?

I think I would hire him, but I would tell him to chill out!

Mia Freedman

Mia Freedman is one of Australia's leading digital entrepreneurs as co-founder of Mamamia Women's Media Company. It is the largest women's podcast network in the world, with a monthly audience of more than seven million women and more than fifty-five different programs. Prior to starting Mamamia, Mia was a magazine editor, newspaper columnist, radio presenter and TV host. She has written four books, hosts the interview podcast 'No Filter', and co-hosts the top current affairs podcast in Australia, 'Mamamia Outloud'. She is also a co-creator and Executive Producer of the TV series Strife, *which was inspired by her memoir,* Work Strife Balance.

Mia, what's your actual role at Mamamia?

I guess you could say I'm the DNA of the business. I have to toggle between being the owner of a media company and being a creator. The part that I've managed to eliminate in the middle is where I'm a manager – I don't manage a single person, even my own EA does not report to me. I've spent so much of my career climbing the ladder, getting to the top, looking around, and then trying to find ways to climb back down, to be back at the coalface, because that's where I'm most comfortable.

That's the hoity-toity answer. But the actual answer is I make a lot of content, I'm behind the business. I identify new growth areas and I oversee how we present ourselves to the world. The thing I've learnt from a business point of view is that I'm most comfortable in start-up mode, getting my hands dirty. The more people between me and an audience, the more frustrating I find it.

Why?

I guess one answer could be that I'm a show-off. I like to perform. In many ways, there's a degree of ego in all forms of journalism. But I want to *do*, not teach. I want to impact women most greatly by *making* the thing, not managing the making of the thing. And I want to learn from the process of making it and the process of seeing how it's received. Then I learn and get better at what I do.

What do you learn from your audience?

Well, when you're a newspaper columnist, or you edit a magazine, or you work at a TV network, so many things are out of your control. It can be very woolly when you're trying to learn what an audience responds to because there can be a hundred different things that affect it. You might have a great column in the newspaper, but the front page will be something that you had no control over, and that might prevent people from buying it and reading your column. Or you might do something fantastic on TV but the show that's leading in might be something, or daylight saving might be something. When you work on the internet, exclusively in digital media, you can't hide from the real-time feedback of your audience. Everything I make is intentional. I can see if you've opened a newsletter I've sent, I can see if you've read an article I've written, I can see if you've downloaded a podcast I've recorded. The numbers can't lie. People's behaviour can't lie. I really like that. I like the real-time feedback.

How similar is your role steering the creative side of a digital business to editing a print magazine, as you used to?

Some things are similar. You've got a team of people and you have to work out how to get the best from them. They're all working under a branded masthead, and you have to stay true to that masthead while still encouraging people to shine in their individual ways. So some of it's similar, but it's the scale. It costs the same amount to produce a podcast that's listened to by a million people as it does to produce a podcast that's listened to by ten people. Same with a written article, an Instagram video or a YouTube video. It's all the same output, whereas magazines, for example, are not scalable. If you want to sell fifty thousand magazines, you have to print eighty thousand magazines. It's a terrible business model, print. So in that way it's [digital] much more liberating. You can have a much greater impact.

You mentioned all these disparate elements that come under a masthead. How precisely do you have in your mind the identity and core value of the Mamamia masthead?

So for a long time, the first few years after I started Mamamia in the lounge room, my husband Jason would say, 'But what is Mamamia?' And what he was getting at is, 'What's your why?

315

What's the core purpose of Mamamia?' I would get really impatient with that – like, 'It's just the vibe, it's for women. It's about being good, supporting women.'

It wasn't until a lot of years later, as we started to scale the business, that he was insistent that we sit down and actually articulate our core purpose. Not just for our audience or our advertisers, but also for our staff, which was growing exponentially at that time. The only way to create a culture and a brand is to have core values and a core purpose. Core purpose is how you create a brand, core values are how you create a culture. And so we articulated that Mamamia is about making the world a better place for women and girls. And it's like, 'Okay, how do we do that?' That's our 'why'. That's why everyone in our company comes to work every day, and that is the filter through which every editorial and business decision we make goes.

I'll give you an example of a business decision. We decided early on that we would not support the paparazzi economy. We would not participate in it. So even though all our competitors in the women's space publish paparazzi photos of celebrities at the beach, celebrities with their kids – taken without women's knowledge and permission – we don't do that because we know it does not meet our core purpose. It is not making the world a better place for women and girls. It's predominantly women and their children who are stalked by paparazzi. Even though that costs us from a business point of view, cos that's traffic we don't get and pageviews that we can't monetise, that is a business decision we've made.

Even though you were a bit irritated by the conversation at the start, once you did identify and articulate your 'why' in one sentence, what effect did that have on the business?

Massive. The most dangerous time for business is going from start-up to scale-up, because it is such a shift – from who you hire to what you create, to how you run anything. They say you should be able to walk up to anybody in the whole business at any time of the day and say, 'What's our core purpose?' And if they can't tell you, you're going to struggle with engagement, because they don't know why they're there. For us, it meant suddenly having a great filter for the editorial decisions we make, for the business decisions we make, for the staff we hire. Everybody's pulling in the same direction. It's been a game-changer.

I assume it also makes it very easy when you're commissioning work or new products and new podcasts to decide, 'Is this a Mamamia kind of story?'

It absolutely does. And it also gives us a unique selling point from the very crowded market of much bigger media companies.

What do you think makes a good editorial leader?

As a leader, it's your job to work out how to get the most out of your people and what motivates them. One of the things that we do when people start with us is say to them, 'What fills your cup?' and we give them a list of examples. Is it public praise? Time off? Being sent flowers? A shout-out in the newsletter? Private praise? Some people love being called out in front of everybody, other people find that absolutely mortifying – it's much more mean-ingful to them if their boss comes and has a quiet word with them and says, 'Hey, I really liked that story that you wrote,' or, 'You did a great job editing that show.'

I think as a good leader, you need to be really self-aware. You need to understand your own biases and weaknesses. A big one for leaders is unconscious bias. As a leader, you tend to promote and surround yourself with people like you. They're the ones you gravitate to because they're the ones you understand the best. Obviously, when you've got a company full of men, that can be a really bad thing, because they'll hire lots of other men. For me, I'm very extroverted, very larger than life, very fast. And I'm attracted to people like that. And you can't have only people like that.

With any new hire, from a junior person to a senior person, are there any particular qualities that you highly seek?

I would say curiosity, more than anything else. That's crucial to me. An evenness of temperament. We put everybody through a psychographic test. It basically shows someone's personality profile. If you've got someone working in the IT department versus sales versus a podcast producer, they're going to need different strengths. Some will need to be more sparkly, some will need to be better at working independently. We've got people in the business across all different kinds of profiles; it's about the strengths they bring to their particular job.

Do you think that the skills that make somebody a great journalist can be taught? Or do you have to arrive with certain attributes?

I know they can be taught because no one starts as a good journo. I remember Deborah Thomas, my first boss, would sit me next to her and rewrite my copy while I watched. It was excruciating but it was a gift. I mean, my god! Back in the day, it used to be great when you would print out your copy, give it to an editor, and they would write all over it with pen. Now, with digital media, a journalist will file their copy, an editor might make changes, someone will choose a headline, it'll go up, and there's no physical trail of what those changes are. I really miss marking up copy. I don't do it anymore much, but I really love working with words.

At Mamamia, do you talk to staff about what constitutes good writing?

If you're a news journalist it's going to be very different to a lifestyle journalist or the host of a pop culture podcast. It's genre-specific. But, you know, I do masterclasses with the team here, as does Holly [Wainwright], who's our Head of Content. She's got a masterclass on tone that she takes every new starter in our business through – even the people in the sales team, because they'll have to put together decks for clients, and tone is really, really important.

I do masterclasses on something called the 'T', which is something I learnt from the editor-in-chief of US *Cosmo*. We used to have these global conferences and all the editors – from sixty-five different countries – would go to somewhere like the Bahamas or Amsterdam or New York, and we'd have meetings and presentations for a few days. I remember the new editor of *Cosmo* gave a presentation and she talked about the T. Apparently on a tennis court there's something called the T, where you've got the most control and ability to place the ball. Her husband's a kids' tennis coach and they start at the T, where they can hit all the shots. But then they'll start to drift and suddenly, they're not in the position of strength for their game. So he'll always be like, 'Go back to the T, go back to the T.' And she talked about us going back to the T as well.

I'll give you an example. The T is your 'why'. Your sweetest spot, the core of your brand, where it's at its strongest. Everyone will go off their T – because your staff can take you off your T, the news cycle can take you off your T. We've come off our T many times. For example, if you do one story on *7.30* about Kim Kardashian's new underwear, people will go, 'Well, that's a little bit weird,' but it won't take you off your T, right? But if you do a story about Kim Kardashian's underwear, then a story about Kylie Jenner's pregnancy, then a story about Nadia Bartel snorting coke, suddenly you're off your T.

The T of Crikey is going to be different to the T of *7.30* is going to be different to the T of Mamamia. And there'll be aspects of Mamamia with different Ts. 'Mamamia Out Loud' has one. With our podcast 'No Filter', we have the T in the intro each time: 'Conversations with people from all walks of life, who tell their stories very candidly and aren't afraid to be vulnerable.' So that's the T, right?

How do you come up with story ideas or new podcast ideas?

From our chats on WhatsApp.

[*laughs*]

I'm not even kidding. I have an insatiable appetite, and the best people in our team do, for consuming things. I am content-agnostic – I will look at YouTube videos, TikTok videos, I'll watch *7.30*, I'll be alive to conversations happening in my group chats, I'll notice my own behaviour changing and what I'm thinking about things. And I've come to know over the years that I'm a basic bitch, in that if I'm thinking about something or doing something or interested in something, a lot of other people are going to be very shortly as well. I'm fractionally ahead. So when I was into podcasts, I just followed my gut; because I'm like, well, 'If I'm listening to a lot of podcasts, that's going to be a thing soon.' I'm not a futurist who knows what's happening in five years, or even two years, but I'm probably about six months ahead of the pack. It's just being alive to the vibe.

You just said something that I think is absolutely key in journalism, whether you're Helen Garner writing literary nonfiction or the most tabloid journo. It was when you said, 'I notice what I think about things.' Noticing is possibly *the* skill in good journalism, other than curiosity, and they're related. It's noticing, 'Oh, that seems a bit weird. That's interesting.'

Yes. For example, I was thinking the other day, 'Where's part two of Barack Obama's book?' I would love someone to go write that story. What's the story behind why Barack Obama's book has taken six years? That's a story I'd be interested to know cos I'm just nosy and curious.

And why is yuzu in so many restaurant desserts now?

It's true. Like, why? They absolutely are stories. It's that thing of 'everything's copy'.

Trying new things comes with risk, and you can't embrace risk without being prepared to accept failure. How do you deal with that?

I try to fail fast. I don't flog dead horses. That's an awful expression. But I don't beat myself up. If something's not working, I just want to keep going, move on and try the next thing. Maybe that means I give up too easily, but I'm willing to accept that something hasn't worked. There've been podcasts that we've started that just haven't kicked. And there've been ideas that we've had in the business that just haven't worked. Sometimes our timing's just been off, sometimes our execution's been off. And I've tried to learn from that and move on and make the next thing better.

What do you think is the most common misconception that legacy journalists have about digital media companies?

Clickbait. I think this idea of clickbait is so reductive. Clickbait is when you manipulate people by having a misleading headline. Magazines do this all the time, which is why it's ironic that it's associated with digital journalism. It'll be like 'Fifi Box's Exciting Baby News', and then you'll look and it'll be her sister's had a baby, you know? A good headline should entice someone to want to know more, to want to read that story. It should never knowingly mislead, just encourage.

I think that the other misconception about digital journalism is that it's somehow lesser; that because it's so often written by young people, it's less worthy. I don't think any of that's true.

Also, from a women's media company point of view, this idea that anything a woman's interested in is obviously dumb and frivolous. Which is not a new thing. That was an aspersion that was cast over women's magazines, and women's magazine editors. That because it was interesting to women, it must be dumb. Nobody says that about sport.

Your business has an audience of more than six and a half million women every month. It clearly has been groundbreaking for digital media in Australia. And yet, I still occasionally see it described in newspapers as a 'mummy blog'. What do you think motivates that condescension?

Oh, misogyny. The same thing that motivates people in the book world to call it chick lit instead of fiction written by women. It's that idea that if you have a uterus and an internet connection, you must be a mummy blogger. It's just really sad and reductive. It's the same reason businesswomen are often referred to as socialites or influencers, when in fact they're running businesses and they happen to have a social media account. It's just pure sexism.

This is the exact reason that I invited you to be in this section of the book. Undoubtedly, you are as powerful and influential as any male newspaper editor in the country, as any television executive producer, and it's mystifying to me that it gets overlooked or dismissed so readily. I guess the flip side of that is, it allows you to operate doing what you're doing and get on with what you like.

It does. I think there's also the idea that because I put on my make-up on social media, or I'll do a post about a top that I've bought, it means that I can't also be serious. But that's why Mamamia's been able to be a success. We were the first ones to come along and say, 'Well, yeah, women are interested in fashion and cooking and make-up, but they're also interested in politics, current affairs, news, pop culture, sport.' A lot of legacy journalists still sometimes find that hard to understand and they'll call us a parenting site or a lifestyle site. But we've got as much news content as any other major media organisation, you know? It's about 360 degrees of content. We're content-agnostic, because guess what? People are content-agnostic. The things that people are interested in are both high- and low-brow.

David Penberthy

David Penberthy was the editor of The Daily Telegraph *from 2005 to 2008, and subsequently edited news.com.au and* The Punch. *He is a columnist with* The Advertiser, The Australian *and* The Sunday Mail, *and is co-host of the popular FIVEaa breakfast program in Adelaide.*

An editor is a romanticised figure in some ways, from powerful crusaders like Ben Bradlee at *The Washington Post* to feared figures around whom everyone tiptoes, such as Anna Wintour at *Vogue*. What is the job actually like?

It's frustrating because so much of the time the thing that got you into journalism is the farthest thing from what occupies your time. You're responsible for the commercial operation of the paper and you end up spending a hell of a lot of your time working with marketing people, circulation, advertising and human resources. I started putting fake meetings in my diary to block out time, which would say things like 'staff development meetings'. They weren't meetings at all, they were just time for me to walk around the room and talk to the reporters and say, 'What are you working on? What have you got coming up? How are you enjoying the round?' Or to the younger ones, 'What field of journalism are you most interested in?' Time is your greatest enemy in the job. I know that editing is seen as a bit of a power trip but you're really there to try to think like a reader. You know, 'Is this a paper that anyone's actually gonna care about?'

'Is anyone gonna care about this?' should be the starting point for all of our journalism. Anything you approach, you've got to try to think, 'Am I just writing this because it's something that I'm interested in? Or because it'll impress my friends? Or is there a greater social interest and purpose behind this, that's gonna grab people and mean something to them?'

When you're working the kind of crazy hours that editors work and earning more than what the average Australian earns, how do you keep in touch with what the regular person cares about?

One thing that I prided myself on, even when I was a senior journo prior to editing, was I'd still always try to get out of the office and cover things myself. And, particularly with political journalism, one thing I was really red-hot on was the idea that vox pops aren't something that you get cadets to do. I think there's a hell of a lot to be said for [the idea that] people who are really senior, if they're gonna say, 'Monaro is a bellwether seat' – to use the time-honoured cliché – should actually go to Cooma and Batemans Bay, talk to three hundred people and work out why it is a bellwether seat.

The bloke I followed as editor, Campbell Reid, had a big influence on me. He used to walk around the newsroom angrily when it was full of reporters saying, 'Why is everybody here? There are no stories at 2 Holt Street, Surry Hills.' He'd go through these periods where he'd write five hundred cab charges and say, 'I don't want to see anyone for a week, just go somewhere, talk to people.' Otherwise, if you get sucked into the vortex of lunch at alternating French and Italian restaurants on Crown Street every other day, Friday night work drinks with the staff, and then do it all again the following Monday, you end up being completely disengaged from what people actually care about.

What's the balance between the editor saying, 'You do this, you do that,' versus the editor being told, 'Here's what our staff has,' and you picking and choosing what to run?

I reckon it was about fifty-fifty. The thing that always got me excited, particularly working in tabloid journalism, was trying to find a unique way, or a comical way, of dealing with an issue that would historically have been covered with a series of thundering editorials demanding a better deal for people. One good example from my time at *The Daily Telegraph* was, there'd been endless stories about delays in the commuter train network. Our transport reporter, Heath Aston, came up to me and said, 'Oh mate, I need to talk to you. I hope you don't mind, I've set something up for next week, but I need to get your blessing because it's going to cost us a little bit of money.' It was one of my favourite moments as editor. He'd arranged for the Olympian [marathon runner] Steve Moneghetti to come up from Melbourne to Sydney, and to run head-to-head against one of the peak-hour trains – I think it was the 8:13 a.m. train – from Petersham to Central. This was in the early days of the internet, and Heath said, 'We're going to film it and take photographs, and we'll see if he beats the train.' And to CityRail's great shame, he beat it to Central by about two minutes. We had this beautiful front page and the headline was FASTER THAN A LOCOMOTIVE, then in big letters, 'Olympian shames hapless rail network.'

It went off online because the video was just hysterical. He was in his running gear, going around the bend through Redfern. It struck me as the ultimate tabloid story. The best thing was, that day the head of CityRail held a press conference saying that the article was clearly stupid and ridiculous. He bought into the story and then all the rest of the media was covering it. It felt like an ultimate *Telegraph* moment, where we'd, quite deservedly, taken the piss out of something on the basis of shoddy service that taxpayers were paying for, and that our readers, more than anyone, had to endure.

If you're commissioning yarns like that, you have to have guts. What kind of personality do you think suits the job as editor and suits the job of journalism?

When I was editor, we would get up to fifteen hundred applications for one cadet job, or one entry-level position, which we had to get down to a workable number. I had a rule. I said to the HR people, 'Look, can we just not interview anyone who hasn't had a part-time job and hasn't listed their part-time job?' I think that working in retail, working in hospitality, working in any kind of environment where you have to talk to people from every single walk of life is a more important skill for journalism than having a degree. A lot of the best journos I know are people who come from non-journalism backgrounds – they're just people who are engaged, they're good listeners and they like people. You need to be naturally into humanity, and curious, and believe that everyone's got a story to tell, in order to do the job well.

How often do powerful people ring an editor or an anchor of a program to complain or curry favour?

Oh, they do it quite a lot. It depends on the politician. John Howard never did. In fact – this is hand on heart – the only time John Howard ever complained the entire time I was working at *The Daily Telegraph*, he didn't do it to us at the paper, he did it to our CEO. And he wasn't demanding, he was just requesting. One of our photographers had been told that his daughter Melanie was trying on a wedding dress in George Street, and he got a photograph of her. It was before her wedding, obviously, and you could see the gown. We had the photos and someone rang the PM's press office and said, 'Look, we have these photos and we're thinking about running them tomorrow,' John Howard rang the CEO, John Hartigan, and said, 'You know I'd never tell you what you should or shouldn't put in your newspaper, but I'm just asking you as a father to respect the tradition that a groom never sees his bride's wedding dress.' And we didn't run the photographs.

All the journos were going, 'Ah, it was such a great scoop.' I was chief of staff at the time, and I was slightly miffed, and then I thought about it and said, 'Well, the upshot of it is, if we run them, we'd probably look like scumbags and a lot of the readers would hate us for doing it, particularly women.' So we didn't do it. That was the only time in his prime ministership that John Howard ever contacted us, as far as I know, and it was in about ten years of dealing with him there. Kevin Rudd, whole other story. You know, sort of like the Shane Warne of politics with his incessant texting. But it varies. I think most of them are generally pretty level-headed about it; they know when to fire up, they know when to take one on the chin.

How do you handle that as the person receiving the call?

I think the big challenge for editors is to handle it with zero ego. None of these people are contacting you because they like you, they're contacting you because you're the halfwit who's sitting in the big chair for your designated three, four, five years. There can be a tendency in the media for people to think that they're big swinging you-know-whats, and I think that you should realise that when you're editing a paper, everything you publish has consequences, and you gotta think through that. I think that's where editors can become deluded, if they not only believe their own BS but start acting on it.

What about the relationship between the editor and the proprietor?

Oh, I must admit, I had pretty frequent dealings with Rupert Murdoch. And I had much more frequent dealings with Lachlan. But I was never actually given specific marching orders. In fact, when the paper ran a pro-Rudd editorial in 2007, the only person I initially dealt with on that, just in the 'no surprises rule' as he used to call it, was [CEO] John Hartigan. I rang him up and I said, 'Harto, I reckon Howard's cooked. I reckon he's gone.' And he goes, 'Yeah, I'm feeling that way, too.' And that was from doing all these vox pops, getting out and talking to people. I had a face-to-face conversation with Rupert Murdoch about our position. In fact, it was the night that John Howard appeared on *The 7.30 Report*, where he gave that on-air promise that if he was re-elected, he'd definitely quit halfway through the term. And I was going, 'Well, there's a vision to lead,' like, you know, 'I can promise I'll definitely do half my term if I'm voted in again.'

As I was watching it, I'd rewritten the front-page headline, and it said, 'Half-term Howard: PM cuts 18 months off use-by date,' or something like that. And Rupert Murdoch came into the room and he said, 'What's your assessment of all this?' And I said, 'It looks like a total shambles, frankly.' And he said, 'Yeah, I agree.' I mean, it was a conversation with Rupert Murdoch, but it wasn't like he came into my office to tell me what to do – he came into the office to find out what I was doing and then went, 'Yeah, you're right, it is a bit of a mess.' I know it jars with the assertion of his critics, most of whom have never worked for the guy.

Equally, though, say you decided the newspaper was gonna launch a campaign to legalise crack, or you were gonna mount a series of campaigns looking at the human side of the suicide bomber – 'What is it that makes these young men make such terribly sad decisions in their lives?' – well, I think there are certain bedrock values. You know there are certain economic and political views that he [Murdoch] has, but I think that they're the views that most people who read our papers also have. Otherwise, they wouldn't read our papers.

How did you feel when you went to bed and you knew that you had a big splash the next day that was going to set off an absolute bomb?

I think it comes back to the point I was making earlier about not believing your own BS. I wanted the paper to be unpredictable. I wanted it to have a sense of attitude. I wanted it to be often a funny paper. I used to say to the staff, and I used to say to my boss, 'You might die of a lot of things working at *The Daily Telegraph*, but boredom's not one of them.' What I actually lived in fear of the most was a boring paper. One story that I often tell journos, and particularly young journos, is that there's a really excellent piece in Tim Flannery's anthology about the best Australian explorers. He had criteria by which he selected extracts from their journals. One of his criteria was, 'Can they write?' And he tells the story of this guy called William Gosse, who was walking through the centre of Australia, and he wrote this in his diary: 'I had been walking for several hours in a northerly direction, where I came upon a large rock, which I named after Mr Ayers.' This guy's just discovered Uluru and that's it?

I remember one night talking to one of our excellent reporters, and he'd interviewed this woman whose son had died in a hit-and-run in Sydney. It was the six-month anniversary of his death, and the bastard who did it still hadn't been caught. This journo had written an amazing story, an exclusive, on the front page. After the deadline, I was walking over the road with him and I said, 'Mate, you've done a really good job on that story.' And he said, 'You know what's the saddest thing? This mum, with all the stress of it, she's lost so much weight in the last six months that she's even lost weight on her hands. And at the end of the interview, she turned around and she went, "My god," cos she realised her wedding ring had slipped off while we were talking in the park. And we couldn't find her ring.' And I said, 'Oh mate, that's so bad. Did you find it?' He said, 'Yeah, that's why I was late back, we were looking together for about fifteen minutes.' And then I said, 'I don't want to sound like a heartless bastard, but nothing you've written tells the story of her grief as much as that story.' And so we went back to work and we rewrote the copy. That's not schmaltz or a beat-up, that's just an indication of how much someone can suffer from something. There was really only one reader who we wanted to read that piece: the guy who killed the kid.

Are there common mistakes or bad habits that you see in written copy, in newspapers or online, that constantly irritate you?

I can't stand a lot of journalese, things like, 'An ugly war of words has erupted after X said Y about Z in an angry attack, comma, blah, blah, blah.' There are so many ways you can write things and so many words at your disposal. I'm not saying you need to force your readers to stock up on *Roget's Thesaurus*, but journalism can, at times, be lazy. You go to the job because you like to write, and there are certain sorts of constructs that people are used to, but I think sometimes it can all look a little bit too templated.

Is there still a line between straight news reporting and opinion? Or is there a bleeding together of those things in modern journalism?

I think there's a bleeding together. Being someone who approaches things in an open-minded and neutral fashion is the most dangerous place to be at the moment. Working in radio now, we build the show as a place where we're not just happy but thrilled to disagree about things, to go, 'Okay, so that's that side of the argument, what's the other side of the argument?' But it seems being liberal – supporting the plurality of ideas, a contest of ideas – is under threat. I think it's threatened by social media, but it's also threatened by what seems to be a more strident editorialising approach, on TV as well. The day that people feel that they can't say what they think is really dangerous.

Justin Stevens

Justin Stevens has been the ABC's Director, News since April 2022. From 2018 to 2022 he was Executive Producer of ABC's nightly current affairs program 7.30. He began his career on the Nine Network's Sunday *program and has also been a producer on* Four Corners *and on the documentary series* The Killing Season *and* Keating: The Interviews. *His work has been recognised with Logie and AACTA awards, and Walkley nominations.*

What does an executive producer do?

The EP is a bit like the coach of a sporting team. You lead everyone in the program team to do their best possible job. You're also the ultimate decision-maker, because any team needs a leader to make final decisions in a cohesive way.

Continuing the sporting analogy, if the EP's the coach, what is the anchor?

The anchor is Michael Jordan, [if] the EP is [Chicago Bulls coach] Phil Jackson. The EP takes decisions that have big ramifications, but the anchor is the front person of the team and the one who the audience sees. If something's wrong, it wouldn't necessarily be the anchor's responsibility, but they're the ones on live TV putting their neck on the line every day.

What other staff on *7.30* help build that entire nightly half-hour program?

Many talented and hard-working people. You've got producers, reporters, researchers, editors, and people responsible for on-air graphics. The production manager does a lot of unsung heroics behind the scenes, pulling off the impossible – getting people on a flight when there are no flights, finding accommodation in the middle of nowhere. Around the EP is the senior team of supervising producers. The anchor generally has an interview producer who is directly responsible for chasing and supporting their interviews. *7.30* also has a political editor, and a producer specifically for that role. Making daily news and current affairs is a big team effort.

Talk me through the routine you had at the start of the day as EP of *7.30*, after you woke up but before you'd spoken to anybody, when the program was a blank slate in front of you.

Any journalist, however senior or junior you are, whatever your role, needs to have a disciplined morning routine around news consumption so you have a good sense of the big moving stories. For me that's about absorbing as much domestic journalism as I can, and then anything beyond that I have time for. I listen to

Radio National from about 6 a.m. until 7.50 every day, check what *AM* has on the early edition and who its main interview is, and try to check what 2GB is doing. I look at all of the key news outlets online.

How early did you start communicating with your staff, and who were generally your first ports of call?

News is breaking twenty-four hours a day, so I feel strongly about making sure there are clear boundaries in regards to out-of-work contact. If you're contacting anyone before 9 a.m., or after the show, there has to be a good reason. It means that they know it requires immediate attention.

You and I were usually talking from around 7.30 or eight because we both had that morning routine. For some interviews, you need to get a bid in early. If you're a reporter or producer and you're going to be assigned a same-day story, you want notice. We had a conference call at 9 a.m. to run through what we already had planned, how the plans might need to change and anything we needed to chase. At the same time, we had to be mindful that we might need to throw that out at a moment's notice.

Hours later, at 8:01 p.m., what would have made you go, 'That was a great show'?

At the centre of a good program is strong, public-interest journalism. It is editorially robust, fair, accurate, entertaining, relevant, surprising, revealing, visually watchable, and produced with integrity. It's when you've interviewed someone everyone else has been chasing and the public want to hear from, and advanced the story beyond what we already knew. When you hear great human stories and see the human impact of policies taken by our politicians. When you break news or do something of substance that matters for the democratic process.

How did you come up with story ideas for a program like *7.30*?

Ultimately, ideas are the difference between a program being good or average, so it's vital to have a robust ideas culture. For any good idea you can guarantee there'll be thirty to forty amazing journalists with the same one, so you have to be at the front of the chase.

You need headspace to dream big with ideas. The most compelling moments on TV are usually because someone landed something that seemed impossible, like the BBC did in getting Prince Andrew's first interview off the back of the Jeffrey Epstein scandal. I bet when they sat around and someone said, 'You know, we should have a good crack at landing Prince Andrew,' they thought, 'We're never going to get him, and if he did anyone, would he really do the BBC?' But someone had that idea. And it was a big idea. They no doubt showed persistence to secure the interview. It was massively in the public interest when it came off.

Other ideas are smaller and you deploy and activate them quickly: maybe doing a comprehensive timeline about something, or pulling out an old piece of archive material, which you remember was rich and is now relevant to this moment.

People need to feel confident they can offer an idea, whether it's a good or a bad one.

Yeah, you have to reassure people that just because we don't say yes to an idea doesn't mean it was a bad idea. It doesn't mean you're bad at your job. We will always have more ideas than we are able to do. The contest of ideas means only a few will get up day to day.

You have the best contact book of anyone I know. There are very few people in Australian public life for whom you would not have a direct number. How important is that bank of people in terms of helping you find stories or land major interviews?

It's essential to have as many as possible and to be disciplined in retaining your contacts. It might be that you interviewed someone in a fairly innocuous story, and five years down the track they are at the centre of the biggest breaking story of the day. Public relations people can see their role as being a sort of dam wall to the media, and more often than not their advice [to a client] will be to go nowhere near a journalist, so the direct contact is critical. Also, in the age of email and text messages, journalists shouldn't underestimate the power of a direct call to an individual to explain what you're about and why they're relevant to the story. It's difficult to relay that in writing if they don't know who you are.

When was the first time you set foot in a television studio?

When I was fourteen or fifteen I did work experience with Peter Overton at Channel 9. At that point in his career he was reading the 11 a.m. news, and he let me shadow him and I got to sit next to him as he read the news. That was amazing and lit a flame in me.

Not everybody is in a position where they can go and do work experience placements. Every bit of your spare time may be spent juggling several part-time jobs. You may not have the connections or the confidence to make the call to get work

experience. How important is it that we offer multiple pathways into journalism so that it's accessible for people from all kinds of backgrounds?

It's vital the Australian media finds ways to broaden the diversity of people coming into the industry and to make our workplaces and newsrooms as inclusive as possible. That isn't tokenism; it's central to making our journalism more relevant and accurate, because it more accurately reflects the diversity of our country. At the ABC we try to ensure we have many pathways for upcoming journalists, and nobody should ever feel like it's a closed shop to them.

Unless we do that, we're going to end up with a monoculture of people who all think the same way about 'What is a story?', and miss a whole range of issues in the community. If you're a university-educated white person who lives in inner-city Sydney, you have a very different view of the world to a working-class person whose parents are tradies on the outskirts of Brisbane.

That's right. We have to park our own personal experience or views to do good journalism, and be mindful of where there might be limitations in our own lived experience when we cover different things. We need to make sure our personal views don't get entangled with what we do and that the journalism is free of any agenda. Often the most important public-interest stories are not being heard because those who are impacted are powerless and don't have a voice – our job is to give them a voice.

When you come into a newsroom as an inexperienced journalist, it can be intimidating to look around and see a TV anchor,

the executive producer, other very experienced people. How do you find your voice and develop confidence?

Through life experience and getting a better understanding of how people do their jobs. You'll gain the confidence to back yourself and be more at ease, feeling like your voice in a newsroom matters. Accept that you're not going to have that straightaway, and don't be intimidated by people who have found it faster. It took me a few years. It's also incumbent on managers of news teams to ensure they foster an environment where all staff feel they get a voice in the conversation and that their ideas are heard – that helps build individuals' confidence.

Don't underestimate how much you can learn from what can seem like boring or dreary jobs. For instance, in a lot of my junior jobs I had to spend a lot of the day on the phone to viewers. I used that opportunity to speak to as many members of the public as possible and to refine the art of listening – to hear someone's viewpoint and to steer a conversation. When I was appointed Kerry O'Brien's producer at *The 7.30 Report*, I think my name came up because one of the supervising producers, Phil Kwok, had heard me do that day after day after day. He was like, 'Give that guy a crack because I've heard him on the phone, he's good at chatting to people and maybe there's something there.'

An executive producer or editor has to be broadly across the news but they also need a depth of detail about ongoing stories. It's a lot. How does one person hold all that in their head?

It becomes somewhat instinctive the more you do it, and it's also about being as highly organised as possible. You need a clear sense of what is and what is not a story. You have to be able to make good, clear, fast decisions. Anyone in a role like that who makes slow decisions or hesitates – you feel the whole team slow down and things start to splutter. So, yes, you are holding a lot of information. But everyone is and it's about moving as quickly as possible on things.

You need to be a leader, but there's also a lot of technical precision. Every big-picture thing you're trying to do with a program or team will involve a host of minor, incremental, technical things. If you don't technically know how to do something yourself – and you won't all the time – you need to make sure you have great people around you who do know.

The quality of what's made for television these days is incredibly high. To stick with our basketball analogy, do Netflix documentary series like *The Last Dance* raise the bar for what audiences expect from daily television journalism?

They show us what's possible and give us visual inspiration. Cameras and technology have advanced so much – and it's affordable, which is exciting, because for programs such as *7.30* we don't need massive budgets to make something look high-end. Another key thing around any program, or sporting team, that has had success for a long period is that success can also be a potential trap. You can trick yourself into thinking it will be sustainable forever. You need to consistently find ways to stop and go, 'Okay, we need to evolve the program in this way. And this is how we're going to do it visually, in a production sense and editorially.' There's a balance between identifying what should never change about a program and the ways we should continue to evolve.

You became the ABC's Director of News in 2022. How do you take all the skills you've learned as a frontline program-maker and turn that into a job managing twelve hundred people?

In the front of my mind is always that I have to safeguard and enhance ABC News' ability to do impactful public-interest journalism, especially the kind that holds powerful people to account. One of the things that's really on my mind is the massive amount of disinformation out there, and I think the ABC has an important role in countering that. What I hope I can do is take all the knowledge I've picked up from all the amazing people I've worked with and stories I've covered and use it to enable those twelve hundred people I manage to do what they do so well – get our audiences the information they need in a way that evolves with technology and adapts to the way people use it.

Acknowledgements

Thank you to Lisa Millar and Annabel Crabb for being interviews #1 and #2 – the lab rats on whom I could test my audio and transcription software. My love to them too for their friendship and wise counsel. I'm also grateful to Antony Stockdale for his helpful technical advice.

Huge thanks to the talented Grace MacKenzie for being a fantastic editorial assistant. Smart, hilarious, kind – my favourite type of friend and colleague.

I'm grateful to all the team at Simon & Schuster and in particular, my publisher Ben Ball, who understood very clearly what I wanted this project to be and asked for nothing more or less than what I proposed. Ben, thank you as always for your immaculate judgement and stewardship. Thank you also to my adored Meredith Rose, queen and copyeditor.

This book would be nothing without the amazing professionals who allowed me to pick their brains. They frequently blew me away with their enthusiasm and knowledge. I'm so thankful that they were prepared to share their time and experience for the benefit of others.

I wouldn't have had my career in journalism without generous colleagues who passed along their wisdom and taught me so much. I don't want to name anyone because I fear leaving somebody out, so just broadly I would like to say how appreciative I am to the wonderful journalism faculty at QUT, Channel 9 Brisbane, the ABC, and to many other friends and competitors I met on stories along the way who've been great sources of encouragement and mentorship, but most of all *fun*. I don't forget it.

I dedicate this work to two consummate professionals and dear friends no longer with us. Journalist Mark Colvin had an unparalleled commitment to accuracy, clear writing and intelligent broadcasting, and cameraman Mick Walter was my nightly dance partner on the studio floor at *7.30* for the best part of a decade. They epitomise the best of the media and I miss them both very much.